Early Celtic
Christianity

Early Celtic Christianity

BRENDAN LEHANE

CONSTABLE · LONDON

First published in Great Britain 1968
by John Murray Ltd
This edition first published 1994
by Constable and Company Limited
3 The Lanchesters, 162 Fulham Palace Road
London W6 9ER
Paperback edition 1995
Copyright © 1968 Brendan Lehane
ISBN 0 09 474490 4
Printed in Great Britain by
St Edmundsbury Press Ltd
Bury St Edmunds, Suffolk

A CIP catalogue record for this book
is available from the British Library

FOR MY MOTHER

Contents

Author's Note

I am grateful to so many who have encouraged and helped me during the writing of this book. Mrs Conor Cruise O'Brien most helpfully read the manuscript. Dr C. H. Talbot put me right on many points and also enabled me to correct more basic errors of emphasis. The Rev. Leo Sherley-Price allowed me to quote from his translation of Bede. The Arts Council of Great Britain, through a Maintenance Grant, made it possible for me to work in Ireland, a period heightened by the kindness of too many Irish to mention. The staff of the National Library, Dublin, and of the British Museum Library were consistently kind. Mrs Osyth Leeston and Mr John G. Murray gave me advice and encouragement at every stage of the book.

Early Celtic Christianity

Introduction

Since Greece, Europe has evolved heavily. Where the Greeks were all verve and inquiry, poetry and caprice, high nobility and spirited debasement, the Romans homogenised the uneven scene with a genius for system. They bought or copied as much as they could of the best of Greece, and preserved it in stone, an orderly language, and a strong and solid polity. In the process, they gave Greece a Roman stamp. Cicero and Virgil were somewhat plastery casts of Plato and Homer.

The Roman talent was for empire and law—sword and conscripted pen. With these they fashioned Europe's future. Both the patrons of the Middle Ages—the Holy Roman Empire and the Papacy—drew for much of their structure and motivation on the bequest of old Rome. Only the break with that tradition, brought about by minds that conceived Reformation and Renaissance, induced a return to a lighter, more spontaneous and varied outlook. National languages, religions and cultures appeared again. Science, and senses of humour, were revived. The Roman spectre at last was shrinking.

Even before the Renaissance, however, the continuity had not been complete. Between Roman dominion and the high Middle Ages several centuries intervened. Labelled the Dark Ages, they were not so dark as old historians nor so bright as modern iconoclasts have painted them. They were a time when the learning that before covered the empire like a sea sank to the level of rivulets.

In this parched period some peoples and places came to unexpected and unlikely prominence—parts of North Africa and Spain among them. Ireland too rose to European importance. Before, she had looked inwards and tired herself with bickering while the world went by. Afterwards, her story was of wrestling with the ambition of England, and a few happy lulls between the deadly bouts. For a few intervening centuries she held and prized the bequest of Christianity and Rome, brought to her by refugees, to be grafted with her own, hitherto isolated, riches. When the chance came, she carried her possessions to continental Europe, willingly restoring a tradition to places where it had been neglected and exiled. 'For the first and so far the last time in her history', James Carney, one of the foremost of a new, exacting breed of Irish scholars, has written, 'Ireland became the most vital civilising force in the West.'

Ireland was more than a custodian. Fervour and apathy, meekness and bravado, kindness and icy cruelty and all the other opposites of the Irish character put a stamp on the new creed and learning that could not be imitated. The combination of her sequestered position, a Celtic homogeneity that is found in no other country, and a poor, sometimes inadequate yield from natural resources, put brakes on her in times of general progress but saved her from many European calamities. When the Continent reeled at the impact of the barbarians, Ireland benefited by boatloads of refugees. In the same way, in more recent centuries, Protestant countries grew rich when the recalcitrance and autocracy of Catholics caused learned men and artisans to seek a more tolerant climate.

To understand Ireland's affluent age it is necessary to follow the tracks of history that lead almost purposefully towards her in the centuries preceding the sixth. The trail from Palestine is most clearly posted. Over the sea and the Alps and across the plains of northern Europe came the creed, ideas and enthusiasm of young Christianity. In subsequent centuries more ideas and observances followed, sometimes faltering on the continent, sometimes stumbling as far as the anomalous western state, where they were able to mature. The new paths made way for other imports, above all the language and thought of Rome, shorn of its imperial flavour. There was never a political tie between Ireland and Rome. But from this time on Ireland had associations with the continent which were to last. She stepped on to the stage of European history, and for a while remained on it, playing a minor but essential character.

Shaken though it was in its later centuries the Roman hegemony did not entirely collapse. There was a zigzag continuity between Augustus and Charlemagne in spite of the buffets of invasion and disorders within. Ireland had little to do with this perpetuation of central and imperial authority. Her contribution was to the spirit of Europe, not the body politic; and a clash had to come at last between Irish interests and the schemes of Empire and Papacy. When it came, and was resolved, the Roman powers were relieved of a minuscule annoyance. For Ireland the effect was quite different.

Through the lives of three Irishmen who were once famous all over Europe this book attempts to describe the country at the time when the duties of guardianship brought her to realise and exploit the intricate resources of her character. The first chapter sketches the imperial Roman world. It tries to show the Europe through which monastic practices passed on their way to the west, and some of the things that enhanced or altered their nature during the long journey. The isolated course of Ireland up to the fifth century, and the arrival of the Christian missions which established permanent links between the island and the continent, are the themes of the second chapter. From that time on, with the two influences amalgamated, Irish Christian culture began to cohere. The rest of the book follows its fitful expansion.

Ireland, in every age, is best known through the lives of individuals—figures sometimes comic, or fanatic, or rumbustious, or humble, never as coldly motivated as an abstract of national trends would suggest them to be. There is, however, one motive common to these three—Brendan, Columba and Columbanus. They are searching compulsively for something unworldly, for their own idea of God, for a refuge from earthly things, for the Promised Land, for perfection. The quest drives each one outwards, far from his home and people, to bring his gifts, oddities and aspirations to other countries and races. So Ireland itself was carried abroad, and the history of the country refused to resolve itself on Irish territory.

Introduction

For the researcher of this period, the guides are a tantalising mixture of the true, the dubious, and the notably incredible. The earliest Irish sources that survive were written in the eighth century, at least a hundred years after the death of Columbanus; and many of them have been shown to be tendentious—from a variety of motives—in their treatment of the past. In this context it is worth pointing out that for the last fifty years more work has been done in Ireland, and elsewhere, on the many codices of Irish literature that survive, than ever before. A scientific style of scholarship has penetrated the curtain of mystical fog that surrounded early Celtic inquiry. Had it begun earlier, the excesses of Yeats' Celtic Twilight might have been avoided, and the fibres of colourful romance set off, at least, by the glint of realism's steel. Now, as sharp brains apply themselves in Dublin, Belfast, Cork and Galway—outside the country too—the assumptions of a thousand years are questioned, and often tipped away. Nothing is certain any more. Doubts extend to some of the most sacrosanct conventions of a country that prides itself on its history and piety. Fifty years more may see harder facts emerging, and scholastic harmony—even cerebral decadence for want of strife. Now, and for some time to come, the problems are being scrupulously analysed and tested.

One of the most salutary effects could be the breaking of a taboo. There are signs already that this is working. History in the British Isles traditionally starts with Caesar, jumps to the Anglo-Saxons, and feels its feet firm only after the Norman conquest. The period between Caesar and Augustine of Canterbury, the interplay of Roman with Celt, and the subsequent movement of both races before the Teutonic invasions, are left, for want of date and certainty, as a vacuum in the history books. The new application may start to fill that void, and open the way to a recognition of this turbulent age. It is a period in which the boisterous and finally tragic history of early Christian Ireland will be seen to have taken a principal part.

4

I

European Background

In A.D. 81, forty years after Claudius the Emperor's troops had begun the occupation of Britain, the Roman commander Agricola considered the advantages of taking Ireland. The project seemed easy, and offered good and well-placed harbours for the shipping route between Britain and Spain. Agricola, called to other affairs, simply bore it in mind; and Ireland remained outside the imperial orbit for all time. It shared the privilege with the desert fringes of Arabia and North Africa, the Scottish highlands, and the daunting wilds of eastern Europe. But being far less troublesome than the latter, it could be left without regret on the extra-imperial shelf.

Rome at the time was at her apogee and, if the symptoms of decline were present, soothsayers were too prudent, and society too preoccupied, to notice. Emperors—Tiberius, Gaius, Caligula, Nero—were generally on the mad side of sane; the silvery strains of poetry and prose, and more caustic styles in art, were to win less respect with posterity than the achievements of two generations back. But from a contemporary point of view Augustus must have seemed a model of dull integrity—like Queen Victoria to a later generation—and the old rounded rhetoric of Cicero and measured hexameters of Virgil had, in the nature of things, to give way to a literature that had more edge, bite and cynicism. Other seeds of decline were hardly noticeable in the cosmopolitan towns of the west. Pressures of space in the Asiatic steppes were felt on the imperial marches in the form of barbarian migrations, but by filling her border armies with conquered troops Rome spared her own youth the troubles of war. Greece, Egypt and the Middle East were well under control, a source of constant pride to Romans who thought that by accepting a salute it was possible to absorb a culture. They licked the icing of the oriental cake. Perfumes, rugs, spices, and silk arrived by ship, sometimes after

5

desert journeys that had brought them from Greek depots in India. Egypt provided vital grain. And for the growing class of wealthy idlers in Rome the Levant was always good for philosophic stimulants. For their purposes the gods and mythical heroes of Greece had become as sterile and traditional as their own pantheon. But Isis and Sarapis and Zoroaster, and a few of the more esoteric Greek cults spiced the tired appetites of refined Romans. They, and the more recently imported Mithraism, offered mystical suggestions of hidden meaning in this life, and opposed the futile finality of Stoic doctrines.

Another—the newest—doctrine offered also a life in some removed world, but in other respects was dull and irritating. Jesus had lived, said his radical say, and paid the penalty. His teachings owed their survival to the rapid growth of towns where they enabled the simple poor to profess a contempt for their masters and surroundings and share an excitement in promises for the future. Christianity spread like a minor plague and would shortly have to be eradicated. It was born and maintained on the level of rabble naïvety, and Roman aristocrats were used to movements passing from top to bottom through their society. Wanting profundity, its appeal would not last. The outlook, as on other fronts, seemed good.

Optimists would have missed other omens of decay that grew as the huge administration of empire became more formalised. The supervising and economy of the Roman world contained elements that would ultimately contribute to their own destruction. The stanchion of the whole structure was the class of peasants, the men who actually harvested the crops on which almost the whole of the economy depended. As time went on their labour, the foundation of empire, became involved in a circle of exploitation and corruption. For their profits on foodstuffs were increasingly subjected to taxes, and the exorbitant rents demanded by patrician landlords, who needed the money for life and luxury in cities. With only narrow profits the countrymen resorted to quick yields, and soon exhausted large stretches of country through erosion and over-production.

Much of the land lost its value for production, and in time had to be deserted. But the borders remained, and it fell on the army to protect remote, unpeopled provinces. In the first century A.D. there were few border disturbances and the army was kept to reasonable proportions. It expanded as threats came from the east, and recruits were drawn from barbarian tribes whose loyalty to Rome, of which few ever came within a thousand miles, was suspect. Again increased costs had to be borne by the remaining peasantry. From their taxes too came the support of growing army and civil administration. But not all this money found its way to the needs for which it was raised. Patricians and civil servants grew richer while the poor grew poorer. What graspers filched, the peasant paid. Only the poor townsmen were guaranteed provisions, provided free by the state. They comprised many disillusioned rustics with too little to do. They had to be kept happy and out of mischief, and the cost of bread and circuses went, like other things, to the taxpayer.

With outlying lands deserted, or farmed by a class of exploited serfs, with a largely foreign army of three hundred thousand volatile souls, and a civil service turned in on itself by corruption and luxury, the empire came to be at the mercy of outside invaders. Later they came, but a long while later. For Romans of Agricola's time there was no obvious cause to worry. They were kept busy with their civic duties, their philosophic debates, their rituals and their excesses. And peripheral problems like Ireland quite passed them by.

The Irish, in their small way, were also preoccupied. They had trade, and perhaps social contacts, with the outer world. But Emain Macha, an earthen mound in Ulster, meant more to them in the first century than the spreading marble splendours of Rome. Emain Macha was the seat of the Ulster kings, who during this period were the dominant royal family. Almost all we know about them, and the rest of Ireland for another four hundred years, is based on guesswork and indirect evidence. Their traditions survive in the heroic tales that began to be written down in the seventh century; but it is impossible to distinguish clearly the overlay, usually tendentious, of historic times.

The dominant race in Ireland was the Celts. For more than a thousand years before Christianity they had been a homogeneous and formidable group that spread from central Europe to Asia Minor in the south and Britain in the north. They had inflicted on the Romans some bruising defeats, and when they themselves were beaten the Romans cherished their victories. Some of their gods had been respectfully assimilated by the Romans. Their artistic achievement, the La Tène culture, was outstanding outside the Mediterranean orbit. Caesar made some notes about them, with a lack of sympathy characteristic of, and probably necessary to, an efficient general. But even Caesar praised the courage of the Belgae, a branch of Celts in the north-east of France, and closely related to the enterprising warriors who frustrated his ambitions in Britain.

From other mentions of Celts in classical writings a cliché picture emerges. To the Roman, on Greek precedent, a non-Roman was a barbarian, with some, though not all, of that word's modern connotation. Thus the Celt was horrible to look at, held bloody human sacrifice, and had little to say. His hair was long and shaggy, and the sounds emitted when he did speak were nasal and jarring—the 'ba-ba's that gave rise to the Greek word barbarian. Yet even from Roman accounts the impression emerges of a people with formalised manners, a rigid hierarchy, complicated religion, and an interest in music and poetry. Till the Romans fought them back, and finally conquered them, they controlled the inner bulk of Europe; and at their European height—perhaps three or four centuries before Christ—they had planted vigorous colonies in Britain, Ireland and the Iberian peninsula.

To what extent the Celts made Ireland Irish is impossible to say. That Ireland had not been an inconspicuous stretch on the world's periphery is evident from both archaeology and early literature, though there is little else on which these two sources consistently agree. The stories and records of the seventh and following centuries draw a romantic, dramatic picture of the island's prehistory. They trace it to the immediate aftermath of the flood when Partholon, a survivor, and direct descendant of

8

Adam, arrived in the country to find a savage, uncouth population who quickly absorbed or destroyed him and his followers. Other waves followed till the arrival of the Tuatha de Danaan, a magical race from the east, who brought with them the archetypal mystical symbols of Indo-European myth: a stone that acclaimed with human voice the rightful accession of a new king; a spear that wielded itself in battle, bringing dire slaughter upon an enemy; a sword that needed no second blow; a cauldron with a never-failing supply of food—the universal cornucopia. Finally the Milesians arrived, at the time of Alexander the Great, and during their ascendancy the heroic age of Ireland began. They defeated the Tuatha in Meath, established the dynasties that survived well into the Christian age, and formed an aristocracy to which all Irishmen till the late Middle Ages liked to trace themselves. From them, in the early centuries A.D., the Ulster kings of Emain Macha traced direct descent, though genealogies could later change, with surprising alacrity, at a switch of dynastic fortunes.

Archaeology tells a different story, though time may reconcile the two versions with little suffering to either. More and more the themes of folklore are being explained, and no longer dismissed, by more palpable discoveries. A short while ago writers—often Irish clerics of an independent turn of mind—delighted to trace the common ancestry of ancient Irish priests and Old Testament prophets, deducing from their theories a special sanctity in the nations of the north-west. Historicism first swept the fancies away. Then more discriminating methods, shorn of nationalism, began to point to similar links, deriving them from tangible remains and the apparent movements of races. Structures and motifs of Mycenean remains in Crete or Greece appeared to share features with the giant funeral cairns in the antiquary's treasure-ground between the Boyne and the Liffey. Irish artifacts of the early Bronze Age turned up in the Middle East, and oriental daggers, and beads of glass and faience, were unearthed in Ireland. From her far-flung connections and her innate wealth and technical skills—the production and design of gold and bronze and jewellery—it

9

emerged that Ireland was a focal point of trade in northern Europe a thousand years before the birth of Christ. How far developed were her connections in ideas and religion can never be known. It is plausible, at least, to claim that they existed.

Trade was carried on between the south and eastern kingdoms of Ireland and Britain, Gaul and Spain. But the Irish Celts, the Gaels, in general approved of the geographical isolation of their new home. Away from the commotions of Europe, they started insular commotions for themselves. They created the heroic age of Ireland, keeping alive the traditions they had brought with them. Kings fought kings, stole wives, massacred herds and flocks. War flared chiefly on issues of livestock, of which the rustling of cows was the general pretext for a call to arms. In the later classification of the heroic themes of poetry, cattle-raids were given equal weight to visions, love-tales, and adventurous journeys over the seas.

Life was lived in the confines of a rigid society, a hybrid of Celtic and earlier Irish conventions that had no exact parallel in continental civilisations. Within each village, or tuath, the king held complete authority. He was advised by the warrior aristocracy around him on points of policy, and by the Druids whose influence was reinforced by the attention paid to coronation and other rituals. Below this composite aristocracy was the large group of bards, scribes, genealogists (of exceptional importance), jurists, artists, historians and skilful craftsmen. Their position was not inherited, though there was a growing tendency for it to be confined to certain families. The class of freemen came next, sometimes owning land themselves but always dependent for their welfare on an aristocrat. They supervised the running of land, served in armies and paid a tithe to the king. Between them and the slaves there was often no clear demarcation; status depended on the indulgence of the nobility. But slaves there were, and there were still slaves when Christianity was brought to the country early in the fifth century. For, once established, the structure of Irish society changed little before the sixteenth century, when Cromwell's troops smashed the fabric of an ancient civilisation.

*   *   *   *

So Ireland and the Roman Empire, if the two can be mentioned in a breath, followed their separate courses, each indifferent to the other. Three centuries after Agricola's appraisal the outer coating of each, while covering the body still, was worn and frayed. Disease had grown inside and the climate was bringing changes. Ireland, a modest region on the world's periphery, having nowhere to topple from, could only gain by change. The superstructure of empire had all the way to fall. To some extent both processes were brought about by the same cause. During the first four centuries of the Christian era the future of Ireland was being decided in Europe and the Middle East.

Until well into the Christian era the eastern Mediterranean went on providing the world with philosophies, cerebral wrangles, and logical nuts to crack. After the theologies of Egypt, Assyria and Persia came the refreshing enlightenment of the Greeks, with its inquiry, originality, lightness of touch and spirited argument. Christianity followed, and for several centuries its heady aftermath continued to flow to the west in the form of heresies, reformations, blasphemies and counter-reforms. The countries of the eastern Mediterranean were always a powerhouse of mental invention and contortion.

To the Byzantine, Rome, though important, did not seem so decisively important as it did to the West; rather it was a place to which the cultural axis swung for a while only to return, fight again for its existence, and perpetuate itself in many minor and two major philosophical traditions, the Orthodox Church and Islam. Nevertheless it was Rome which during this period catered for the cultural needs of northern Europe and the Atlantic seaboard. Most of the originality of the Levant was distributed to western Europe marked with the heavy stamp of Roman system.

One of the Empire's great legacies to Europe was, as a result, a hybrid culture comprising the inspiration of the Greeks and the method of the Romans. Another paired the Roman system with the new religion of Christianity. In the process, naturally, both Greek and Christian philosophies were somewhat diluted. All the same their Roman foundation ensured them a more permanent strength in the West than in any other part of the world.

The lasting quality that Rome added is best described as an intellectual discipline, a system of logic, a kind of mental code of laws—arbitrary perhaps to unattached philosophers, but of a superb and enduring practical value. Greek and Judaic ideas, percolating west from Byzantium, Antioch or Alexandria, were moulded into a compact, comprehensible shape by the outstanding minds of the West. Some of the oriental cults from Syria and Persia, comprising mysteries and irrational concepts of the world and existence, attracted and diverted the Romans for a while. But, since they could never conform to the Roman mental discipline they died, after a space, a western death. Christianity was unlike these. Even in the East it was peculiar, based on the tradition of a race which had kept itself surprisingly secluded from the hotbed of peoples and ideas around it. In the words of Jesus there was indeed mysticism and paradox enough to keep the East in ferment for hundreds of years. The important point, though, was that the problems were expressible in words, and not only in strange symbols and occult ritual. When the minds of the West took Christianity to themselves they found logic and system to satisfy their Roman outlook, and an optional overlay of mystery to keep them interested and respectful.

To most modern western minds, still willy-nilly in the confines of Roman discipline, the first argumentative centuries of Christianity are difficult to understand. That heresies could be based on such apparently casuistic tidbits as they were, and that they could cause wars and alienation, affronts our common, or Latin, sense. The answer lies again in the East. Whether Christ had one or two natures, whether he was one or two persons, whether Mary was the mother of Christ the God as well as Christ the man, or only of one, or the other—wrangles of the sort were the daily fare of a region which had produced more sects and cults than modern America. The preoccupation was not the concern of any one class. Buying bread in Alexandria might involve a traveller in prolonged discussion on Monophysitism with the baker.

Among the educated such disputes were often the expression of differences in current scientific and philosophical thought. They were of first importance, and naturally took on the dimensions of political issues, to which they were often linked.

Rome, once she had accepted the framework of Christianity, could not reject out of hand the subsequent servicing offered from the East. She had to absorb the new objections or counter them. In different cases she did both, and she was fortunate in having minds equal to the challenge. The important condition was that things that were accepted should be adapted to the system. And as time went on this process of adaptation built up an unprecedented central religious authority, a parallel to the centralised civil government which it succeeded.

It was of course the need for universal government that had developed the Romans' universal system, and the government itself followed from the military skill which brought them an empire. In the later imperial period, after the emperors had moved to Byzantium, they found it necessary to keep Christianity under their thumbs as a support of civil authority. In Italy the Church was more independent, so that there were frequent wide gulfs between the religion of Rome and Constantinople. But if the bishops of Constantinople were tied to politics, those of Rome were confined by the heritage of an organised framework throughout the western world. As the threats to that world grew, the need for conformity grew. God and Caesar were never quite incompatible. Even while the Visigoths were drinking victors' draughts after their sack of Rome in 410, Augustine, the greatest Christian thinker since Paul, was vindicating the policy of a Christian state in his *City of God*. And because of this authority, and its awesome reputation, the Europe that emerged two centuries later from the great movements of races known as the barbarian invasions was still technically Christian, owing allegiance to newcomers who had assumed, and not destroyed, the institutions they had found.

Nevertheless there were Christians who could not square their beliefs with the priorities of a vast and ordered society. Some would say they were the kernel of the religion's adherents—men who looked for personal perfection and renounced material things without regard to comfort, family, town or state. While the body of the Church took on the structure of the empire it served, a scattered class was resisting the alliance of mundane and spiritual forces. It was a class with notable forbears. They were the ascetics, who turned to practice their belief that a Christian life neither was nor should be anything but an interval of tears. 'If any man would come after me, let him deny himself and take up his cross and follow me', Christ himself had said; and again, with insistence: 'If any man come to me and hate not his father, and mother, and wife, and children, and brethren, and sisters, yea, and his own life also, he cannot be my disciple.'

In the early centuries, because of the hostility of the world, Christian asceticism had taken a violent form. Those who left all to follow Christ openly professed their religion and died as martyrs. Martyrdom had been the ideal, it was praised in prayer and poem, and admired as the supreme offering by those Christians who shrank from it. In a worldly sense it had fulfilled a purpose, helping to establish Christianity as the religion of the empire. By the fourth century the enemy was no longer persecution. It had become official apathy and universal materialism. So ascetics turned their backs on all the practices and pleasures of the world, took to secluded places, and came as near to God as mortal life would allow them to be. Hermits were the antithesis of imperial citizens. Their aim of life was to train the mind and body for the exclusive adoration of God in the world to come. And while much of their following was due to the filth, turmoil and dangers of city life, with devotees preferring the quiet, if frugal security of the desert, their real attitude was rooted in convictions about the distracting uselessness of the world. That the sands of Sinai were no less the world than God's creatures bursting the city seams is a thought that was understandably overlooked.

Two traditions began in Sinai. The first grew only on the strength of example, the second built its own structure for survival. Antony of Egypt, when he took to the desert for prayer and self-discipline, wanted to be alone. He ate bread and salt, and drank a little water, and examined his soul during intervals from praying and reciting psalms. 'I kill my body, for it kills me,' said one of his successors.[1] Antony, and most of all the later Simeon Stylites whose aerial penance was denounced by Gibbon, have provided easy material for the acid pens of those historians who applaud the social life. What Lecky called 'a long routine of useless and atrocious self-torture' was indicted as denying all the virtues of friendship and family and social obligation, and serving absolutely no civilised purpose. But the hermits made no claim of material usefulness, and like most extremists they had chapter and verse to justify their attitude. To them the social world was simply such a sinful and corrupt place that any involvement in it was sinful and corrupting. Moreover Gibbon and Lecky chose as their examples the most obviously repulsive hermitic stories from the mass of accounts that have come down. While Simeon became a scabrous sight for prurient tourists, Antony preserved an agile mind that could be useful, in his old age, in theological disputes, and a fit body that carried him through to the age of a hundred and five. 'It is forgotten', wrote Helen Waddell, 'that inhumanity to oneself had often its counterpart in an almost divine humanity towards one's neighbour. . . . The Desert has bred fanaticism and frenzy and fear; but it has also bred heroic gentleness.'[2]

Moreover the hermits added to their discipline and austerity a quiet humour and an awareness of nature that correct the impression, more often handed down, of emaciated fanatics. The hermit Pior always ate walking about, and, asked the reason, said 'I wish not to regard my eating as a serious occupation, but as a superfluity,' a sentiment worthy of a Roman Stoic. Pambos, an illiterate, left his retirement to hear a teacher discourse on the psalms. The teacher began with a text, the thirty-ninth Psalm; but after the first line—'I said, I will take heed unto my ways, that I offend not with my tongue'—Pambos was away. Asked why he left, he replied that he would practice that first lesson before going on with the next; and he had not returned twenty years later because his tongue still occasionally let him down.[3]

Whatever the merits or demerits of the hermit life, it led to a second movement which caught popular fancy and thrives to this day. The desert had limits, and for some hermits solitude was unbearable. As a solution to both problems the monastery was devised, and people began to retire in groups. Company gave greater contentment, and at the same time opportunity for practising Christian virtues towards others. Where the first movement had inspired mainly admiration, the second brought recruits in thousands. Five thousand settled on the desert between Cairo and Alexandria alone, many more in Sinai. These camps had no official status in the Church, but a need was soon felt for codified discipline. So monastic rules were drawn up, the first by Pachomius, a later one by Basil. Basil's less stringent code is still followed in most Greek communities. Again the ordered historians of the eighteenth century have jibbed. To them the monasteries, though a step higher than hermit isolation, had no place in any economic, cultural or social system; and being historians of the Roman heritage they placed system above all. On any chart of the imperial organisation a monastery could only be marked as a cul-de-sac, the end of a social road. Except, that is, where the errors of monastics produced monastic children who went back into the world, and on such deviations the historians alighted with relish. But again those who went into obscurity renounced any obligation to system. They had learned to hate the cramping confinement of dirty and demoralised cities, whose inhabitants were pawns for leaders to feed and play in political games.

The movement spread through the Middle East, and as quickly it came to Europe. It was introduced by missions and by western pilgrims returning from the Holy Places. Athanasius, born in Alexandria and forced from it in the middle fourth century by one of the politico-religious shifts that made partisan life precarious, brought to Rome the ideas that Antony and Pachomius had made reality among the plains of the Thebaid. Athanasius had known Antony as a friend. It has been said of his *Life of St Antony* that 'no book has had a more stultifying effect on Egypt, Western Asia, and Europe'. [4] Credit is given to him for introducing monasticism into the west, but there was so much ideological traffic in this direction that it is hard to single out one man for the distinction. He was certainly followed soon by others, and before the end of the century Jerome and John Cassian had breathed vigorous life into the new practices in the west. Jerome, an Italian, had grown up with the resolute aim of living as a hermit. Near his home in Aquileia he began with friends a community of ascetics before setting off for eastern deserts. His success, at least his reputation, can be judged from his popularity among Renaissance painters, who often used him, a lion, a desk, a scroll and other scholarly properties in a bleak and sandy scrub to depict their image of the old ascetic spirit. But his spell in the Syrian desert lasted only five years and he was tortured always by pain, loneliness, and memories of Rome, Aquileia, and—in his own words—of 'maidens in their dances'. At last he returned to Rome and became the Pope's secretary. He preached and wrote of the virtues of asceticism, and thundered and blustered to the end of his days. The *Vulgate* and translations from Hebrew into Latin were his most enduring memorials, but he helped to establish the creed of the eremite in Italy, and so all over Europe.

News of the monastic life was the immediate cause of Augustine's conversion, and he spent what time he could in seclusion for the rest of his life. It spread up through Italy, and into Gaul, where among many others Martin of Tours and Honoratus of Lérins gave it powerful impetus. We read of people founding monasteries by the ten, sometimes by the hundred, and when we consider the simple recipe the numbers are not so surprising. Everywhere people were tired of the repressions, threats and deprivations caused by remote governments and remoter wars. Throwing up the few advantages of city life they took to the security of a religious community. Individual abbots made rules, which were sometimes adhered to and quite often not; some monasteries became lively centres of learning, some took on the duties of social service. There was no central authority, no unified aim, and the story of each community is different from that of others.

Recruits arrived in hundreds. Gallic monasteries became

17

famous for their proselytising and their scholarship, and for the sturdy individuals who ruled them. St Martin brought monasticism to Tours after a youth spent in Dalmatia and Italy. He travelled by any available means—foot, water, donkey—to bring his message to the remotest parts of north-west Gaul, and people crowded to hear him. He made a name by his miracles and his temper. He smashed heathen idols and withstood and reproved marauding chieftains. After his death a cult attached to him, and he was one of the first Christians to be canonised without martyrdom. After Martin others developed what amounted to a fashion for the communal life. John Cassian brought his rule direct from Bethlehem and Egypt to the two monasteries he founded at Marseilles, and his writings influenced most medieval monastic theories. Honoratus of Arles built the monastery of Lérins that spread its arms over the Continent and the British Isles. Germanus of Auxerre, Hilary of Arles, Eucherius of Lyons, Lupus of Troyes were other pioneers in the overspill of the ascetic tradition in this new western environment.

Quite often the theme of the monastery was simply escape. There was reason enough for this, for the fifth century, when the movement took root in Europe, opened on a changed continent. New peoples were coming in from the east, pressed by expanding Huns in the south Russian steppes, and able to overrun the weakened defences of the Empire. Not that the invaders comprised the flood they are often supposed to have done, nor that the Empire was incapable of shrewd and forceful resistance and absorption. The last hundred years had seen a firm recovery from a period of decline and anarchy that went before, and in some cases even an expansion of the western borders. But the army had never lost its power over the civil authority since Septimius Severus put into force his dictum 'Enrich the soldiers and scorn the rest'. While the army gained in power it changed in character. Recruits came largely from border tribes, Germanic peoples who took a pride in the Empire but never quite lost sympathy with their close relatives over the border. When those relatives rose to march, jostled by tribes to the east, they found less ruthless opposition than a strictly Roman army might have given them. Besides, the Germans within the borders were providing some of the highest officers of the Empire. One of them, Stilicho, by the division of his loyalties allowed the advance of Alaric and the Visigoths till it was impossible to keep them from Rome itself.

Up till this time the population of much of north-west Europe —Gaul, Britain and parts of Spain—still comprised the Celts who had swept across from the East in the last great immigration, a thousand years before. The Rhine border divided them from Germanic tribes outside, and when these tribes managed to cross over to the west, they were absorbed without difficulty into the Empire as federated groups. In most cases this was what they wanted. Generations beyond the border, glimpsing the order and benefits of the Empire, had made their prime aim to partake in and not destroy that order. But now a great unsettlement, tracing its source across the Russian plains to China, and equal to the concentrated force that originally brought the Celts to Europe, pressed these fringe tribes on. Increased population, perhaps unusually expansive leaders—the reasons are not known —turned the nomadic Huns into a whiplash of migration. From the Rhine to the Danube the Germans were forced to press on. Visigoths harried the eastern Empire, then passed along and swept into Italy. Vandals desolated France and Spain. Franks moved into north-east France, Allemanni took over Bavaria, Burgundians occupied the region that still holds their name. Their practice was to loot, then treat. Rome fell to the Visigoth Alaric in 410, but he was soon enrolled on the Roman side and sent to deal with the Vandals in Spain. By superb diplomacy the Roman court played off tribe against tribe, helped always by the respect for Rome felt by all invaders. By the middle fifth century, when the Huns themselves appeared on the scene threatening final chaos, the new races had been sufficiently assimilated to drive them back in a swift, harsh campaign. But troubles were not over. From North Africa, where the Vandals had set up an independent dominion and disrupted Italy's corn supply, came an invasion by sea and another sack of Rome.

After a fashion, the West recovered; but the real empire was in the east, where an appearance of unity remained after the hundred years of sabotage. In the sixth century Justinian was even to recover Italy for a while, through the patient skill of his general Belisarius. But fundamentally West and East had long been separated. Lip-service and conventions were maintained, but they often covered rifts and at times aggression. From now on the West was left to its own devices, and the West was an uneasy mixture of many parts. Ravenna was yet to see its age of splendour, but even that was a glory cut off from the realities of Italy. Catholic authority centred on Rome, the court on Ravenna. But power and influence came north, and settled jerkily on the Frankish tribes who had appropriated Gaul. They grew in strength, and when the concept of Europe again became a reality it was built around their successors. The barbarian raids changed the face of Europe.

The fifth century warped the religious pattern of Europe out of recognition. Italy, and those races which came under Rome's civil jurisdiction, were still ostensibly Catholic. Some of the barbarians, and especially those in the north whose contact with Rome and Byzantium was minimal, remained pagan. The rest had adopted the heresy known as Arianism. Not that a Teuton free-man-warrior would have argued for long or with conviction against the divinity of Christ. Heresy, like orthodoxy, was used primarily as a political weapon. Nevertheless Arianism had become the Christianity of the barbarians. In the early fourth century an eastern priest had gone out to teach a tailored version of the scriptures to the Goths. Christ, they were told, was not God by nature—only by virtue of God's award after his impeccable life. He was a sort of demigod, a designation they could understand. Mary had no miraculous sanctity, for she had not given birth to a god; that they could understand too, and liked better than other explanations. The idea meant more to them than Catholic teaching and it spread, and moved forward with their movements across the west of Europe.

In Gaul, the Franks themselves were heathen, but tolerant of

Christianity. After their first incursions, when the world seemed to be tottering, Catholics and Roman officials alike came out of hiding to find they could resume their lives under a different leadership. Catholic, Arian and heathen confronted each other in every town and village. In parts there were persecutions of Catholics, but neither Arian nor heathen appears to have been over-zealous. Their main concern was to find land to live on, and if those they deprived still held to their faith it was, in two senses, immaterial.

The currency of Christianity, however, became highly inflated. Amid all the turmoil the Catholics found, in the presence of their new conquerors, a valuable ticket to survival. Up till now the barbarians had lived on plunder, sailing across the Rhine for fresh food, cattle, gold and slaves. The way of life implied vulnerable neighbours, which the weakened Empire had provided. Now, with the sea on two sides and tough tribes on the other two, the Franks had to settle for a self-sufficient economy. There to instruct them were the Catholics, whose organisation had been parallel to the Roman civil structure and was thus ideally suited as a model. Priests and bishops instructed in the ways of administration and civilised behaviour, and they took every opportunity to convert their pupils. As the fifth century advanced the Catholic authority did not diminish. Its subtler spokesmen could easily outwit the apologists of Arianism, and they continued to play an important part in politics. While the German tribes still maintained their structure, based on the loyalties of kinship and the leadership of a tribal chief, the Catholics were better able than anyone to handle the diplomacy necessary to international bargaining. So that in the second half of the century the Gallic chief Syagrius, for all practical purposes an independent ruler, took pride in the title Rex Romanorum, though in the Empire it would have been a meaningless label. And, until the time of Clovis, the Franks remained officially a federated ally of Rome.

In 482 Clovis succeeded as king of the Franks. His territory was still small, corresponding roughly with modern Belgium. He had visions of empire, and before his death he had realised them, using a combination of military skill, daring, subterfuge, deceit, alliance, marriage and murder in the process. On his accession, France north of the Loire was held by the Gaul Syagrius; Aquitaine, the southern French coast and most of Spain belonged to Visigoths; the Alemanni spanned the upper reaches of the Rhine and the Burgundians held Burgundy. Clovis quickly took northern France for himself. He married a Burgundian princess, a Catholic, who tried to convert him. At first he saw nothing to gain; then decided his soul could buy a kingdom. After expedient bargaining with the Catholic hierarchy, he brought himself and his Salian Franks under the papal mantle. Baptism worked, and he promptly trounced the Visigoths. At the end of his reign only the Burgundians and a Visigothic remnant on the south coast remained free of the Franks in France; and twenty years later Burgundy too had been won. From then on France's problems were internal ones.

Outside the monasteries Christianity had turned political and lost meaning. Now the monasteries themselves were in danger. Their traffic with the east, the source of their ideas and progress, was being interrupted. For one result of all the movements of the fifth century was to close effectively the imperial routes of old Rome. More important, the monks were living in a time and space which could less afford the social luxury of unproductive recluses than the age of Roman dominion.

New boundaries stretched across the main highways. Everywhere the conquerors were too busy sorting their local affairs to bother with roads that had been imperial arteries. On the Mediterranean, Vandal dominion in North Africa had made sailing a dangerous occupation. Pirates were plentiful, and the East too was preoccupied with her own problems. Trade never entirely dried up, but it was riskier now, and the free flow of ideas that had accompanied it was all but choked. Christianity had always been refreshed by the originality of Eastern thought, and now it was left to its own devices. As an administrative body it flourished under the new régimes. But as a spiritual force it counted for less and less. The monastic movement lost its energies, sinking into the torpor of materialism which was the fashion of the times. Abbots became the hirelings of ruffian chiefs, or, grown rich through threats and specious promises, took on the trappings and ethics of chiefs themselves. Monks of integrity went away, to die as solitaries or to emigrate north.

In only one remote corner of the western world did Christians have the time and freedom to develop and mature the creed. The corner was Ireland, happily uninvolved with all these continental machinations, though never entirely cut off from them. It was only lately that anyone in Ireland had been much interested in such connections. The interest was not sparked from within, where there was considerable vested opposition to immigrant ideas. It came in part from Gallic refugees, arrived to build a Christian world beyond the borders of a decadent empire. And in part it came from Britain, which curls round the east coast of Ireland like a mother nursing her child. To the great annoyance of the Irish, Britain has often tried to fulfil her geographical role. To their greater annoyance she has sometimes succeeded.

*   *   *   *

Britain had turned Christian two hundred years before, accepting the decision of Constantine as she had acquiesced in most other orders, benefits and demands of her Roman overlords. There are many tales of Christianity arriving before this date, some claiming an apostolic foundation for the British Church, others—Bede among them—reporting that a British king, Lucius, was baptised at his own request in the second century, and that his example was followed by his people. Bede's early history is an unreliable patchwork, and it is certain that whatever Christians were in the country before Constantine's Edict of Milan they were not favoured by authority. At the opening of the fourth century St Alban stood in for an outlawed priest, refusing to offer prayer and sacrifice to the official gods of Rome. He was beheaded beside a Hertfordshire river, having first, in the manner of Moses, caused its waters to halt, to allow the execution party across.

Then came the official imperial adoption of Christianity, and for a hundred years after Alban's martyrdom Britain played a part in the development of European religion. British bishops attended and contributed to councils held in Gaul, even in Asia Minor. They sent missions to try to convert the pestering Picts, and they successfully evangelised some Celtic tribes in Wales. Through the barbarian movements on the Continent the Arian heresy arrived in Britain, and earned a popularity that worried the Catholic establishment. Then at the end of the fourth century a Briton, claimed Irish by those Irish who venerate thundery eccentrics, began an influential heresy of his own. As the doctrines of Pelagius spread he was to attract the attention of the greatest Western thinkers. 'That great mountain-dog through whom the devil barks' was Jerome's description of him, and most of the leading clerics of the day agreed. A revealing comment came from Prosper of Aquitaine, who linked his colourful indictment of this 'slandering serpent' with a slur on the country that gave him birth—the only country, says Prosper, capable of doing so.

Britain, a risky though prosperous colony throughout the Roman occupation, was certainly held low at the time. Twice soldiers stationed there had been proclaimed emperor by their troops, and set out to realise their claim. Neither succeeded, though one did great damage during the attempt, and Britain was getting a name for sedition. Britain was expensive to keep up, for plundering tribes of Picts, Welsh and Irish demanded numerous and well-equipped garrisons. Pelagius had not helped the country's reputation. He denied original sin, and claimed that Adam would have died whether he succumbed to the devil or not. He took his beliefs to Rome and gathered a strong body of supporters. Several missions had to come from Gaul to Britain to wipe out traces of him there. Germanus of Auxerre led one, and another some years later. They appear to have done their work thoroughly, and fifty years later orthodoxy was re-established. But Pelagius showed two things clearly: that in the remoter reaches of the Empire new ideas could be strongly planted; and that even in those times there was a wide streak of pragmatism in the intellectual life of the islands. In the uncharted seas of Protestantism, Pelagianism seems a very natural current.

By this time the Roman influence was ebbing. The barbarians caused regiments to be withdrawn to prop the weakening borders. Then the borders fell and Rome herself was overrun in 410. The western Emperor wrote from Ravenna that the British must see to their own defences; and though he had every intention of re-occupying the country, his chance never came. Irish raiders continually looted points on the west coast, and there were settlements of Irish in both Wales and Scotland which marauded on their own behalf. The Picts now found unmanned Hadrian's Wall no obstacle, and made life in northern England precarious. There were rebellions against romanised families who now had no buttress to their former privileges. And worst of all, there were the Saxon raids, which had continued in a small way for over a century but now broke into flood. A legend tells that a British chief, Vortigern, called in the Saxons to help fight the native risers, and so began the Anglo-Saxon occupation. It is an archetypal story of unwitting treachery leading to the death of a nation. In Ireland a chief similarly invited the Anglo-Normans to settle an Irish quarrel, and his name is still cursed. Whatever the causes, the Anglo-Saxons came, and during the next two hundred years pushed their way across the country. In the late fifth century there was some efficient resistance in the south and south-west. When all appeals to Rome went unanswered the British at last found a leader in a Roman-trained Briton, Ambrosius Aurelianus. He checked the Germanic advance in the Dorset region, and revived British morale. From this swing of fortune emerged another leader, who entrenched the British position for fifty years or more by his victory at the Battle of Mount Badon— possibly in Dorset, or farther north near Swindon. Arthur is the most shadowy and inspiring British figure of the time. History tells us nothing of him, while later legend raised his achievements to a global, even a godly, scale, as it did those of Charlemagne and Theodoric. All we know is that he checked the tide, temporarily.

Unlike the Romans, the Saxons had no need of tact in subduing a people. It was want of space that brought them, and they had no intention of allowing native life to continue uninterrupted. The result was mass migration to the west. To the west went the upper classes of the old society, and most of the middle group, the traders and bureaucrats. Latin went, and the Roman way of government, and the craftsmen and writers and artists. Christianity too was swept back in favour of Odin, Thor, Woden and Frig. All these civilised traditions went beyond the line of Arthur's watershed to Cornwall, Wales, Cumberland and the north. The Britons had been pushed to the edge of Europe, the mountain ridge where sheep survive better than cattle, and the climate is harsher. Some took to the sea, many arriving in Brittany to bolster that anomalous, unconquered refuge of Celts. In Wales Christianity settled more firmly than elsewhere. A powerful monastic tradition began, born among the communities of France and so owing its existence to the Sinai foundations. From Wales it spread west, in the direction of refugees.

So Christianity penetrated to Ireland. It came across the sea from Gaul, and across the narrower channel from Wales. It was not a predestined trip. No anchorite in the desert could have imagined his image and example travelling over land and sea, through the wavy plains of desert and the foetid stalls of Alexandria, across the Mediterranean in vulnerable ships that stopped sailing in October because of winter squalls, through marbled complacent Rome and the crushed and clamorous markets of Marseilles, across the terraced vineyards of Provence and the Massif, down to the starker, colder plains of northern France and finally into the foggy unknown of the English channel—to ignite, after four thousand miles, an isolated culture set in the northern seas. No one could have imagined it, but so it happened.

Ireland had a barbarous reputation, but sometimes small disorderly states are washed up on the beach of history, to sparkle for a while till the myriad bubbles of foam burst or evaporate. Now it was Ireland's turn to shine so, as, far away and simultaneously, the receding waves of other civilisations gave an hour of glory to Ethiopia, and to Japan. Europe was convulsed in the waves, but she had—casually enough—given Ireland thoughts and people that were to help her through her task. These influences worked on a strange and old civilisation, and produced a strange and vigorous reaction. Ireland began to expand along three paths. The first led to the province of imagination, with officious St Brendan guiding his obedient monks towards the land of Promise. The second was more real—across to the rugged landscape of north Britain, with hardy St Columba founding his mission posts along the west of the Highlands. The third took the Irish to a Europe fraught with the aftermath of invasion. It was to Europe that St Columbanus was to carry his unwavering belief that he and Ireland could put a continent's troubles to rights.

II

Pagan Ireland

Brendan, Columba and Columbanus were born into a country left far behind by Romanised Europe.

Writing was not known in Ireland till the sixth century. There was a form of script before then—the ogham alphabet, which corresponded to Roman letters but was marked in horizontal and diagonal lines—but it was too clumsy for continuous texts and only used on memorials and inscriptions. Strictly, Ireland before that century was in its prehistoric period.

When they colonised the country, however, before the time of Christ, the Celts had been at a comparatively advanced state of civilisation. Their pantheon was as elaborate as that of the Romans, and the powers and vagaries of individual gods as diverse and unpredictable. For an unlettered people, they were mature in other aspects of their culture. Surviving artifacts indicate their skill and ingenuity, and the comforts they enjoyed. Their art was lively and decorative. Each community was divided according to an elaborate social scale. That they did not write seems to point to a positive rejection of writing, for they were certainly in contact with races that did, and showed in other spheres that they were willing to absorb what was useful to them. The idea of rejection gains support from our almost total ignorance of the ways and beliefs of Druids, the leaders in their various cults, and important advisers of the kings of tribes. Everything seems to point to the fact that the Druids, to preserve their isolated privileges, resisted the introduction of writing. Their lore was passed by word of mouth, and learned through long years of training. It was secret to those outside the order. Writing would have led to leaks.

Myth and legend were also a class's exclusive preserve. The *filid*, or bards, kept alive the ancient stories of the race, dramatised new events, and entertained the courts with their long, stylised narratives. The tradition lapsed only a few hundred years ago— even continued, in a debased form, to this century. Certainly it was strong when the monasteries rose up with their thirst for all knowledge and culture, and monks began to write down the old poems and sagas. Because the old Celtic religion was not such a formidable enemy as the paganism on the Continent, the monks had no fear or horror of old heathen sagas. They garnished them with Christian extras, sometimes substituted a Christian theme, but never tried to eradicate completely what they had inherited. So that our knowledge of prehistory is greatly enhanced by the survival of tales which often incorporate the fortunes of the race. Though it is necessary to extract the interpolated Christian elements.

Even then we may not arrive at the facts. The sagas were aimed at the aristocrats of the day, not at posterity; and to a large extent they told those kings and courts what they wanted to know. We may find out what sort of thing they enjoyed hearing, but whether this tallies with the actual doings of their ancestors is another matter. Archaeology can help a little in confirming or rejecting the stories of the bards, but it goes to such an opposite extreme from romances—all pots and pans and tombs and earthworks— that it may give quite as distorted a picture. It may tell as much as one unspoilt, unpeopled Woolworth's and a preserved crematorium would tell future generations, standing alone amidst the rubble of the twentieth century; a little but not much. The truth must emerge probably half-way between myth and potsherd; and from this median we must look for a moment at the antecedents of Christian Ireland.

The Celts had arrived during Ireland's Bronze Age. They brought the use of iron and other metals, and they admired the way of life of heroes. They were tall and fair, and the race they conquered was short and dark. They imposed their language (the modern version of which the Irish government is trying to restore) and their art and law, and where possible they enslaved the local population. But they found an old and not negligible culture in the country. Over a thousand years before, when the Minoan civilisation of Crete and Mycenae was at its height, there had been a less glorious parallel in the British Isles and Brittany, whose memorials include the megaliths of Stonehenge, Carrowmore, Carnac and the vast earthen sanctuaries of Newgrange, Dowth and Knowth, west of Drogheda in the Boyne valley. They were probably constructed by related peoples of Indo-European stock. And where Mycenae and the Cretan palace of Cnossos gave rise to much of the heroic myth of Greece, so the old neolithic and Bronze Age cultures of the North left their legacy of gods and epic heroes to the Celtic invaders.

The older inhabitants were not eliminated, nor even conquered at first throughout the island. There had been a trickle of Celtic, and other continental influence for hundreds of years before the main body arrived, and from this trickle the native population had learned the latest methods of defence, as well as ways of building and decorating. They managed to preserve themselves intact for hundreds of years in the north, and in the south-east. It is a mark of the high development of the earlier race that it is often hard to distinguish the achievement of the Celts from that of their predecessors. They included among their number many rich families, as can be seen from the remains of farms where a large variety of animal bones have been traced—cattle, pigs, sheep, deer as well as domestic dogs—and of brooches, pottery, and leather and cloth goods.

Neither in time nor space, therefore, was the Celtic immigration a suddenly effective *coup*. It was more an assimilation by the native race, and by the beginning of the Christian era the Celts had blended with the scene. From that time for a thousand years the political groupings in Ireland were more settled. One province succeeded another in the prestige of leadership. But the life and possessions and economy of each group—even each individual—hardly changed at all. If we knew more of early Irish history we might well find that the social scene on the eve of the Anglo-Norman invasions was one familiar and recognisable to men of the early Bronze Age. A continuity, unique in Europe, is the hallmark of early Irish history.

Courtly life

By the first century A.D. Ulster had become the most powerful
of the five existing kingdoms—the 'Five fifths of Ireland'. The
remains of the mound of Emain Macha evoke some of the
grandeur of the Ulster court in primitive times, the old tales more.
Half the riches of the early literature were composed around the
royal house of Ulster, and the names of its characters are among
the best remembered. There was Conchobar, the petulant king
raised from his grouses by the feasts and quarrels of his Red
Branch knights; and Maeve, his wife, who left him for the King of
Connaught, then plotted to steal the Brown Bull of Cooley from
the Ulster men, and so initiated the most colourful saga of the
whole collection. Cuchulain, young and brave, alone withstood
the Connaught forces, straddling a ford where, like Horatius or
the picked defenders of Thermopylae, he could take on his opponents one by one. The war ended—an incidental fact in a pic-
torial tapestry—and new dramas began. Deirdre, brought up to be
Conchobar's wife, shirked the dull prospect of duty and flew with
the three sons of Uisneach to Scotland. There the matter was
different; the growing awareness of beauty in a rugged land, sighs
for home, the pretty happiness of young love, till the four were
brought home, through a ruse, to be killed. Deirdre's lament
before she died breathes the doleful evocation of these early tales:

> Three heroes who were not good at homage,
> Their fall is cause of sorrow—
> Three sons of Cathba's daughter,
> Three props of the battle host of Cooley. . . .[1]

Knightly heroism, pageantry, love, risk, tragedy, and a per-
vasive flow of subdued humour were the fabled mark of the times.
It was apt that the arrangement of society was tightly feudal.
Kings themselves were the commanders of armies and the
ultimate arbiters of justice, their powers sanctioned at their
crowning by a symbolic marriage to the local earth goddess. The
king's palace was the centre for a baronial way of life; and hunting,
courtship, warring, feasting and story-telling were the ingredients
of an existence that caught the fancy of later Norman troubadours.

Pagan Ireland

Below the king were his nobles, the warrior aristocrats. Bound to him in strict allegiance, they were an extension of kingship. They lived off their vassals, and paid and maintained the privileged, but dependent, men of wit and learning. In return, genealogists dutifully traced their ancestors back, through the first Gaelic settlers, to Adam. The Brehons were their main administrative assistants, and in them rested the whole anomalously complex and particularised system of law.

Brehons and genealogists belonged to an accomplished class between aristocrats and freemen. As with middle classes of later days, their power lay in their brains. They made up the professions —the *aes dana*—and were sometimes picked, sometimes born to the vocation. They included poets, doctors, musicians, historians, clerics and story-tellers. For amusement and cerebration and the assurance of pedigree blood, kings and lords were in their debt. And the account was feudally honoured by prestige and privilege, life amid royal families, a broad authority, and a place far higher in the scale than those next beneath them, the freemen.

As in other societies the commoners, freemen owning small plots of land, with sometimes slaves as part of their farming equipment, were the bole of the feudal tree. Their labours were the sowing and harvesting of crops, the tending of livestock, winning or losing, in the ranks, wars against neighbours, and buttressing the king's finances with a tithe of such profit as they made. They were the vassals of noblemen, but with rights and standards that lifted them above slavery. Slaves were ciphers, without privilege or respect from the law, and so they continued to Anglo-Norman days. Freemen counted for something, their lives were guarded by religious sanctions, and they could count on all the generations of their families for the enforcement of redress or revenge. Crime was regarded as an affront to all four generations of the family—often as many as a hundred kinsmen.

This framework of society held together over the centuries, steeped in conservatism. At the core of its reaction were the Druids, the most enigmatic ingredient of all. The laws of Brehons have been preserved, copious and meticulous; the creed and aspirations of Druids, never set to paper, have eluded historians ever since. It is known that they arrived in Ireland with the earliest Celts, bringing a new religion which in time became fused with the old; and one measurable result of the Celtic immigration was to confuse the religious pattern of the island into a shape peculiar to itself.

Some of the sagas tell of battles between semi-divine heroes, and so symbolise the struggle between Celtic Druids and the Tuatha de Danaan, the race previously dominant. When a conquering race came with its own gods its members did not, as Christians or Muslims would, deny the existence of their enemies' gods; they would simply want their own to prevail, so reflecting their victory. If the struggle was protracted, celestial bargaining might go on, whereby some of the lesser gods gained a place in the newcomers' hierarchy. Rationalising the early myths, it is possible to see that the Celts eventually had to allow the old gods of the Tuatha to stay. Some were consigned to mounds and barrows that became associated with their cult. Their dominion extended only over the other world, hardly touching the issues of this life.

There they remained, occasionally allowing a visit from some king or hero of the world outside, spirits of darkness, and perhaps more to be feared than in their prime. They have lived on too, diminishing in size and influence, but real enough to the minds of many. They are the fairies, the little people of the earth, and their females the *banshee* still have the most malevolent powers. They inhabit the hillocks and streams and lakes to which they were originally consigned.

Others of them were adopted by the Druids, and stayed to influence the lives of men. Chief of these was the Dagda, the most accomplished god of all, a patron of everything. Gods were seldom specialised, as their Roman equivalents were. Dagda was the father of the gods, and beneficent provided he was appeased. He mated with territorial goddesses whose association was with a particular area, and produced heroes, or demi-gods, who exercised a special influence on that area. So Oengus was his son by Boann, the goddess of the River Boyne, and Oengus's palace was at Newgrange, from which he worked his spells. In Leinster the Dagda's spouse was the Morrigan, a horrid spectre whose lair was the region of Glendalough and to whom are attributed all misfortunes in the area. In Connaught he took the goddess Maeve (linked with the cattle-raiding queen, as Arthur, Brendan and other Celtic heroes are blended with regional gods), whose spirit is evoked in many names over the province, and buried—it has always been told—under forty thousand tons of chipped stone jutting from the flat summit of Knocknarea in Sligo.

*   *   *   *

It is impossible to draw a line between the old and new mythology, just as it is impossible to give a date before which Ireland was pre-Celtic and after Celtic. Outlines blur at the edges. Race itself becomes only a vague term when it is seen that most invasions are made by men arriving in large numbers in the land and taking, as part of the spoils of victory, the womenfolk of their victims, so evenly mixing the blood of their successors.

There can be nothing but speculation, then, over what the Druids brought and what they found. Their religion is inscrutable, the subject sometimes of fanatic speculation. At Caesar's time their headquarters was the Isle of Anglesey, and they were strong throughout Gaul, Britain and Ireland. Shortly before Agricola rejected the project of conquering Ireland they were banned in the empire, and their Anglesey stronghold was eradicated in a dramatic campaign by a Roman general. In Ireland they lived on, as mysterious perhaps to the inhabitants as they have proved to posterity. Their lore may have contained historic traditions of the race, and doctrines of life and the cosmos close to the similarly guarded teachings of Pythagoras. If they inherited the knowledge of their British predecessors their understanding of astronomy and mathematics was remarkable; for recent researches at Stonehenge and other megalithic sites have suggested that these are uncannily precise instruments for measuring heavenly movements. All that can be ascertained is that they awarded numinous power to number, riddle, and paradox; and that the oak tree and mistletoe played some part in their rituals. They had considerable powers over people, and are shown in different stories producing insanity or an enervating sleepiness in those who opposed them. Their rites are said to have included the sacrifice of war prisoners and some criminals.

The Ulster dynasty did not keep its lead long into the Christian era. The tale of the Brown Bull of Cooley and Cuchulain's solitary stand recorded an actual change in the political balance. By the end of the second century Conn Ced-Cathach had founded a dynasty with authority over the larger part of Meath and Connaught. His successors were to claim the overlordship of Ireland for a thousand years, and they grew in power as Ulster shrank. To their capital in Tara—now a bleak and dented hilltop twenty miles out of Dublin, once a sounding point for the musty nostalgia of Tom Moore's ballads—ruling families came from the whole island every three years for parleys, contests and banquets. Though the lords of Munster disputed the claim, the Tara king styled himself *Ard Ri,* High King of all Ireland; and since his land included the most fertile plains of the country—those of the east and west midlands—the title was more than a formality.

Cormac Mac Airt, Conn's grandson, brought Tara to its highest prestige. He built halls and schools for history, war and law, and roads spreading out across the country. He fought his neighbours to make a peace that suited him, and succeeded in quieting the country for forty years. But the hostilities broke out again in his son's reign, and Ireland resumed the sporadic bickering to which, for want of a common enemy, her inhabitants were generally given.

The ethic of the time, a century or so before Christianity began to seep in, comes through clearly from two works inspired by Cormac's reign. One is a ninth-century collection of aphorisms purporting to be 'The Wisdom of Cormac the Wise'.[2] If true, they give a rare glimpse at the period. Cormac is asked a variety of questions about life's values, and prefaces each answer with a confident 'Not hard to tell . . .'. Among the best things for a king are firmness without anger, keeping hostages in fetters, honouring poets, importing treasure from over the sea, and an abundance of wine and mead. Best for the good of the tribe is the meeting of nobles and questioning of the wise. The sweetest things include a paean after victory, praise when earned, a lady's invitation to her pillow. Worst for the body of a man: sleeping with a leg over the bed-rail, new ale, gazing at glowing embers, dry food, bog water and rising too early. The worst things he has ever heard are the groans of disease, and a womanish quarrel between two men.

His utmost rancour is reserved for women. 'Crabbed as companions,' he seethes, 'haughty when visited, lewd when neglected, silly in counsel, greedy of increase, steadfast in hate, viragos in strife, niggardly with food, quick to revile, eloquent of trifles, tedious in discussion . . . woe to him that humours them, better to crush than cherish them.' It may have been the interpolation of a ninth-century monk with neuroses of his own, for it goes ill with the remainder of the king's pagan common sense. And it hardly tallies with the other work describing Cormac's time.

The king's army, the Fianna or Fenians, was the most efficient the country had yet seen, and the first standing force of a High King. Around it grew a body of legend of which much has survived. It was the Finn Cycle that first attracted eighteenth-century romantics to Celtic myth, inducing the purple tales of gore and repentance abounding in James Macpherson's Ossianic apocrypha. Most of the original tales tell of heroism and the constancy of fine warriors, of doomed love and tragic divisions of loyalty. The poet's relish is in florid descriptions of the splendour of pageantry, and the rising tension of long combats, sustained by minute observations on scene and emotions and by a vital imagery. The effect is of all the jousting colour and the toned sensitivity of the courts of Aquitaine. And the characters of Finn MacCool, the ascetic, dedicated leader of the Fenians, of Dermot, his brotherly friend and an epitome of romantic valour, of Oisin, the kindly poet, possessing in Christian eyes the highest virtue to which paganism can aspire, and Grainne, Cormac's graceful daughter—these were the archetypes of heroic legend, and became models for many medieval myths, those of Wales and the Languedoc among them.

Niall of the Nine Hostages

Such legends, though, remove us from the facts, if not the spirit, of the time of Cormac. By the end of the third century he had imposed his rule over a third of Ireland and his influence over it all. To the south of his kingdom, the province of Munster, advancing fast through trade with Gaul and Spain, grew in wealth and power, and the palace of its kings commanded the height of the most imposing of old royal sites, the Rock of Cashel. But Meath was still in the ascendant, and late in the fourth century a new High King, Niall of the Nine Hostages, brought a new expansiveness into his line.

Niall was half-British by blood; his mother had been captured in a raid on Wales. During his reign, which covered the first quarter of the fifth century, Britain was becoming increasingly exposed to attack as the Roman legions withdrew to their continental problems. Niall took energetic advantage of the situation, and led several raids on the coast of Wales. Later Irish historians sent him much farther than the west coast of Britain. He was said to have crossed Gaul on an expedition to take Rome, and to have turned back at the Alps because of the pleas of a Roman mission sent to placate him. Nor was he, in executing this ambitious plan, without good Irish precedent. Rome, conqueror of Europe and the Mediterranean, lay more than once at the mercy of a Hibernian army. The explanation for these accounts probably lies in the well-founded traditions of Irish attacks on Romanised Britain, and in the fact that later Irish chroniclers, used to Britain being a country of Anglo-Saxons, confused the Roman element there with the real Rome. Niall was no Hannibal. His successes were limited to Britain, and in Wales, on one of his affrays, he received a mortal wound. Before that, in Ireland itself, he and his sons pushed the languishing kingdom of Ulster right back to the north-east of the country, to what are now Down and Antrim, adding central Ulster to their dominion under the name of Argialla. As a safeguard against rebellion the new territories were forced to provide hostages, and from these Niall took his name. Possibly in this campaign the Tara dynasty was subduing the last independent remnants of the pre-Celtic population, a race having strong ethnic ties with the Picts of Scotland. From the new conquerors sprang the dynasty which was once again to unite Ulster. Until the time of Queen Elizabeth the lords of Ulster were of the O'Neill family, and since with Niall we come for the first time into a period that can be fairly accurately recorded, their claims of ancestry were probably correct.

Two incidentals during Niall's reign were destined to have a profound effect on the future of Christianity in the British Isles. On one of his pirate expeditions, Niall brought back a boy named Patrick as a slave. Patrick's family were well-to-do under the Roman administration, and his new masters were boorish. He came to think he had a mission among them. Secondly the raids on Scotland that had been carried on for hundreds of years stepped up in intensity. Irish began to colonise the western islands and the mainland up to Dumbarton. Although they were effectively countered by British resistance, there seemed the possibility at one time of Niall including a wide strip of Britain in his kingdom. Thirty years after his death part of Scotland did come under Irish rule, when Fergus Mac Erc sailed over to set up the kingdom of the 'East Gael'—Argyll. The Irish brought their name with them; for they were known then, and for several centuries after, as the Scoti, or Scots. Ultimately the Roman name Caledonia was to give way to that of its colonisers; and the Irish in Ireland altogether dropped their old name.

After Niall the system of succession in Ireland, whereby authority passed to all the sons of a chief or king and not solely to the eldest, soon broke up such large kingdoms as were established. Connaught, traditionally linked with Meath, had by the fifth century fallen away from it, leaving the high kingship at Tara with dominion only over Meath. For a short while, after 463, Aillil Molt again joined the two thrones, but he was killed in battle twenty years later, and Connaught again was left to itself. So this period, at the level of royalty, continued the strife of previous generations, and the previous pattern of dynasties expanding, then cutting themselves off from their forebears, and so leaving as much of a political chequerboard as ever there was before. This was how it was when St Patrick arrived to—as the old annalists had it—convert the whole country in thirty years.

Christianity arrived and soon throve in this atmosphere of skirmish, chivalry, primeval valour and squalid brutality. It is hard at first to see why it should have done. It is hard to see why it so easily replaced the esoteric dominion of the Druids, whose authority pervaded every aspect of life and society. The answer must lie in two phenomena. One was the refined variety of the new religion that reached Ireland—the monastic form from Wales and Gaul. The other was—must have been—the character of the Irish. It was in the substance of this character that Christianity was to act as a fermenting yeast. Some of the traits enable us to see why this was possible.

For five hundred years the Irish had been left alone by the world outside, except for a trickle of contact through trade and buccaneering. In this isolation they had developed a high opinion of their own race which was, for most practical purposes, the only race in existence. They had frittered away energy and time on internal commotions, which seldom seem to have altered the state of things as much as the bloodshed would warrant. But they had left time, amid their fighting, for something that may be called racial introspection. It can be seen in the legends that they liked to tell each other, tales of supernatural heroism, of moral and religious dilemmas, of the deaths of lovers, and of such distinguished people that it is hard not to think of them as gods. The subjects of these stories were their ancestors, the stuff from whom they were bred. They developed, for their small size, a colossal national pride, in spite of their country being, on the European scene, of no significance at all.

The Irish had a bureaucrat's love of classification, well seen in the ordering of their stories. Every tale had to fit under one of the many headings available—Cattle-raids, Wooings, Feasts, Deaths or Massacres. And it always did fit, and observed the conventions of the class. This tidiness of division is seen in other ways, in a rigid adherence to protocol, and a great love of formulating things according to abstract codes and specially significant numbers. Of these, the number three had the most potent properties. It may have derived from Druid formulae. The story of Deirdre and the sons of Uisneach was one of the 'three sorrowful tales of Ireland' although there were hundreds more than three. Most beloved was the triad, an arrangement of three statements which summed up a thing or person or quality or mood, or simply linked otherwise incompatible things. Three false sisters were said to be 'perhaps', 'maybe' and 'I dare say': three timid brothers 'Hush', 'Stop', and 'Listen'. The three keys that unlock thoughts were drunkenness, trustfulness, love; and the three signs of a dandy were the track of his comb in his hair, the track of his teeth in his food, and the track of his stick behind him.[3] If there were paradox or pun in a triad, so much the better. They were close in spirit to the riddles of early English, and the Irish had their liking for riddles too.

Sometimes this mental neatness disconcerts, it is so finicky and often carried to absurd extremes. But the Irish were, before all things, paradoxical. As fixed in their character as pedantry was the contrary quality of rash, persistent adventurousness. It is shown in one of the classes of tale mentioned above—the Immrama, or voyage-tales. In these tales the Celtic imagination leaps into the western sea and travels miles across it to the Land of Youth, or the Plain of Pleasure. Here all is young and beautiful and rich and happy. Passionate desire takes a hero to it, sometimes carried by a lovely maiden on the back of her winged horse, sometimes in the swift boats of skin and wood, the curraghs, which fishermen still use in the west. Usually the hero is forced to return. Oisin the poet goes, full of love for the princess Niamh who carries him there. He stays what seems to him three years, but in reality it is three hundred, so quickly and delightfully does the time pass. When he returns Finn and the companions of his youth are all gone, and the country is peopled by a race that is mean and diminutive compared with the giant heroes of his day. Christianity has arrived, and he spends long hours with St Patrick arguing the merits of the pagan life.

Always the sea journey takes a hero past islands of great beauty and animals of amazing talent. For the Irish, neither armies nor immigrants ever arrived from the west, as they did from other directions. The sea was a misty bleakness, but when the sun split the cloud there were rainbows and the frothy caps of waves and deep blue water stretching away into the infinite. They peopled this unknown eternity with characters of their imagination, and the idea of an earthly paradise to the west lived on into Christian times.

These apparently contrary qualities, the practicality and the dreams, were deeply embedded in their character. To some extent they enabled Christianity to take root in the country. For the glories of God's kingdom were to be achieved through an ascetic strictness—an obedience to precise rules—rare on the Continent; yet the journey was fringed with unimaginable beauty and poetic delights. It is a polarity which lies behind the energy, endurance and persistent humour that pervades the character of archetypal Irish Christians.

If the success of Christianity was helped by the nature of the Irish, it benefited no less from the form in which it reached Ireland. The monastic variety of the religion was quite different from the hierarchical, diocesan structure of the established Roman church. It kept more of the simple, explicit prescriptions, and more of its attractive, half-mythical content than the judicial hand of Rome encouraged. Moreover, monasteries did not obtrude on the lives of those who wanted no change. They were self-sufficient communities of men, or women, under the rule of an abbot or abbess. They preached virtues that were not far removed from the respected standards of Irish society—Christianity was always adaptable—and like the monasteries of Egypt they offered a welcome change to those who were tired of squabbles. Most important, they were organised, apart from a division of the sexes (which was perhaps not universal) much like the units of the society they came into. A tribal group under a chief with a fairly fixed territory was in form not so different from a monastic community. Most likely the ancient, esoteric and unchallenged status of the Druids was becoming a drudge to younger people, and was itself running out of enthusiasm. Christian monasticism was a refreshing alternative. Open to all, it kept no secrets from anyone, and had as its aim the happiness of the whole population.

Allied to the monastic rule was the life of the hermit. It too was spread by refugees and missionaries from Gaul and Wales, and by Irishmen who had gone to Gaul to learn under Martin at Tours, Honoratus at Lérins, Germanus at Auxerre and others. It put greater strain on a man, but again it could not offend society. As in the Egyptian desert, it taught that salvation was through renunciation, and the idea was easily absorbed. The values of the sagas taught much the same thing, that heroism and honour were achieved only through hardship, sometimes death, but they were rewarded somewhere beyond mortal life, in the deeps of the earth perhaps, or over the western sea. Now the hermit was to pit himself against the hostile powers of nature, and his rewards, like the hero's, were to be the joy of the challenge and the delights of the after-life. Though the two often mixed, for nature could be quite as kind as chastening.

Learning was a third quality which endeared the religion to the Irish, who delighted in the importance the Church gave it. Memorising and reciting legends had been the function of one of the highest classes in the land, and was imitated by others far away from the comfort and splendour of royal courts, the *shanachies* who kept the imaginations of humble people awake and alive around the glowing embers of an evening fire. Now there was a new source of tales, the lore of the Old and New Testaments. And there were comments to make, and meanings to be dug, and subtleties to be explored and exploited by the burrowing minds of recruited monks. The race that had devised the exquisite complexity of the Brehon law and took an almost perverse delight in mental system and classification turned to Christian theology with refreshed vigour. Irishmen learned and recited the psalms with ease, took in and extended the tables and classes of saints with a mature aptitude, and through their trained awareness of the numinous powers of nature relished the symbols and mysteries of the new creed. The tellers of triads adopted the Trinity with a ready instinct. Patrick is said to have explained the concept with the use of a shamrock leaf. He had no need. In these and other ways the new religion captured the people's imagination. They took a proprietorial interest in it. Before long they even learned to identify themselves with the chosen people of Israel. There is more than one hint of their belief in themselves as a race of special importance to God, and that belief was enhanced by the conquest and suppression of later days. It is echoed still; the Irish are the only nation whose national independence is celebrated on a moveable Christian feast-day. Sometimes this identifying went to strange lengths. In the past, old gods had become entangled with their successors—both gods and heroes—in the minds of poets. Now some of the early saints of Ireland were given the attributes of Semitic originals. Christ and the Virgin Mary were half-reborn, woven into the fabric of Celtic divines; much in the way that Mary had taken prominence in the Mediterranean world, combining the maternal, nourishing and spiritual qualities of Artemis, Selene, Hera.

Besides, Christianity came at the best time possible, with refugees who brought other arts and distinctions which were welcomed in the country. As Germanic invaders overran Britain, so the British sailed to the west bringing the tested benefits of their Roman heritage. Writing came, and the Latin language, in which the liturgy of the new religion had matured. The Irish learned it fast. New ideas of science and cosmology came, so that in the dark years that followed in Europe the Irish never forgot, for instance, that the world was round. Methods of farming changed radically. Suddenly the country became a ferment of new ideas and beliefs, as the indirect impact of Rome was felt for the first time. Women could play as great a part as men in the new religion, and did. Even hermits seldom remained alone, but used the habit of retreat to purify their ideas and develop them, and returned to the world to contribute to it. Life had not been hard before, and there was no need to stress the escapist side of Christianity.

There was a final reason for the success of the creed. It was the

absence of a reason for failure. Nowhere else in Europe had the
Celts been able to impose their culture on all levels of society.
On the Continent Rome had suppressed Celtic culture and made
its races part of the great Roman system. Though the Empire had
made a lesser mark on Britain, there was little chance, when troops
were called away, for the old Celtic traditions to revive; new
conquerors saw to that. Only Ireland had had something like a
thousand years for a powerful class of Celts to imbue the whole
land with their ideas, their art and their political forms. The Irish
alone, during all this period, had never learned to suspect foreign
creeds, since they had experienced none. There was no fear that
God might be a subtle front for Caesar. If the new religion appealed, it was given a fair hearing. And it appealed.

Thus, because the new missions were peaceful and anxious to
please, their message brought not so much a conversion as a
blend of traditions. In a country which, though no Utopia, was no
less happy or healthy than any other, they could lay less emphasis
on the aspect of retreat from the world, and more on the enrich-
ment of earthly life through divine blessing. The kingdom of
heaven became something near. It was this change of emphasis
that enabled the Irish sometimes to locate heaven on earth,
not in some ethereal paradise beyond the clouds. In many other
ways they adapted the new creed to their own elaborate myth and
lore and ethic, enriching both traditions.

The first progress of Christianity was in the south and east of
the country, where the contacts with Europe were strongest.
Some remains, and a few dubious traditions indicate its course
there; and it can be seen that there was much activity among the
followers of the pioneers—Ailbe, Declan, Ibar and others. But
the only documents of real value refer to the north. For it was in
the north that Patrick, at some period of the fifth century, arrived
from Britain on his ordained mission, and began his tenacious
campaign to win the Irish to God.

How crucial Patrick was to the conversion of Ireland is a
debatable point, and over the last thirty years debate has raged.
His special sanctity in the country, his position as apostle of the

The Patrick problem

Irish, make it essential to acknowledge and describe the question, though there is no chance of solving it. The Problem of the Two Patricks will draw the erudition, the wit and the malice of scholars for many years to come.

Popular tradition, which is tradition of the strongest kind, has it that Patrick was the first man to come to convert the Irish. 1961 was held to be the fifteen-hundredth anniversary of his death, and during that year the Irish remembered him with worship, celebrations and a great deal of publicity. But as critical scholarship applies itself to the fifth century, it grows more possible that the celebration was a mistake. For a theory has emerged that Patrick died towards the end of the fifth century and not, as was previously assumed, in the year 461. His mission, in this case, would belong to the second half of the century rather than the first; and his position as pioneer would be strongly challenged by those many Christians who were known to be at work in the earlier period. For the spiritual purposes of ancient or modern Ireland this matters as little as the fact that Christ was not born on the twenty-fifth of December. Historically, however, it is able to raise partisan spirits high.

J. B. Bury, an English historian with a Teutonic dogmatism, who surprised many by feeling as much at home in Irish history as he had previously in Greek, set the conventional fashion early in the present century.[4] Patrick arrived in 432 and died in 461. Official Ireland agreed, and celebrated centenaries accordingly. Then, from the more recent race of critical and meticulous Irish scholars, whose thundery apostle, T. F. O'Rahilly, died only a few years ago, came the reversal of fashion. 'Bury is generally unfortunate in his incursions into Irish history', wrote O'Rahilly. Analysing Irish and continental sources, and trying to reconcile conflicting records of Patrick and his contemporaries, he updated the Saint by thirty years.[5] He conceded that another Patrick had existed earlier, generally referred to as Palladius. But this was not the Patrick whose *Confessions* have survived. Meanwhile another Celtic scholar, C. Plummer, had satisfied himself that there was never a Patrick at all. The Irish always overlooked the nationality of their patron saint, but none before or since have gone as far as this.

Patrick's status in Ireland was a matter of considerable importance. Consequently scholastic civil war began, and continues today. A climax was reached in the year of the alleged centenary, which Dr D. A. Binchy chose to publish a conscientious, slightly acid article in which he set out to prove that a final answer was out of the question on the evidence available.[6] The dearth of facts was in itself proof that nothing could be proved one way or the other. War had become anarchy, and Patrick was left floating without chronological anchor somewhere in the fifth century.

In 1966 an English professor of theology, Dr R. P. C. Hanson, entered the field.[7] He introduced some new items and some old ones in new combination. From isolated references to Patrick's father, a British deacon and decurion in the Roman service, from imperial edicts about tax-evasion and the chastity of clerics, and from careful dating of the texts of Latin quoted by Patrick, he decided the saint must have been born around the year 390. This made his arrival in 432 more plausible than other conjectures. And Bury, and fifteen hundred years of tradition, were right after all.

In the long campaign, which is not yet over, many scholarly minds have been sacrificed in intellectual martyrdom, no doubt making the academic world a better place, and enabling some of its issues to stand clear and comprehensible. It is typical of the robust spirit now applied to early Irish matters, and not unlike the German and English critical assault on the classics in the nineteenth century. As for Patrick, he was tentatively restored to the status of a pioneer.

Patrick was born in Britain—Wales or Dumbartonshire, it is not known which—and at an early age he was captured during one of Niall's plundering sorties. He was put to work as a slave on a farm in Mayo, where he tended sheep and was confirmed in his Christian convictions by a series of dreams. After some years, one of his dreams revealed to him a means of escape. He was to join the crew of a certain ship and sail away to freedom. But the dream put a bond on him too. He was to return, in maturity, to Ireland, to evangelise the country. After years of wandering he did return. He was ordained bishop, though there were those who did not approve then or later of his appointment, and faced once more the hazards of the pagan western land. His mission, as his reputation testifies, was a great success. People were converted by the thousand, including royal families who brought with them whole tribes. But Patrick speaks of spending large sums of money and giving valuable presents to the kings, suggesting that their faith was venal. He had other problems too. Pelagianism thrived for a while in the country, as it did in Britain. A bishop had been sent specially by Pope Celestine to stamp out the heresy, and though he returned just before Patrick's arrival it would not be unlikely that that, and other heretical variants, persisted. There were also Druids to contend with, who objected to the new faith and its popularity. But Patrick, and the funds of the British church, seem to have spoken louder in kings' ears than the affronted imprecations of the old priesthood.

Patrick's work was mainly in the north and west of the country. He says he travelled far, and sometimes he came across communities where Christianity already existed. In these cases he organised the religion, probably ordained priests, put out the Catholic beliefs that he himself had absorbed in the Roman state of Britain, and satisfied himself that the flock was on the increase. His use of episcopal funds, and the spirit which runs through his writings, suggest that his main concern was the primary step of getting people to acknowledge his God. It is the proselytising disease. That the Christian ethic did not get far during his campaign is shown by the undeterred warring habits of the generations that followed. Once he heard of the massacre of some decent converts. 'The Lord's sheep are around me,' he wailed, 'butchered and spoiled by robbers'.[8] The case was not isolated. Patrick himself had once been Irish booty and wrote that he was always in danger of murder, capture or slavery. He was once kept in chains for two weeks.

The most important effect of his and other missions was in the cultural field. He managed to induce the same respect, not without struggle and setback, for Christian learning and culture that had previously been given to the *aes dana*, the thinking and creative classes of the pagans. And of course the achievement was not made single-handed. Other bishops accompanied him, and at the same time other missionaries were at work in other parts of the country. The vagaries of history deprive us of knowledge of these contemporaries, but a combination of myth and fact has come down as witness to their presence. One tradition has it that fifty scholars landed at Cork from Gaul, chased from their monastery by a usurper. Before a generation had passed Ireland was in a ferment of ostensibly Christian activity.

Later tales elaborated Patrick's achievement. He was said to have had dramatic confrontations with the pagan, lighting the first Paschal fire on the hill of Slane when a Druid festival the next day forbade all fires; or causing the death of a king's magician who had insulted him and his religion. These tales are written in the style of Old Testament accounts of the miraculous doings of prophets; and it was in all likelihood the Old Testament, rather than the historical Patrick, which served as their model. Still, he must have been an impressive figure. It was told that his former owner, on hearing of his approach and his success with others, took his own life rather than submit to the intruder creed.[9] And his own words are injected with a tenacious, obdurate honesty. Patronised by a few chieftains, he began to found a Catholic organisation, and Armagh claimed later the distinction of being his headquarters, and so the prime see of Ireland.

He spent thirty years in the country, by the end of which Christianity was the dominant religion, though paganism persevered for centuries more. He speaks of monastic communities both for men and women, but his own main work was in diocesan organisation, since that was the framework of the British Church he knew. Meanwhile others were spreading the monastic idea, and throughout the country monasteries were springing up. It was the combined work of possibly hundreds of Gallic and Welsh missionaries that sowed the seeds of the later bloom. Only Patrick has survived as a composite figure, and he appears to have stolen the thunder of his contemporaries and those who went before him. There was even a tradition of hostility from existing Christians to this foreigner who tried to impose a national organisation on the small groups which had already been established. That he helped to secure Christianity is not to be doubted. But perhaps no more credit is due to him than to a hundred nameless missionaries. For throughout this time there were wine-boats arriving from Spain, and refugees from Wales and the Frankish occupation of Gaul, many of whom brought with them a Christian message. From Wales particularly came monks with no other purpose than to evangelise. By the end of the fifth century they had achieved a faster conversion than any European country had seen.

Because of the ease of conversion, the differences within Christianity itself were more apparent. To talk now of the rift between the Roman and Celtic churches is to anticipate a much later split. But from the hints of early animosity between groups of converts it is possible to assume the beginnings of the friction even at this time. The Roman Church—Patrick's church—was based on the structure of the Roman Empire, and this in turn comprised numerous cities and towns upon which local life centred. Wherever the Romans had gone, if they found no towns, they built them. And the Church, taking its cue from the lay administration, evolved an urban hierarchy, adapting the names of Roman officials to its own uses.

Ireland had always been outside the Empire. Towns were unknown, and the whole country was split into hundreds of tiny units based on family ties. No Roman soldier ever landed on Irish shores to enforce the civil framework on which the Church had been constructed. The basic theology percolated into the character of the nation; some of its ideals did too, the love of scholarship and the idea of material renunciation. But the centralised authority was not to find roots for hundreds of years. Ireland remained a country of scattered clusters, and took monasticism to itself like an heirloom.

Alien Christians had brought the message. But before long the base of these missions was cut off by the character of the new barbarian invasions. They lost their authority, their funds, and their Roman organisation. As Britain was engrossed in the century of defeat that led to full Anglo-Saxon occupation, Ireland was again isolated, not as before to nurse her old Celtic habits and sentiments, but livened by the new presence of Christianity. For a long period of incubation she developed Christianity in her own particular way, suited to her own character, not that of a relinquished Roman colony. Those who insisted on the Roman way of doing things, just because they were Roman, found little sympathy. Patrick's diocesan organisation was not a natural bedfellow for a nation of tribal cliques. So diocesan organisation faltered and fell. When Ireland again emerged, many years into the sixth century, monasteries were spread wide in each of her five kingdoms.

III

The Awakening of Ireland

The seed was planted. The flowering would follow. But for a hundred years there was little palpable change in the life of Ireland. Cows were milked, dogs coursed, kings and peasants hunted deer and boar, pirates raided, slaves were sold, brown bulls and white bulls were rustled, and in the evening romancers told the great legends of the past, according to their rank and company. Borders changed from time to time, depending on the mood of a king and the strength of his soldiers. Christianity advanced, and priests held mass, chanting mystical formulae to a god who was invisible yet manifest in all the variety of nature, and telling good stories of the precursors of a far-off race. There was more gusto in the new religion, and young people felt a call to it, even giving up the comforts of ordinary life for a rigorous existence in the confines of cells. But there was not much change from old to new. The past was still rich and important, made more so, if anything, by the new faith. Druids were being ousted, not without protest, but they were a run-down class and their influence had long waned.

There is nothing to say that Christianity changed the habits of the Irish people except in the culture of the educated classes and in ritual, which was the outward form of a theology most of them, most of any nation, could never understand. It was Christianity itself that changed, as it did in most places to which it came, adapting to the customs of its hosts. After a long incubation it would begin to affect those who claimed it, but even then only in superficials. After hundreds of years slavery would be abolished, and women exempted from service as soldiers. But if the women were spared war, still their husbands went on fighting.

The changes came in culture, among the individuals who were

alive to cultural things. Christianity fed the minds of those whose minds hungered. There had always been such people in Ireland, the privileged, revered classes of thinking men, and it was these whose imagination was caught. They came in the main from the high classes of their society, because they were the classes with time to spare for the mind. A series of historical chances, the lottery of events, had brought them fare that stimulated their enthusiasm for everything. Part we have seen. It came from Byzantium, Sinai, the monasteries of Provence and Aquitaine, from the harsh mountains of Wales and the hampered plains of Britain; Roman dominion had spread it, Roman decline left it to take firm root. Balkan battles and the tidal rush of men from the central plains of Asia; hermits languishing in desert drought, Levantine merchants plying a far-flung trade, clerics copying manuscripts in Rome, and the seething confusion of oriental politics; all these were planks in the ship that brought a cultural revolution to Ireland. And just as important were the factors of Ireland herself; the high place of letters, the scrupulous love of scheme, priority and place, the love of facts, the closeness to nature, the values and virtues of the pagan Celt, the streak of whimsy and the unforced vein of poetry in him.

These were the ingredients, mixed by Patrick and the first order of saints. Then there was a long silence in Ireland. For fifty years there are no records of the maturing of the new spirit. And then the mind woke, and wanted to break out of its confines. For two hundred years the cultural story of Ireland is full of event and expansion and the searching for something transcendent, something that might or might not exist. Communities of saints sprang up over the country, and provided the base from which this expansion could take place. The pioneering was left to individuals, and others followed in their wake. The story must be told through these individuals. In Brendan, Columba and Columbanus is seen the insatiable questing that was the core of the character of the new Ireland. Though life went on, and there was little change for the ordinary man and woman, reflections from these archetypes were glanced down through the strata of society. People heard of the doings of the individuals, and approved them and where there was a chance they helped them. Only Drake and a ship's crew could circle the world and trounce the king of Spain, but they made the character of the England of their day.

Brendan stands for the expansion of the imagination of Ireland. With him, as with others, we are at the mercy of texts which have not survived from his day, but were copies of works which may, in some cases, have dated from near his time. Hardly any Irish literature exists in its orignal form from before the tenth century. Of that which does, little appears to have been copied from models earlier than the eighth century. What comes down from them was written by monks in monasteries, often no more than clerical copy-writers, whose duty in writing the lives of past saints was not so much to check their sources as to earn a reward, earthly or otherwise. So most of the saints' lives are an amalgam of pagan and Christian, fact and fiction, ancient and comparatively new. As long as the recipe was for the greater glory of God, and the higher sanctity—and so heavier profit—of the writer's abbey, it was fit for publication.

All the same, creative monks could interpolate only what was compatible with the known facts and the spirit of the age. People believed in miracles, so they created frills to the lives that raise a modern brow in question. But to catch the spirit of the age, to see the charm and delights and imaginings and aspirations, it is important to read what they wrote without excess of cynicism (though never ruling it out altogether—that would be to miss the point). If much of St Brendan is a myth, it is a myth created by those who knew what they wanted to tell, and chose the best method for telling that they could. The myth becomes the age that gave rise to it.

*   *   *   *

One day in the year 484 a prosperous Kerry farmer saw a bright light shining in the sky over Fenit, a village on the coast a few miles west of Tralee. The same night thirty cows brought forth thirty calves in his barn. Next morning, guided by the light, he walked to the village, and found a new-born baby in a cottage. To the babe, St Brendan, he offered the thirty calves. And so, in a manner suspiciously akin to the birth of Christ, St Brendan was born.

From Tralee, on the other side of the bay, the Dingle peninsula stretches out into the Atlantic, topped by the humped line of the Slieve Mish range of mountains. Fenit itself is flat and duny, with white sands reaching for miles to the north and bordering the stream-cut green of west Kerry. On these beaches Finn, King Cormac's lieutenant, and his companions raced by day and slept by night under an open sky. The prospect is mountains and sea, and these two giants, imbued with legend and the awe of peasants, watched over Brendan's early years. The livelihood of the people came from fishing and farming sheep and cattle. It was sheep, three of them miraculously springing from the well where he was baptised, that paid the priest's fee. When he was two the boy was put out to a foster-mother. Christians had taken over an old custom, putting their young children in the care of a monk or nun, to educate them with the necessary stress on religious doctrine. Brendan was removed to Kileedy, where St Ita took him in charge. She herself had founded the nunnery, and it is told of her that she had, besides her high measure of sanctity, a fair knowledge of the world's backsliders through girls who made renunciation a passing phase. In a poem attributed to her, but probably written centuries later, she sings of her delight when Jesus comes to her, as an infant, to sleep on her bosom; and mentions in passing the unwanted attentions of ill-minded monks. Monastic conditions, especially in the early formative days, must have led to many abuses. Some of the virulent opposition to the new creed may have come from those who saw the monastic life as the common man's equivalent to the imperial court.

Brendan was too tender to notice the hemming temptations. He learned from Ita, in triad form, the things that were most displeasing to God—hating others, embracing evil, and trusting riches; and those which found his favour—steadfast belief in him, the simple life, and generous charity. He absorbed self-control by example; Ita kept an enormous stag-beetle on her body as perpetual chastening. And after five years spent learning the rudiments of the dedicated life he returned to his family and the mountains. A local bishop, Erc, was taking an interest in him, and a little while later removed him from home again to foster him more directly for a divine vocation. Erc is a mysterious figure in the early church. He may have accompanied one of Patrick's assistants to the west, the first mission to Kerry, and remained as the first bishop. But he later turns up as a fiercely ascetic monk living alone by the Boyne, north of Dublin, and daily immersing himself in the waters of the river to chant the psalms. This tough master made his pupil tough, and so able to respond to later calls to adventure at which a lesser spirit would certainly have balked; though at times the young novice appears to have taken strictness too seriously. One day, it is told, Bishop Erc went to preach in country districts, and allowed Brendan to accompany him and his assistants in the carriage. As he preached, the boy, who was now ten, was left alone reading the psalms, till he was interrupted by 'a young maiden, gentle, modest, flaxen-haired, of a princely family who came close to the carriage and saw his face beautiful and bright; all at once she makes a sportive bound into the carriage, in order to play her game with him'. But Brendan refused the call. 'Go away home,' he cried, 'and curse whoever brought you here.' And so saying he took the carriage-reins in his hands, stood up, and brought them down and about her till the royal young lady was bruised and bawling.[1]

Psychologists would see a suppression here, and rightly so. It was shared by others of Brendan's calling, notably St Kevin who threw his own succubus over a cliff into Glendalough in Wicklow, where she unhappily drowned. But in Brendan's case, Erc, reappearing, was quick to rebuke the deed, and the lesson of Ita was realistically brought home.

These men of iron had a warm side too; so much is seen from the many animal stories that crowd their lives. One is told of this time of Brendan's life:

Now Bishop Erc had no milch-cow, and on a certain day Brendan was asking milk from his foster-father. 'God will do that,' said Bishop Erc. Thereafter came the hind every day from Slieve Luachra with her fawn, and she was milked by him, and after milking she used to go back alone to the mountains. [2]

Erc's guardianship lasted a further five years, at the end of which the young man had proved himself a worthy disciple of Christ. It was time for him to start religious training in earnest, and to this end he was sent by Erc to learn the rules of the saints. Then the Bishop would be able to ordain him. The new course meant staying in an educational monastery, and Brendan set off north to Galway to study under a man who is no more than a name to us, St Jarlath. There was little hardship in travel, whether on foot or in horse-drawn cart, since Christian priests had inherited the privileges of other professional classes, and were allowed to travel freely. There were exceptions, where a king had a personal dislike of the new religion. But Brendan came across no such opponent. The only disbeliever he encountered was a distinguished poet from the courts of the kings of Munster, at Cashel, whom he left, after a roadside debate, converted to the faith.

Rules of saints form a complex literature. They summarise the ethic of the monastery, and the penitentials contain stern sanctions for disobedience. The surviving rule of St Ailbe is one of the early rules in which Brendan would have been instructed. [3] The intense legalistic complications of later codes—derived partly from the Brehon outlook—had not yet appeared. Ailbe's text is a quintessence of common sense, general maxims for behaviour, and an occasional hint on etiquette: the priest or monk, for instance, is to genuflect three times on approaching the altar 'neither with frivolity nor excitement'. Ailbe was of the old school. At dawn each day he lay outside his cell on a cross of stones to chant the psalms from memory. Brendan would also have learned as much Latin as had penetrated to this Connaught community—it may not have been much, apart from Jerome's *Vulgate* which was in universal use. And here he would have been

A monk's training

expected to learn the psalms in their entirety, as Ailbe had done and every monk did, and probably found quite easy to do through constant hearing.

As a result of his learning Brendan was in a good position to frame his own rule, to which he now applied himself with the help of an angel who came to dictate. Clearly he had by now formed his ambition to found a monastery of his own, and as soon as Erc had ordained him he collected a band of monks and took over—or was given by a compliant king—a piece of land five miles or so from the village of his birth. This was Ardfert, where nowadays the hoary, graceful ruins of a medieval cathedral mark the site of the first foundation. His thoughts were already turning towards the hermit life, and he looked with longing on the sea, the steel-grey, hard agent that brought winds stronger than a man, and menaced with hostile mists that swept across its surface and up and down the distant hills, and then cleared and was blue and deep and soft and beckoning. He would go off by himself and plan isolation, a long journey, unbroken contemplation of the work of his God. But for the most part the work of the monastery required all his efforts.

In its long journey from Egypt, the monastic idea had changed its shape. In the beginning it had been a retreat from the turmoils and evils of the urban world to what was regarded as the natural world of God. It was a personal dedication that took no heed of the rest of mankind. In Gaul it had fitted more into a social pattern. Monks went out of their confines to preach, convert and help the poor and sick. And they began to bring people in, not necessarily for similar dedication, but to learn about the religion, to read the Bible, and to hear the great truths explained. In Ireland the purpose again was expanded. Learning of any kind, Christian or pagan, was encouraged. By drawing no clear line between, say, Augustine and Virgil, or David and Cuchulain, they managed to allay suspicion and animosity in the minds of ordinary people. Many of the monks themselves were laymen, bound not by oaths but by genuine respect for and love of the new learning.

Monasteries were to become virtual factories of scholarship.

The Awakening of Ireland

The spread of a new culture demanded a great deal of copying of manuscripts, and to this task monks of all ages, who sometimes found the work very tedious, had to direct hours of every day of their lives. There would normally be a special hut for the purpose, equipped with desks and pens and inks of different colours, where the dreary task of transposition would take place.

> My little dripping pen travels
> Across the plain of shining books
> Without ceasing, for the wealth of the great—
> Whence my hand is weary with writing [4]

laments a scribe of later days, but his sentiment is not confined to his age. In addition to copying there were other menial tasks which depended on the wealth and situation of the monastery. The garden had to be cultivated, since as far as possible food for all the monks came from the land around their buildings. In a lonely island sanctuary like Skellig Michael, off the west coast of Kerry, and even today approachable only on a few days of the year because of rough seas, the few square yards of earth would have taken little time in the tilling. In bigger institutions the work involved was far greater, and much depended on the attitude of the abbot. Oxen were a common gift from local kings who desired good relations with the monastery. But there were those who despised any aid to manual labour. Thus Enda, the uncompromising abbot of Inishmore in the Aran Islands, insisted on weeding beds with his own hands, and dug ditches without implement, and forced the policy on his underlings. Elsewhere life was easier, sometimes comfortable. A comparison of the diet sections of monastic rules shows all the variants between beans and water and an ample allowance that included meat and wine on every day except official fast days.

Brendan's monastery at Ardfert soon became famous. It was on the strength of his foundations that he was later put among the 'twelve apostles of Ireland'; and in the course of his travels and learning and exchanging ideas he met several of the others. Brigid, ageing by now, came to visit him. He, amongst others, paid calls on Finnian of Clonard in Leinster, sometimes known as the 'tutor of the saints of Ireland', who prepared hundreds to become the missionaries of Ireland, and firmly established the scholastic tradition of the monasteries. More is known of Finnian than of many other monastic founders, since Clonard was centrally placed and many of the most famous later saints went through their early training there. Both Columba and Columbanus were his pupils. Finnian had a strict ascetic rule, derived partly from St David's monastery in Wales where he had spent some of his youth. He himself ate no more than barley bread and water, though he allowed himself fish and mead on Sundays. He never wore anything but a coarse wool habit; and though the monks were allowed milk from their own cows to dilute their porridge ration, most of the cattle produce went to needy locals. Typically, the monastery was planned like an ordinary hill-fort of the time, an addition being a church of stone or wood set in the middle of the sparse low huts. Now and again the master himself would take up position on a boulder by the site, and as well as the monks crowds from miles around would gather to hear him preach. These crowds now came under the spiritual guidance of the abbot, for the diocesan organisation of Patrick's day had quickly dissolved in face of the social conventions of the country. To Finnian therefore, or other abbots and priests, the converted Christians would confess their sins and receive suitable penance, usually much lighter than that imposed on the monks themselves.

Importance was attached to appearances in the monastery. There was a different punishment for crimes committed with and without publicity. Monks moreover had to be examples, and for that reason the sanctions against their backsliding were greater than those against the laity. A monk guilty of murder was sentenced to ten years of exile, existing for the first three on bread and water; he must besides recompense the family of the victim. A layman who had committed the same crime had only to fast for forty days and pay the compensation. Of serious crimes, it seems to have been sexual offences that occurred most often. Long lists of nicely differentiated penalties are set for fornication, imagining fornication, offences against men or women, and worst of all against nuns. Laymen guilty of such offences were generally deprived of the company of their wives for a period of years.[5]

Two very Irish elements emerge from the penitentials. One is the private nature of confession; hitherto the churches of Gaul and Britain had laid heavy stress on public confessions and atonement. The other is the confused idea of chastity. The notion of sexual restraint must have come hard to people accustomed to fairly free morality. It was not altogether new, for Christianity had only extended a practice kept by Roman Vestal Virgins, priests of Diana, and sects and religious officials in every society, of sublimating physical love in a dedication to a deity. Nor were the bishops of the Church altogether clear about their own policy. St Peter himself had been married before his conversion, and nothing conclusive remains to show whether, or how soon, or on what grounds, he broke the relationship. In the fifth century clerics under the rank of bishop in the western Church were not forbidden to sleep with their wives, though the practice was discouraged. In the eastern Church there has never been a bar. Another early custom, officially banned by the Council of Nicea in the early fourth century, was the spiritual marriage between monks or hermits and ascetics of the opposite sex. There is some reason to think the habit reached Ireland, and may have been continued in Brigid's foundation at Kildare, which included both men and women living in strict, though perhaps not permanent, segregation. Not everyone was quite clear about his obligations, whether to reject entirely the attractions of the other sex, or partially to accept them. For some the question did not arise: rejection of the other sex amounted to a sustained phobia. And among those who drafted rules there was general agreement that unequivocal sins of the flesh were to be condemned, and painfully atoned for.

There was a close fellowship between abbots, and their lives are full of references to chance arrivals, finding the cupboard bare, miraculous conversion of bread into meat and water into wine. Brendan would have been so welcomed at Clonard; he brought news of politics and manuscripts and the progress of the Church in his part of the country. These were still the days of expansion, and the news of another chief or king brought over was cause for celebration. The result of journeys of this kind would be a great deal of new information for the home monastery. Mutual influence of widely separated monasteries is seen in the similarities of rules, of styles of art in manuscripts, of liturgy and the buildings of monasteries. Art in particular was a lively concern. More than most things it shows an inherently Irish trait, an unrepentant whimsy.

The antecedents of Irish art were much the same as those of Irish Christianity. Styles were a rich amalgam of old Irish motifs and the themes and design of Middle Eastern models. A clear open script, the Celtic half-uncial, was developing which makes early Irish manuscripts more easy to read than any contemporary documents from other countries. Letters were generously rounded, stems firm and sometimes slightly curved to add to the flowing effect. At this period the decoration of manuscripts was only beginning under the influence of scrolls imported through Spain and Gaul from Middle Eastern sources. Capitals began to sway and curve and grow appendages, usually abstract designs which filled a gaping space. Scrolls and twirls appeared, very similar to the ornaments on pins and brooches that have been found. As time went on, and copying became more of a business (literally a business for increasing monastic funds), greater elaborations were introduced. The main aim ceased to be legibility; visual effect took precedence. The men of God, as they sat on hard benches in draughty ill-lit cells, began to doodle. They drew animals where there was no call for animal drawings, they moulded initials out of serpents and birds and composite creatures with bird-heads and serpent-bodies. They drew rows of dots, and squiggles and coils and interlaced patterns like the weft and warp of fabric. Facility of reading was more and more forgotten as words were split or bent or stretched or squeezed to fit the demands of pattern. And as an artistic crowning glory the carpet page evolved, a whole page of colourful abandon with simply no relevance to anything around it but without question for the greater glory of God, and a welcome perquisite for the wealthy buyer of books. But that was in later days. Now the demand was graceful simplicity. These books were for reading. It was the Irish who first created pocket books, smaller than a paperback, to fit in a satchel and be carried on their frequent journeys. The Stowe Missal, a relic of some time later, measures roughly four and a half by five and a half inches.

Brendan's journeys may have taken him to Skellig Michael, off the coast of Kerry and perched precariously atop a gaunt jut of rock. Life was different here. These monks gave nothing but example to the people of their homeland. They lived in unimaginable hardship, cut off from the mainland by a turbulent sea and almost constant winds and mist, confined on a few square yards of approximately flat summit. They had brought their earth in curraghs, across eight miles of sea to their natural pyramid; and here they built huts of stone and oratories for prayer and walls to form a bed for the earth. For the most part their food must have been fish, but they kept goats to supply milk. Their routine was unremitting hardship, yet the foundation remained into the ninth century when the Vikings cut it back to the bones.

Already Brendan had been attracted by the hermit life. The sea beckoned him, as did the old legends of the paradise in the west. He had strengthened the religion of his community, and now he retired to contemplate in isolation. His chosen site was another lofty nest, now called Mount Brandon and in full view, when the mist abates, of his native village of Fenit. Here he went alone, built an oratory, and dwelt. His view was the sea, the jagged coasts of the Dingle peninsula pierced by creeks and bays, soft greens and browns of the sloping bog and forest, and the steely sheen of high mountain lakes. His company was a bird or two, a wandering sheep or goat. And his diet was meagre. He had come because he wanted to reduce life to its simplest terms, and to suppress everything in himself but an awareness of God and God's creation. His mind was more able to concentrate on single themes than any mind involved in a group of people. So his mind experienced things not given to others. He saw visions and the manifestations of miracles, and animals gave him their trust and affection. It is a terrible effort to overcome the stone-firm attitudes of a refined and intricate civilisation in order to glimpse the mind of a hermit, much easier to laugh at him or call him quaint. He was real, and his world was as real as a child's or a poet's. 'What's aught but as it seems?' asks Troilus. The world is the world perceived, and perceptions differ.

Will changes things. The hermit wanted to see the divine expression in the world. But other conditions change things too. Food and the shortage of it induces visions and hallucinations. Still, though mind and stomach and the chemical components of food eaten are all connected, they are not equated. The vision exists, whatever induces it. 'I have myself', Robert Graves has written, 'eaten the hallucinogenic mushroom *psilocybe*, a divine ambrosia in immemorial use among the Masatec Indians of Oaxaca Province, Mexico; heard the priestess invoke Tlaloc the mushroom god, and seen transcendental visions'.[6] Berries and herbs and mushrooms were undoubtedly eaten by the hermits when they found them. Cold, hunger, long hours of prayer all contributed to the effects. These were as real as a town of brick and concrete.

The hermit tradition had a long influence on Ireland, and probably its origins go back before Christian times. It is part of the syndrome that includes a passion for travel, a restlessness, a will to self-denial and a happy dependence on only the simplest things. Simplicity is paramount. Preoccupation with a few things led to a fantastic inflation of those things. Instead of looking with wonder on the complexity of the whole scene, the Irish hermit looked at one object and let his mind add complexity to that. For him, a flower or a bird was invested with incongruous attributes and rare powers; but what makes these attributes easy to accept is that the gap of incongruity can be jumped by a short leap. Anyone can make the leap, if he is willing to allow the possibility.

Brendan had visions, to which we shall come. They are grandiose and take us, with him, out of the country. But the mind was projected in little zones as well as great. In men who moved no more than a few miles in a lifetime there were restless mental searches and convoluted imaginings. Nowhere is the ascetic perception seen more clearly than with animals. An animal was company, and as such his attributes began to grow. The beginnings are seen in the life of Ciaran of Ossory, a saint who died before Brendan was born.

> Now when he came there [to his site near Ossory] he sat down under a tree, in the shade of which was a boar of savage aspect. The boar seeing a man for the first time fled in terror, but afterwards, being tamed by God, it returned like a servant to the man of God. And that boar was Ciaran's first disciple and served him like a monk in that place. For the boar immediately fell to before the eyes of the man of God and with his teeth stoutly severed branches and grasses to serve for the building of the cell. . . . Then came other animals from the waste to the holy Ciaran, a fox, a badger, a wolf and a stag. And they abode with him as tame as could be.
>
> Dissension came when the wily fox turned false to his vow, and carried off Ciaran's slippers to his lair to eat them. The badger was sent to fetch back the booty, which he did, and the fox too, much the worse for the fight he had put up.
>
> And the holy man said to the fox: 'Wherefore, brother, hast thou done this evil thing, unworthy of a monk? Behold! our water is sweet and common to all, and our food likewise is distributed in common among us all. And if thou hadst a desire of thy natural craving to eat flesh, the omnipotent God would have made thee flesh of the bark of trees at our prayer.' Then the fox, craving forgiveness, did penance fasting, and ate nothing until the holy man commanded him. Then he abode with the rest in familiar converse.[7]

Animals and birds were quick to learn the sacred mission of their new companions, and generally did their best to help. Columbanus was aided by bears, Columba by a heron and a faithful horse. Sometimes a divine message was brought by animals.

64

St Gobnet, a nun of Munster, was to know where she should found her church in the Aran Islands as soon as she saw nine white deer grazing. Brendan founding Ardfert was corrected in his siting by a dove. The dove appeared as the saint and his followers were studying their plans, snatched the papers and flew with them to the place which God had granted. Sheep sprang out of the well to pay his baptismal fee, and deer came to provide him with milk. Another bird dropped a feather for a hermit in need of a pen. St Ciaran of Clonmacnois, an influential foundation close to St Brendan's most famous monastery, was assisted by a fox which carried his psalter for him, and a deer whose horns served as a lectern at services. A wild boar cut sticks and grass with his tusk, to help him build a cell.

A touching story is told of the animal friends of one of the many St Mochuas:

Mochua and Columcille lived at the same time and Mochua, being a hermit in the waste, had no worldly goods but only a cock, a mouse and a fly. And the office of the cock was to keep the hour of matins for him. As for the mouse it would never suffer him to sleep but five hours, day and night, and if he was like to sleep longer, being weary with vigils and prostrations, the mouse would fall to licking his ear till it woke him. And the fly's office was to be walking along each line of his psalter as he read it, and when he was wearied with singing his psalms, the fly would abide upon the line where he left off until he could return again to the saying of the psalms. Now it came to pass that these three precious ones died soon. And upon that Mochua wrote a letter to Columcille in Alba, sorrowing for the death of his flock. Columcille replied to him and this is what he said: 'My brother,' he said, 'marvel not that thy flock should have died, for misfortune ever waits upon wealth.'[8]

These tender relationships were not one-sided. The hermits were supreme in their gentle and courteous behaviour towards animals. So Giraldus Cambrensis records the legend of St Kevin, that at Glendalough he was one day praying and:

According to his custom he put his hand (in raising it to heaven) out through the window, when, behold, a blackbird happened to settle on it, and using it as a nest, laid its eggs there. The saint was moved with such pity and was so patient with it that he neither closed nor withdrew his hand; but held it out in a suitable position without tiring until the young were completely hatched out. In perpetual remembrance of this wonderful happening, all the representations of St Kevin throughout Ireland have a blackbird in the outstretched hand.[9]

It may be regretted that his patience did not work for the girl who attended him by his cliffside cave, even if her purpose was not pure. Another saint was so long in praying with arms outstretched that two birds built their nests in his hand during the recital. And there are many records of the misery of animals when their patrons died. An abbot at Lismore came across a bird weeping by the path, and stood musing until an angel came to explain:

'Hail, cleric!' says the angel, 'let the trouble of this vex thee no longer. Molua, Ocha's son, is dead. And for this cause the creatures lament him, for that he never killed any creature, little or big. And not more do men bewail him than the creatures, and among them the tiny bird thou seest.'[10]

Though they came from the hermit traditions, all these stories were written, and a lot invented, in the monasteries. Like the artistic designs they became in time more involved, and a literary doodle grows up to match the artistic one. Sometimes these whimsical comments develop into poetry. They grace the margins of many weighty manuscripts, and have sometimes commanded greater attention than the central matter. 'Wondrous is the robin there singing to us, and our cat has escaped us' a scribe informs the world in his margin; while another, before laying down his pen, allows himself the groan: 'Alas! my hand'; and another: 'Let no reader blame this writing for my arm is cramped through excess of labour'.[11] But it was nature that brought solace to the busy monk, as it did to the hermit:

Nature poetry

> Ah, blackbird, thou art satisfied
> Where thy nest is in the bush:
> Hermit that clinkest no bell,
> Sweet, soft, peaceful is thy note.[12]

The awareness of nature, starting with the musings of the exiled ascetic, gradually grew to the beautiful finesse of mature Irish poetry, through

> A hedge of trees surrounds me,
> A blackbird's lay sings to me;
> Above my lined booklet
> The trilling birds chant to me.
> In a grey mantle from the top of the bushes
> The cuckoo sings;
> Verily—may the Lord shield me!
> Well do I write under the greenwood tree.[13]

to the exquisite economy of this poem on the parting of summer, often quoted:

> My tidings for you: the stag bells,
> Winter snows, summer is gone.
>
> Wind high and cold, low the sun,
> Short his course, sea running high.
>
> Deep-red the bracken, its shape all gone—
> The wild-goose has raised his wonted cry.
>
> Cold has caught the wings of birds;
> Season of ice—these are my tidings.[14]

These were the poet's thoughts; his words were Irish. Part of Ireland's luck in escaping the Romans was in being able to keep her own tongue and develop it in a literary way. The Irish kept their spontaneity in their vernacular literature, though they took willingly to Latin for scriptural and scholastic purposes. Freed by the new Christian culture from the heavy duty of court eulogies and false genealogies, the Irish poet created not only one

67

of the oldest European literatures outside Latin and Greek, but one of the most sensitive and appealing. Its misfortune later was that, having few obvious links with Latin, on which most present European languages were based, it became isolated and remained almost undiscovered till recent years.

We are far from Brendan in his mountain-top sanctuary, but it is worth following the course of this refreshed and lively poetry a short while more. It will never be known how much of the tales of old heroes, written from this time on in the monasteries, derive their style, as well as their themes, from the cultural rebirth of the sixth century. Much would certainly be accurate transcription of the old legends. But the habit of inspired particularising, of picking a little detail and blowing it up to great and colourful proportions, seems to owe its influence more to the single-minded attentions of the early hermits and scribes. The tales are scattered with these evocative details enlarged; stories of men fighting 'until the blood reached the girdles of men'; or the uncanny powers of some of the characters, like Lug who could 'leap on a bubble without breaking it'. And the characters of Welsh myth, often derived directly from the Irish, who could hear an ant walking fifty miles away, or run along the tops of trees, or shoot an arrow through the legs of a bird standing on the other side of the Irish Sea. And the similes, in which hen's eggs become 'the gravel of Glenn Ai', a leek the 'tear of a fair woman', and seaweed the 'mesh of the plain of Rian'.

Another development was far more cerebral, and certainly went back to the mystic beliefs and experiments of the old Druids, though it is again indicative, in a rather vexing manner, of minds that fixed on a single thread, running through a web of complexity. It is a kind of flirtation with the obscure. We have looked at the riddle (popular in early England too) and the triad, which are all examples of this bent, and some of the preoccupation with numbers and abstract qualities that mark the Druid doctrines. These all came through to the Christian age, augmented by translations from Hebrew apocrypha, and trying to combine the lessons of Christ and Paul with an arcane symbolism in words, numbers and qualities. Some hold that the old heresy of Gnosticism found a new plot in Ireland, and that from it much of the folk superstitions of the Middle Ages sprang. In its simplest form this preoccupation is a love of wizardry; books, the containers of wisdom, are given far more than instructive powers, so that Bede can report the belief that people 'suffering from snake-bite have drunk water in which scrapings from the leaves of books from Ireland have been steeped, and this remedy checked the spreading poison and reduced the swelling'.[15] Then it becomes a play on letters, A having chief place 'because in the name of the Creator and the principal creatures the letter A is placed first: Adonai, Angeli, Archangeli, Anima. And the name of the first man, Adam, and of Abraham, who is head of the faith, is also spoken through the letter A'. And there are further references to 'Almus, Ageos, Alleluia, Amen', the words of praise reserved to God.[16] Matching Patrick's shamrock lesson, the letter is explained as symbolic of the Trinity—three strokes making one primal letter.

As in the early laws, and the social divisions, a clear love of classification can be seen in all this. As time goes on, meaning becomes divorced from form, and a hotch-potch of names, symbols and words from different languages become wrought together in formulae that have no logical sense and very little apparent merit of other kinds. The qualities of numbers are developed in a clear progression that owes its conception to Pythagoras; each cardinal number representing some basic relationship, as One —the unity of God; Two—the bond of marriage. The longest, and most baffling, of the relics of literature of this sort, is a work known as the *Hisperica Famina*.[17] It discusses such commonplaces as Sea, Fire, Earth, Wind, Clothes in an inverted style of Latin, propped with inapposite and misunderstood words from Greek and Hebrew, as well as some native Irish. It is a very laboured linguistic surrealism, and appears to get nobody anywhere. But it again illustrates a trait in the Irish mind, and brings associations of doodles paradoxically wrought by over-attention. The *Hisperica Famina* has been called, with some restraint, 'perhaps the most extreme thing in medieval Latin'.[18] It does not enhance

69

Irish literature. But the spirit it exaggerates produced, in moderation, some of the most beautiful fantasies of early literature. Among these are the seafaring legend of St Brendan.

Brendan's legend is an allegory of the pains and pleasures of the ascetic search for God. The two are not clearly divided, as they never can be. The loneliness of the desert places was compensated by the heightened awareness of little things round about, and the delights of coming to know them. Commonly enough, the enjoyment of this dedicated life led hermits to pray for mortification and suffering, and to go out of their way to find it. The belief in salvation through suffering was a deep one.

> God give me a well of tears
>   my sins to hide;
> for I remain while no tears fall
>   unsanctified. [19]

For some, leaving family and friends was enough, since the warmth and secure rights of the small community were a big sacrifice. For others there was a need to intensify their exile. They would seek out lepers to minister to them. St Finnian purposely caught the disease from a child as a means to perfection. Of the same order were those who immersed themselves in running waters to say their psalms, winter or summer, like Brendan's own patron Erc and many others. The stricter rules of some monasteries enforced these practices, ordering an almost intolerable number of genuflections, prostrations and fasts. An unusual torment was devised by one hermit, the son of Tulchan, who, in an age of uncontrolled pests when the blight of fleas was often referred to, conceived a penance to last a lifetime:

> that his pain might be the greater here,
> he never scratched himself. [20]

Another sat seven years on the backbone of a whale. And so of course things went too far, and sober voices had to advise moderation to those whose pain was becoming indulgently masochistic: like the anchorite who:

used to make two hundred prostrations in the morning and a hundred at every canonical hour and a hundred at matins. Seven hundred prostrations in all he used to make in the twenty-four hours. That was told to Mael Ruain. 'I give you my word', he said, 'that he will be for a while before his death and he won't make any prostrations.' That proved to be true, for his legs became cramped so that he could make no genuflections on account of making too many before that. [21]

The wise virgin Samthann of Clonbroney told a hermit desiring to follow the fashion and look for God in foreign lands: 'Were God to be found overseas, I too would take ship and go. But since God is near to all that call upon him, there is no constraint upon us to seek him overseas. For from every land there is a way to the kingdom of Heaven.' [22]

To Brendan, however, a long journey was permitted, was even pressed upon him through a divine vision. He was no fanatic torturer of the body, wrenching grace through unnatural want or strain. He had served his people in his own light and gone away from them alone to become close to God. All the stories that are told of him while he remains on the land of Ireland indicate a kindly energetic man, with an occasional lapse into temper and silliness. His aspiration was one that was common to many of his contemporaries—and to earlier and later generations—to go into that ocean which brought his country its winds and mists and dazzling sunsets, and to see what lay beyond, the source from which these things came. Others before him had been vexed and some—Oisin and Bran—had been spirited to the unseen land beyond the waves. Those who wove the tale of Brendan undoubtedly had earlier ideas in mind, and Brendan, like Brigid, is a composite character with pagan threads woven into the Christian pattern. It is another example of the vigour of Irish Christianity, which had no reason to hate or suppress the ideas and desires of generations before the gospel came. Brendan's name, and the variation used in the later naming of the mountain where he sat—Mount Brandon—are close to that of Bran; so are some of the tales of the journeys, though Bran went in search of a fair lady, a motive for which Brendan would have had contempt. Bran means raven, a bird of antique sanctity in the island. And ravens play some part in the tales of the hermit-sailor.

* * * *

'And he heard the voice of the angel from heaven who said to him: "Arise, O Brendan," saith he, "for God hath given thee what thou soughtest, even the Land of Promise." Then Brendan arose, and his mind was glad at that answer, and he goes alone to Sliabh Daidche, and he saw the mighty intolerable ocean on every side, and then he beheld the beautiful noble island, with three trains of angels rising from it.'[23]

It may have been the starving and the intoxicating herbs, but he knew the island was there, a real projection of the mind, or a real land of bright abundance. He was not alone in visions of angels or of lands that half equate with the world after death. Fursa, an Irish monk in Britain later, took leave of his body for the space of one night and was conducted in the period round heaven and hell where he was scorched—and the scar remained—by a splash of flame from some sinner being thrown to his punishment.[24] Both accounts have some reflection in, if not influence on, the work of Dante, though grotesquely exaggerated claims have been made by nationalistic Irishmen. Brendan's story has far more in common with that of Bran than with apocalyptic works. His story is one of the Immrama, a division of the tales listed in those scrupulous classifications of later scribes. Immrama are voyage tales with a colourful supernatural element in them—encounters with monsters and mystics and other-worldly landscapes. There is too a common quality in the motives of them all, a desire to attain some intangible ideal that is difficult to express, a need to escape for a while from the world's realities. Bran sailed out to an Eldorado to find an island of restful delight and sensual pleasure, where wailing and treachery are unknown, a 'distant isle' where there are

Into the West

Golden chariots on the plain of the sea
Heaving with the tide to the sun[25]

and all the pastimes of heroes are well provided in beautiful settings. Maelduin sets off with his warrior companions to take revenge on the man who killed his father. Revenge itself is a quality that brings no real relief; and he finds a greater satisfaction in renouncing his legal claims. Other Immrama have aims as passionate and ideal. The O'Corra go to find the 'Lord on the Sea'; Snedgus and his companions to rescue a man from death by fire.

How much of Brendan's voyage is historical, how much spontaneous or derivative myth is impossible to know, our sources are so meagre and so late. The similarities in episodes make it clear that the tales are closely linked, though the generations of relationship will remain unknown. For the time being, Brendan is a saint and a sailor and a man of flesh and blood. Fired by his vision, he recruits a crew from his monks. They equip a boat, a curragh of wicker covered in stretched hide, and they sail from Brandon Creek, a narrow inlet below the headland formed by the mountain where he had lived alone. Other hermits, in ones or twos, were accustomed to sail off in a boat without oars, trusting to God. Few stories survive of their journeys; perhaps all shared a fate with criminals who were likewise exposed to God's will. Not so with Brendan's crew. They took oars and sail, and they brought back a story.

'So Brendan son of Finnlug sailed then over the wave-voice of the strong-maned sea, and over the storm of the green-sided waves, and over the mouths of the marvellous bitter ocean, where they saw the multitude of furious red-mouthed monsters, with abundance of great sea-whales.'[26]

73

IV

The Sailor Saint

This is the outline of a story that was later translated into English, Welsh, Scottish Gaelic, Breton, French, Saxon, Latin and Flemish. There is a ninth-century Latin version, and a later Irish version which comes probably from an earlier source. Both of these are the surviving key sources. The Latin story is quite polished and sober; the Irish version from the Book of Lismore is more colourful and, in a sense, Irish. The thirty monks and Brendan sailed for seven years, following a roundabout route and returning each Easter to the same place. There are discrepancies between the different versions; they would matter more if any of the versions were completely true stories. The biggest difference is that the Latin tale makes the voyage continuous while the Book of Lismore breaks it into two. The crew have to return and build a new boat without animal ingredients. Ox hide went against the pacific ethics of the Land of Promise.

As they are about to sail three of Brendan's own monks run up to the boat and beg to be part of the crew. In a mysterious manner he allows them to come but forecasts doom for two of them; there is no explanation why, and one is left to guess that the warning may have to do with a *geis*, or tabu, possibly connected with the lucky number of sailors on board, and perhaps a relic from some other pagan tale where the episode has more meaning. They sail away, and for fifteen days winds help their progress. Then comes a still period when it is necessary to row, until buffets of wind bring the sail into play again. Just before they run out of food (after forty days, which means no more than a long haul, as three days means a short one) they sight an island with steep and rocky sides. Stepping ashore, they are greeted by a dog which leads them to some buildings. In one of them a table is laid with enough bread and fishes for them all. But Brendan, whose

caution and prescience are much in evidence during the trip,
warns them to be on their guard against temptation. Again one
wonders why, in this deserted but hospitable island; until, after
they have eaten and drunk, and are resting, a rather shivery and
quite unexplained passage ensues; involving one of the latecomer monks.

> When the brethren had gone to sleep, St Brendan saw the
> demon, in the guise of a little boy, at his work, having in his
> hands a bridle bit, and beckoning to the monk before
> mentioned: then he rose from his couch, and remained all night
> in prayer.[1]

Three days later they prepare to leave. Dramatically Brendan ex-
poses the monk who fell a prey to temptation and now conceals the
silver necklace in his bosom. As the rest fall on the ground to pray:

> St Brendan raised up the guilty brother. They all saw the
> little black boy leap out of his bosom, howling loudly: 'Why,
> O man of God, do you expel me from my abode where I have
> dwelt for seven years, and drive me away, as a stranger, from
> my secure possession?'

The wraith is damned, and the monk, says Brendan, must prepare
to die. After the last offices he does so, and his soul, redeemed,
is borne to heaven by flights of angels.

They take their leave and sail, until on Easter Thursday they
reach an island of fat white sheep 'so numerous as to hide the face
of the land'. Here again they are lavishly provided by a man who
prostrates himself at Brendan's feet in gratitude for the privilege.
He also tells the group their immediate future as they are filling
the boat with provisions. They are to cross to a nearby island for
Easter Sunday, and at midday, after mass, to sail to the Paradise of
Birds. Brendan, with a keen eye for detail, asks the reason for the
massive size of the sheep around them and is told: 'There is nobody on the island to milk them, and since there is no winter to
make them go thin they stay out at pasture the whole year round.'
There is no grass, very little wood and no sand on the shore of

the island to which they now cross. The monks are in for a surprise; but not Brendan himself, who a little tepidly—in the light of his clairvoyance—spends the Saturday night on board while the monks sleep on the smooth surface of the islet.

'When morning dawned he bade the priests to celebrate Mass and after they had done so, and he himself had said Mass in the boat, the brethren took out some uncooked meat and fish they had brought from the other island, and put a cauldron on a fire to cook them. After they had placed more fuel on the fire, and the cauldron began to boil, the island moved about like a wave; whereupon they all rushed towards the boat, and implored the protection of their father. "Fear not, my children," said the saint, "for God last night revealed to me the mystery of all this; it was not an island you were upon, but a fish, the largest of all that swim in the ocean, which is ever trying to make its head and tail meet, but cannot succeed, because of its great length. Its name is Jasconius." '

When the culture of Ireland, invigorated by essences from abroad, was to start moving along the same paths that had brought those influences in—paths now derelict or in decline—Jasconius was to reappear in Middle Eastern waters as a feature of Sinbad's Arabian tales, and a frequent theme in the sagas of Scandinavia. But for the present he turns on his side and washes into the ocean, till his back is needed the following Easter. His services are given willingly. Only the scorch of a bonfire on his back can break his indulgence. From the whale the monks row to another island, as directed by their guide, set firm in the sea and covered in woods and grass and flowers. This is the Paradise of Birds. At the point where they landed there is a tree, of which not a leaf is visible because of the number of large white birds clustered on its boughs.

The saint is vexed by the problem—one might feel inordinately so, for he throws himself on the ground weeping loudly and praying God for an explanation. Thereupon one of the birds flies down to his side—'his wings in flight had a tinkling sound like little bells'—and explains:

Paradise of birds

'We are partakers in the great ruin of the ancient enemy, having fallen, not by sin of our will or consent, but soon after our creation our ruin resulted from the fall of Lucifer and his followers. The Almighty God, however, who is righteous and true, has doomed us to this place, where we suffer no pain, and where we can partially see the divine presence, but must remain apart from the spirits who stood faithful. We wander about the world, in the air, and earth, and sky, like other spirits on their missions; but on festival days we take the shapes you see, abide here, and sing the praises of our Creator. You and your brethren have now been one year on your voyage; and six more years' journeying awaits you.'

Bird and man at once are friends. It is another contribution of birds to the literature of the Irish, as these refreshing creatures partake heartily in the religious offices of their new company.

'On the approach of the hour of vespers all the birds, in unison, clapping their wings, began to sing "A hymn, O lord, becometh Thee in Sion, and a vow shall be paid to Thee in Jerusalem"; and they alternately chanted the same psalm for an hour; and the melody of their warbling, and the accompanying clapping of their wings, sounded like unto a delightful harmony of great sweetness.'

From now on the birds join in all the responses and psalms and offices of the monks until Whitsun, the season for the men of God to depart.

They travel in all directions, with delightful and forbidding encounters on the way, now sailing three days at a stretch, now forty. Storms shake them and waves soak, but whenever they tremble, far from land and short of food, Brendan reminds them of what they should have learned not to forget—God's bountiful attention; for they are never short for long. Once they are entertained on a remote island by St Ailbe, St Patrick's contemporary who must have outlived his natural span by a hundred years. Ailbe was one who clashed with Patrick over details of administration, and finally submitted to him. His monastic rule had been part of Brendan's education. He too has a voyage legend, in which he is said to walk over the sea from Corcumruadh in Clare, and return carrying a fruit-laden branch from a tree on the Land of Promise. There is no reference to his present extended exile, but there is seldom much correlation between the different lives of saints.

The rule of Ailbe's island is silence, and this calls forth an unusually schoolmasterly rebuke from the abbot to his monks: 'Keep guard over your tongues,' he says, 'or you will destroy the spirit of recollection of the monks here with your buffoonery.' But if tongues are still, the spirit of hospitality is not absent. The hosts wash the sailors' feet in token of welcome, and provide them with a sumptuous meal of roots and white bread. Then, as the company prepares for mass at an altar of crystal, a divine flaming arrow shoots through the window, lights all the candles, and flies out again. Brendan, curious as Alice, wants to know the reason why; Ailbe, having relaxed the rule of silence for the first time in eighty years, answers shortly: 'Have you not read of the bush on Mount Sinai, how it burned and was not consumed?' It is a slender contact between the two abbots, but as much as they are allowed.

On they sail, months growing into years, with as little acknowledgement in the texts as in the minds of the anchorites. On one island some of their number, flouting the advice of the forewarned abbot, are drugged by toxic water, and fall into a sleep of two or three days. Later they are becalmed for days in a stretch of ocean so sluggish that it seems curdled. And a little farther on a furious sea-monster—'bigger than a brazen cauldron was each of his eyes; a boar's tusks had he; furzy hair was upon him'—gives chase to the boat, but is happily diverted and killed, in the nick of time, by another. They sail past the carcase of a giant flaxen-haired girl; 'huge in sooth was the size of that maiden, to wit, a hundred feet in her height, and nine feet between her two paps, and seven feet in the length of her middle finger'. Brendan brings her to life and baptises her, then asks about herself. 'Of the dwellers of the sea am I; that is of those who pray and expect their resurrection.'

He asks her plans, and shows no distress at her wish to die again. She has already heard the choirs of heavenly angels and now, after final unction, she passes away, again and finally.

Some time later the exiles pass over a sea so shallow and clear that they can discern great shoals of fishes swimming heads to tails. The monks tremble again; they are easily vexed by now. But Brendan without pause proceeds to choral mass on board:

> 'And the fishes, when they heard the voice of the man of God, rose up from the depths, and swam about the boat in such numbers, that the brethren could see nothing but the swimming fishes, which however came not close to the boat, but swam around at some distance, until the Mass was ended, when they swam away in divers directions, out of the view of the brethren.'

Then comes a strange and picturesque experience, picked on by those who like to chart the route the monks took as clear evidence of an original discovery. They see a crystal column rising out of the sea, so vast that when they think they are approaching it they still have three days' travelling to reach it. When eventually they come near they find it hollow—the boat passes through an opening quite easily—and all is light inside and the sea is miraculously clear. Sailing through and round they find its measurements symmetrical, each side taking a day to pass along. At the end of these researches they come across a chalice and paten lying in a niche. The discovery inspires Brendan to a sleuth's verdict: 'This miracle,' he says, 'is the work of Our Lord Jesus Christ. These two gifts have been given me so that the story of our travels may be widely believed.' He does not see that it is just this detail which will make belief difficult.

Many more islands entrance their eyes with exotic marvels. Returning annually to their Easter service on the back of Jasconius, they go out again each time for fresh diversions: an island with three choirs, of old men, young men and boys, each dressed in vestments of different colours; an island of fruits in which the grapes are as big as apples, and a smell like the fragrance of pomegranates pervades the atmosphere. But now the years have passed, and they are close to their reward. However, before they see the Island of Promise, they must witness a little of the anguish of hell. The experience calls out the most eloquent and vivid passage in the whole story, and the only pity is that the narrator did not save his resources for his description of heaven, or the Land of Promise. Not long after the excitement of the crystal column:

'On a certain day they were on the sea the devil came in a form inveterate, hideous, foul, hellish, and sat on the sail of the vessel before Brendan, and none of them saw him, save Brendan alone. Brendan asked why he had come. Saith the devil "to seek my punishment in the deep enclosures of this black dark sea". Brendan asked of him "Where is that infernal place?" "No one can see it and remain alive afterwards." Howbeit the devil revealed the gate of hell to Brendan. And Brendan beheld that rough hot prison, full of stench, full of flame, full of filth, full of the camps of the poisonous demons, full of wailing and screaming hurt, and sad cries and great lamentations and moaning and handsmiting of the sinful folks; cores of pain, prisons of fire, streams of the rows of eternal fire. On sides of mountains of eternal fire, hosts of demons dragging sinners into prisons foul, stale, musty. Worms curved, hard, big-headed, and monsters yellow, white, great-mouthed; lions fierce; dragons red, black, brown, demoniac; scorpions blue; vultures rough and sharp-beaked; leeches crooked, bone-mouthed; cats scratching, hounds rending, demons yelling; stinking lakes, far swamps, dark pits, deep glens; quarrel without cease. Snow frozen, flakes red and fiery, faces base and darkened, demons swift and greedy, tortures vast, various.'

Only two small episodes keep them now from the object of their journey. First, another of the latecomer monks—so inexplicably sinful—is drawn like a homing pigeon to the precincts of hell, condemned to all the torments listed. Brendan regrets his going, but wastes no time. He draws a moral on the wages of sin and sails again. Then they make out an uncanny figure across the waves, marooned on a rock and battered by the unsparing sea. As they draw closer this turns out to be the archetypal sinner:

'When they came near they saw the form of a man sitting on a stone, and the likeness of a cloak or other garment suspended on two iron forks before him, and he was being tormented among the waves, the cloak smiting him under the eyes, and he being one time dragged off the rock, and another tossed on to it again.'

Brendan asks him 'Why are these torments inflicted on you? And who are you?'

'I am that evil chapman Judas,' comes the doleful reply, 'who delivered the Lord Jesus Christ into the hands of the Jews. But it is not this place which is my requital, but by the mercy of the Lord, in honour of the Resurrection, I have this ease. And to me this state is like Paradise compared with what will be inflicted on me this night in the fiery mountain you saw, where is Leviathan with his companions. There they assail me, and I am smelted like lead in an earthen pot, but I have great ease on Sunday and at certain other feasts. But all other days I am racked and tormented with Pilate and Caiaphas and Annas in hell.'

The officiously merciful Brendan wants to help in some way, and prays for an extension to Judas' furlough. This, granted, infuriates the devilish imps who wait like vultures for Judas' immunity to expire, and they chase Brendan with stings and abuse which fail to pierce his sanctity. The monks sail on, meet a lean hermit on a lone rocky island who can address them all by name, go through for the seventh time their whalebound Easter routine, and finally set off in earnest, with an agreeable guide from the Island of Sheep as companion, for the Promised Land. They sail forty days, and pass through a thick fog towards the end of the journey, emerging finally on to a ravishing landscape. An old man steps down to meet them: 'Search ye and see,' said the old man, 'the plains of Paradise, and the delightful fields of this radiant land, a land odorous, flower-smooth, blessed; a land many-melodied, musical, shouting for joy; a place where ye shall find health without sickness, delight without quarrels, rest without idleness, freedom without labour, luminous unity of angels, delights of Paradise, service of angels, feasting without extinction. . . .' The island, they are told, is intersected by a wide river, and forty days of walking would not bring them to the far side. What they do attempt we are not told in any detail. The Latin text talks of them filling the boat with fruits and jewels, and sailing back to Ireland. Some manuscripts break off; and in one, of the twelfth century, the scribe through excitement or ennui continues without break and inadvertently into a quite unrelated manuscript. This is not the pagan paradise of Oisin and Bran, echoing to the jousts and feastings of knights and maidens of the heroic mould. Nor is it the apex of Dante's paradisal spiral, a summit of perfection wrought by the architecture of the medieval mind. It seems more the conventional conclusion to a tale, by a man who has enjoyed an expedition, related it with a mariner's augments, and laced it with piety to suit the tastes of his audience.

That is the essence of the journey. It is full of the spirit that was passed down by early Christian adventurers to scribes confined uneasily in their scriptoria. It tells of the dreams of men, and their love of the sea, the unknown, the uncanny, the grotesque, and the horrible. It is a Celtic *Odyssey*, though never a patch on Homer; and it has been inflated with the wind of all manner of theories since those early scribes, inserting a good deal of their own invention, put pen to paper. A glance at those theories is profitable in two ways: it shows some of the influence—albeit unintended— that Irish literature had on later ages; and it helps to clarify the influences at work on the Irish themselves.

In the eleventh century, when the marriage of Henry II and Eleanor of Aquitaine brought together England and a large part of France, the Gaelic and old British literature, that had been dispersed by the Saxon raids, was beginning to revive. It spread to the continent, where it sprouted in the rhymes of minstrels and troubadours. The Arthurian legends, which already had roots in Brittany, held pride of place, and it was French poets who brought them to a high pitch, and removed them far from the original models. The same process moulded other legends and traditions, and the name of Brendan was spread through the popularity he was given by French storytellers. In England too, Caxton translated and printed the Brendan story. But England never shared continental enthusiasm for it, and after Caxton English interest declined. Elizabethan literature eclipsed it, and although Tennyson refers to it, and lesser poets filched from it, the popularity of the Brendan legend was never restored.

In Ireland things were different. Brendan's reputation as a religious adventurer assured him of immortality. His story is still taught to the children, and his elevated hermitage on Mount Brandon has been a destination of pilgrims for over a thousand years. But he was popular for more than obvious reasons. In the course of centuries his voyage became invol˙ed in the immense and complicated lore of the Atlantic. St Brendan's Island—the Land of Promise—became the Gaelic version of the universal myth about a land in mid-ocean, Atlantis, which originated—perhaps—with the Greeks and spread through every national mythology. It was an elemental island hidden in Atlantic mists.

Plato's Atlantis, not far west of the Pillars of Hercules, was a continent which had, nine thousand years before, reached a higher plane of civilisation and enjoyed more power than any land since. Then it was washed by a gigantic wave and lost to the world. But the theme continued. Sometimes Atlantis became one of the actual Atlantic islands, one of the Azores or Madeira, and sometimes it was given a place of its own. The location could be real or phantasmal. Lyonesse, Avalon, the Greek Fortunate Islands and Portuguese Isle of Seven Cities were incorporeal abodes of a spiritual after-life, though they occasionally took on substantial form to admit a hero or saint.

With the Renaissance more weight was given to the stories. Atlantis and its versions were assumed to exist. And St Brendan's Island, linked with other Irish legends that spoke of it, began to preoccupy actual navigators. Columbus is said to have visited Ireland, and Iceland too, in search of information about the geography of Brendan's voyage. He took Irishmen with him on his great expedition. And he made scrupulous inquiries about the island in the Azores, after hundreds of people there had sworn they often saw the place on fine days, far out in the west. The Portuguese in particular were concerned with the existence of this potential island colony, and sent several expeditions to find it. The latest one, in 1721, came back with the same negative results as those before; so that they grew cynical and wrote the thing off as a mirage.

This was final renunciation of the idea of an island; but not of a physical parallel to Brendan's landfall. For by the nineteenth century Irish patriot scholars had decided that, if they could not place the island between Europe and America, they would go to the other side and make Brendan the discoverer of the New World. The idea was stimulating to those with knowledge on related subjects, and soon the evidence began to pile. In the course of their researches they produced some feasible arguments.

Some of the evidence came from America itself. It was stated that white men had arrived as missionaries in the central part of America hundreds of years before. Certainly the ease of Cortés' occupation of Mexico was due to a belief among natives that a fair-skinned god, Quetzalcoatl, who after his visit to Mexico had sailed away over the sea, would return one day from the east. The Mexicans identified Cortés, at the head of his resplendent navy, with the god. Now scholars, in their turn, turned the god into a Christian missionary, an Irish missionary, St Brendan.

Other material appeared to support the theory. Traditions of white settlers were found among North American Indians, particularly the Shawnee of the eastern seaboard, who preserved memories of white men using iron implements. None of this evidence, however, made specific reference to Irish missions, nor of course to St Brendan. Singling out the Irish was to come from a separate source that gave remarkable strength to the arguments.

'Ari Marson was driven by a tempest to White Man's Land [Hvitramannaland], which some call Great Ireland [Irland-ed-mikla]; it lies to the west in the ocean, near to Vinland the Good, and six days' sailing west from Ireland.' This passage, from the Icelandic *Landnamabok*, made a breakthrough. The record, written in the twelfth century, described one of the several Norse journeys to Vinland, the Land of Wine. Vinland was supposed, and is now virtually proved, to have been the fertile eastern seaboard of America. And the Norse gave it the title Great Ireland. Why, asked the optimists; because for sure Norsemen had found Irishmen on the continent when they arrived. And they soon produced other texts to stress the point.

Once the link was accepted—albeit by a few—renewed efforts were made to place St Brendan's Land of Promise in the American continent. To make this more plausible the journey story was searched, not for its poetry or whimsy, but for sound geographical data. Here too there was some success, and the efforts still continue. Much is acceptable, though based more on hint than fact at the best of times.

Without doubt there are features in the story which appear to resemble actual places and landmarks around and in the Atlantic. If we cannot decide from the similarities that the Irish first colonised America, there is ample evidence that they travelled far. The most striking example in the story is the account of the crystal column, enormous, translucent, and showing the sea clear and blue underneath it. It takes no special pleading to make it a literary representation of an iceberg. The paten and chalice that Brendan finds at the end of his search are part of the literary aspect. The main description is near enough the real thing to make its provenance clear. Anyone who had seen an iceberg—and especially such a large one—must have travelled far to the west to do so. Icebergs float down from Baffin Bay along the coast of eastern Canada and occasionally reach as far as Newfoundland. They come farther east too, but not as far as the Iceland region. Anyone who had come across an iceberg would almost certainly have called at Iceland and sailed beyond. The Irish, then, had sailed beyond.

This established, it is possible to link other, and less obvious, features of the story with geographical reality. One version of the hell story speaks of a gigantic smithy by which giants worked. On the approach of the pilgrims, one giant ran to the shore and started to fling molten lumps at them, which they escaped by quickly turning back. His companions followed his example, and the boat was surrounded by sea fizzing with the red-hot embers. The inference can be drawn that this is a personalised volcano, and is fittingly placed either in Iceland or in Jan Mayen Island, to the north-east of Iceland. Both sites have persistently nursed volcanoes.

The curdled sea on which Brendan was becalmed is aptly identified with the Sargasso, a vast stretch of sluggish waters in the western Atlantic. While the transparent sea in which he saw and performed to shoals of pious fish could well represent any of the flat reefs abounding in the area of the West Indies, particularly the Bahamas. On smaller details identification becomes more hypothetical. But serious researchers have managed to fit in the Azores, the Canaries, Cape Verde Islands, Greenland, the Faeroes, Hebrides, Rockall and the Orkneys—most of the main features of the northern half of the Atlantic. The Land of Promise is called an island in the tales. Nova Scotia and Florida are peninsulas, easily taken for islands by those who landed, crossed them and found sea on the other side. Florida is made possible by the rich and lush vegetation of the Everglades. Nova Scotia is given backing by the presence of thick fogs from which these pilgrims, and others in other tales, emerge into the blissful landscape. Between them, New England presents a perfectly apt alternative, but for the want of any similarity to an island.

It is not unlikely that knowledge of some or all of these features had been passed down among the Irish. When one considers the distances involved, and the known trade routes from Ireland to Spain and the Mediterranean, the jumps from the British Isles to Iceland, thence to Greenland, and thence again to eastern Canada are feasible. The Vikings were to make them some time later, though their boats, broad-breasted and driven by vast rectangular sheets of sail, were vastly superior to anything that had gone before. Even so, the beautiful gold objects exhibited in Dublin's

National Museum include a model, pre-dating Brendan's time by about five centuries, of a large boat with benches, sail and fourteen oars. No remains have been found of actual boats to correspond with the model, but wood perishes quickly, and this does not rule out the possibility. Even if the model were one of a Roman or other Mediterranean boat imported to the country, it could have given the Irish ideas which led to similar constructions.

That is as far as Brendan's case can be taken. There is neither proof nor disproof. But from this point the voices of detractors are heard. In the first place the earliest known version of the story is a ninth-century one. Brendan lived and sailed in the sixth century. In the course of that time any amount of colour could have been added to what might have started as a simple, not very ambitious journey. It is known that during the latter centuries the Irish reached and colonised many of the northern islands, including the Faeroes and Iceland. It is possible that their discoveries and those of adventurers from different nations were woven into the story. Additions could derive also from earlier records. They could include stories taken from Mediterranean myth and processed for Celtic conditions.

It is always, in this period, difficult to see what is Irish and what is not. Many of the Palestinian traditions around Christ and the Virgin Mary were shamelessly adopted by the Irish for their own archetypal Christians. Brigid became a second Mary, Brendan was born in conditions similar to those of Christ, with a light in the sky, the presence of cattle, and the important locals coming to pay their respects. These cases are far from isolated. In the same way the early Christian Irish adopted and transformed legends and customs that were originally pagan. Now we have another possible example of plagiarism. The Irish certainly borrowed widely from classical myth.

It is important to remember that most of the legends and poems did not begin to be written down before the seventh century. During this time new contacts had been established by the Irish missionaries who penetrated Gaul, Germany, Switzerland and Italy, and brought back cultural returns for their religious offerings. The continental Church had preserved parts of classical culture alive during even the worst barbarian deprivations, in spite of their distrust of pagan survivals of any kind. It is not surprising therefore that much of this classical legacy was imported into Ireland at the same time. Some had arrived before, and it is not possible to know how much was familiar to Irish of the sixth century and how much was kept from them till the seventh and later centuries. What we can be sure of, however, is that the monks who wrote the manuscripts of the Brendan story *which survive* would have had a considerable knowledge of classical literature, mainly in Latin but including Latin translations from the Greek.

In this light, the smithy story of Brendan's hell goes through another shuffle. It may be the tale of a volcano, and Iceland or Jan Mayen are the most likely situations if it is. But the story has a ring of Odysseus' encounter on the island of the Cyclops. Here the Greek wanderer and his crew are the victims of the cannibalistic fury of the giant Polyphemus. Escaping by guile, they are pelted with boulders by the Cyclops whose only eye Odysseus painfully scorched the night before. The stones land short of the boat, and the travellers escape; just as Brendan does. To dismay the literalists more, there are as many plausible parallels in the Homeric story as there are physical features to match the sights that Brendan sees. There is an echo of the land of the Lotus Eaters in the story of the island of drugged water. And some of the description of the Land of Promise seems to be reminiscent of Calypso's seductive island. Nor do parallels stop with the story of Brendan. Plenty of the heroic tales have apparent borrowings from classical authors. The themes of weeping horses and a chopped-off hand found often in the Cuchulain sagas are exactly, and more than once, paralleled in Virgil. Descriptions of palaces seem to be taken from Homer, while some of the tales of early kings are very close to those of the Greek myth and history. The 'Fate of the Children of Tuireann', one of the 'three sad tales of Erin', has strong links with the story of Jason and the Argo. It might be possible—perhaps when Irish scholarship begins the constructive phase of systematising all its researches it will be possible—to create an Irish *Odyssey* or *Iliad* set in an Irish scene, with not only the poetic greatness of the original but a good deal of close relationship in content.

Brendan himself is being left out in the cold. A case seems to be emerging for saying that most of the details of his journey are borrowings from literature made long after he died. But this is an overstatement of the case. A reprieve for Irish originality comes from the fact that in some cases Greek, Latin and Celtic—and even Teutonic—myths share a common source; that anyway some of the literary conventions are not seventh-century and later borrowings but traces from a very distant past shared with other civilisations. The common link of course is the Celtic civilisation which spread all over Europe and the Middle East before the Romans rose to European power and the barbarians pushed the Celts to their western sanctuaries. Modern research is showing that there are clear parallels in the development of most of the major cultures, caused either by contact or by the common evolution of societies facing similar environments.

Still Brendan does not fare well. Either way, or both, his attributes appear to be anachronistic. If he is not what he is explicitly said to be, he becomes a Christian sailor whose memory is shrouded in the attributes of Odysseus; or in those of pagan Celtic heroes; or an amalgam of both. And if the attempts to trace his actual journey are based on literary evidence that is shown to come from earlier or later sources, they are seen to shed very little light on the man in question.

A tenable conclusion is that the Irish in later days sailed far, certainly arrived in Iceland, and possibly in Greenland and some part of America. The main support for this position comes from Icelandic sagas. Equally the Irish, or other races, may have reached America long before Brendan's time. That claim is based on more intricate evidence, none the worse for being so. Ironically it gives the saint himself a possible reprieve. If the journey had been made before it would have given a sixth-century hermit ample incentive for trying it again. So that Brendan, lame from analysis, can after all emerge still as a possible candidate. And in tentative vindication, it must be remembered that the story of this pilgrimage to a promised land hangs on his name. Just as, when we discard the miraculous circumstances of his birth and early life, we can still, without being credulous, believe in a saint of great devoutness and energy; so when the critical apparatus of comparative myth and geography is put away, we still have a man who was famous for his journeys. And even if we withdraw altogether from the dazzling lights of Celtic make-believe, we can account him a godly sailor of no small distinction; and give him credit for being the central theme in a story of great charm, that owes its spirit, if not its total content, to him and the men of his age.

Nor is his case necessarily closed with an indulgent acknowledgement that he might have been a proto-Columbus. Norse claims to American discovery were only recently stamped with the authority of the Vinland map. Brendan may yet find palpable evidence.

*   *   *   *

Brendan returned to Ireland, and the more credible phase of his life. He was still to travel, to risk his life in restless searchings, and to play the autocrat among his erring monks. But from now on he keeps to an undoubtedly mortal plane.

He was greeted warmly by the monks who recognised his leadership. And without delay he set about the more practical side of a pioneering abbot's life. He travelled about the country, doubtless amazing and inspiring everyone with the wonders of his experiences, and turned to the important task of founding more monasteries. Christianity was still in its earliest phase, and the battle for souls was not won. Keeping mainly to the provinces of Connaught and Munster, he took up the threads of his proselytising missions.

Islands were still the acme of spiritual life. So he founded a monastery at Inisdadroum on the Shannon estuary. On Inishtooskert, at the end of the Dingle peninsula, and with Brandon

Brendan in Ireland

mountain in clear view, there are still remains of an oratory where Brendan founded another small monastery. More exist at the foot of the mountain itself, and farther north on the island of Inishglora, off the coast of Mayo. Here the remains are extensive, and until the last century a wooden statue of the saint stood in the corner of a ruined church. It also preserved a typical tradition. It was said that, because of the dedication to Brendan, no corpse buried in the precincts of the monastery ever decayed. More than that, hair and finger-nails continued to grow. There are other places with the same attributes. In the crypt of St Michan's Church in Dublin bodies are displayed awaiting the last judgment, in their pristine forms, though there is nothing to show that hair and nails do not die with the rest. The explanation is in the healthy bog air, very damp but not decaying. It has helped to preserve Christ Church Cathedral on a foundation dating from the twelfth century, which rests much of its weight on original wooden wedges.

He had lost none of his old ebullience, nor the slightly priggish quality that marks his utterings during the Atlantic journey. A characteristic story is told of him at this time—though its outcome is not typical. At work on Inisdadroum, a monk came to tell him that a novice, minding the boat under Brendan's orders, was in danger of his life because of the fast rising tide. Brendan resented the gratuitous advice: 'Do you love this brother more than I do?' he asked pettishly. 'If you do, and desire to show more compassion for him than I have, go to him now, and die in his stead.' The monk went and was drowned in the waves. It was partly as penance that Brendan set out on his travels to the other provinces and Britain.

Meanwhile he went on to found a convent in Galway—Annaghdown by the shore of Lough Corrib. As abbess he installed the only woman he is recorded to have tolerated, his sister Brig. Nothing is told of her. It can safely be assumed that she was both placid and pleasing. And it was to Brig at Annaghdown that he later came to die. Now he pressed on indefatigably. He had other foundations to make, and he soon found the site where he was to plant his most famous house, the abbey of Clonfert.

91

Clonfert today—a dainty church of the twelfth century that styles itself a cathedral and caters for the handful of Protestants remaining in the area—belies its old prestige. It drew recruits from all the central plain of Ireland and became noted for scholarship, devotion and the rigours of a strict rule. It was linked with the saint's name even when his journey was not. St Brendan of Clonfert became one of the twelve apostles of Ireland, and the monastery was among the half-dozen best known houses. Today it is distinguished by its west doorway, one of the best remains of Irish romanesque, and that is all. Nearby the Shannon winds up to the more impressive remains and situation of Clonmacnois, founded by Brendan's contemporary, Ciaran, to whom, during Ciaran's short life, he remained devoted.

Ciaran, like many, had been trained by St Enda on the Aran Islands. He was unusual among founders as being not an aristocrat but son of a carpenter. There is a suspicion here that the record is but one more Messianic association, but the truth will never be known. In his pious novitiate he performed customary miracles, one day feeding a new-born calf to a starving wolf and restoring the calf immediately afterwards by a prayer on its bones. Learning his mother had refused meat to beggars, he ran home and threw out all her food to dogs. Leaving Aran, he founded one monastery at Hare Island on Lough Ree, then moved down the Shannon, beyond Athlone, to Clonmacnois, where he founded his most lasting institution. He was noted for energy and generosity, so much so that a nearby community to whom he gave his help found themselves corrupted by abundance of riches. 'Go away,' they said. 'We cannot let you stay with us.'[2] He died soon after the bare wattle buildings of Clonmacnois began to take shape. 'I do not know of any of the Lord's Commandments that I have broken,' he said, 'but even David son of Jesse and Paul the Apostle dreaded this road.' He was thirty-three. Brendan had wept at his going, and paid regular calls at the monastery, the nearest neighbour to his own, and one that later vied in position with the primatial see of Armagh.

Brendan also stayed with Finnian of Moville, whose achievement was as great and fame spread as far as his namesake of Clonard. Finnian was friendly with Columba, who was at one stage his pupil, and Finnian himself had strong links with Scotland. He studied at Whithorn, at the influential monastery called Candida Casa, founded earlier by Ninian. While there he indulged in a little chicanery that goes ill with his subsequent reputation, but hardly a saint has been recorded whose early life was without blemish. A chief's daughter at Whithorn was in love with another pupil, and asked Finnian to aid her plans in exchange for a number of books. He, a bibliophile, agreed, but deceived her by sending the wrong man to her cell at night. There was a child, threats of vengeance on all sides, and a murderous brawl. Finnian, coming out of the whole episode unscathed, seems to have had reserves of cunning and initiative.[3] They were equally useful in the climate of Ireland, still far from Christian. But his zeal was extreme. At his first foundation seven monks died of hunger and cold; and his curse of a man interrupting the liturgy brought down a literal hammer on the felon's head. Later he went to Rome, was ordained priest, and returned with a new Latin translation of the Bible. He founded the settlement of Moville, near Belfast, which towered above most other houses in scholarship. His great love was books. It was a love as possessive as human passion and it had unexpected effects on his friendship with Columba. To that we shall come in time.

To the north of Moville, on the coast, lies Bangor, founded in 558 by St Comgall. It was another stopping place for Brendan during these final journeys of his life. Bangor's influence was greater than any of its contemporaries'. It was Bangor that stamped the broad but harsh training on Columbanus which he subsequently, and successfully, imposed on his foundations through the Continent. Comgall, like most of his distinguished contemporary abbots, came from an elevated background. As a boy he found his teacher, who had a mistress, incompatible, and with haughty assurance left him. His strictness became proverbial, but he always demanded greater asceticism of himself than of others. He was graced with miraculous saliva. His spit could shatter a rock, and more than once a gobbet turned to gold. He was of the number which prayed in the water, summer and winter, with arms raised in the posture of the cross. He studied for a while under Finnian of Moville, then began his own foundations. These included Bangor itself, where four thousand monks are supposed to have resided at a time, and an untraced location on the island of Tiree in the western isles of Scotland. But Bangor was his greatest achievement, and the number of mentions of it in the lives of different saints is adequate proof of its influence. [4]

At this time the north of the country was gaining in importance. There was no decline in other parts, but the activity in the north caused by constant comings and goings with Scotland, where there was still pioneer missionary work to be done, made it a more fertile area than the rest. That Comgall taught, Columbanus learned, and at the same time over the water Columba founded his Scottish foothold at Iona, are witness of this activity. Brendan went to Scotland, and may have penetrated far. Little is told of him there, but enough memories of his name survive to show he made some impact. His name lives on in places like Kilbrennan (cell, or church of Brendan) in Mull, and in Lorn, Islay, Bute, Barra and St Kilda in the Outer Hebrides. [5] By this time Irish (still called Scottish) missionaries would have penetrated as far as Caithness, and there was probably a chain of communities through which visiting churchmen could pass, getting guidance and sustenance on the way. Brendan's name has been linked with the Orkneys, and Shetlands. Certainly the Irish did reach these islands at about this time, and not much later they arrived in Iceland, whose peripheral islands—the Westmann—take their name from the Norse word for Irishman, or west man. There are still remains of their buildings along the south coast of the country, and the Icelandic sagas speak of Irish hermits living in the country when Norsemen arrived.

With Comgall, Brendan is reported by Columba's biographer Adamnan to have come to Columba's Iona monastery. [6] And after a mass in the church he told his companions that he had seen a bright and fiery light shine above the head of Columba as he officiated at the service. It is somewhat disturbing that Adamnan, who has a high reputation as an early source—though his long catalogues of his hero's miracles, which are generally dull in the telling and the substance, mars his record—says nothing more of Brendan than this. But an impression comes through his work that he is not much concerned with Columba's contemporaries, and he makes a point of telling that any extraneous detail is left out for want of space. This being so, those who claim that Adamnan's neglect shows all Brendan's exotic achievements to be invention are not necessarily correct.

Officious and tireless to his dying day, Brendan now made for Wales, a country with special sanctity among Irish Christians for the debt they owed it. But in the first half of the sixth century, while he had grown up, trained and sailed miraculously over the ocean, the Church in Ireland had grown from strength to strength. The greatest contribution of Wales had subsided, and now the contact between the two countries came mainly from Irish missions over the sea, though a few Welsh continued to arrive both to teach and learn at different monasteries. Irish monasteries were developing a learning that could match the most distinguished continental parallels. By this time the barbarian intruders were well established in France, Italy and Spain, and the Catholic Church, while never in any danger of extinction, had to concentrate more on politics than culture to maintain its power. In England itself, with Arthur dead, and the temporary resistance to Anglo-Saxon invasion overthrown, the Germanic intruders were wiping out any trace of Christian worship and culture. Their own gods came in their place, to flourish for half a century or more before the recovery of Christianity sent them to the darker regions of men's minds. Only Wales, still controlled by pre-Saxon peoples, had a welcome for the Irish. It was a welcome conditioned by the new Irish character. Instead of looting parties, missionaries now filled the boats that sailed between the coasts of Wexford and Cornwall, Meath and Wales, and Ulster and the Irish-Scottish kingdom of Dalriada.

In Wales, Brendan met one of the most remarkable Britons

of his time, and the only one to have left any sort of historical record of the events he saw around him. Gildas had been to Ireland himself, and was later to die in Brittany. (The busy connections within this shrunken Celtic world are constantly referred to.) But his main concern was the troubled climate of his native Britain. Born at the turn of the century, he had lived through the heroic and squalid events in the final resistance of Briton against Saxon. He had seen his own people courageously stem the invaders; but his most vivid impression was of the futile disorganisation of their armies, their want of true faith, and their inability to sustain any effort. Flickers of glory there may have been. The general scene was of dying embers. And Gildas was not of a sanguine disposition. He was of the mould of Job, and the name of his surviving work is *Concerning the Destruction and Overthrow of Britain*.[7] It is a diatribe against the feckless character of his countrymen in the face of challenge from four points of the compass, and their fickle desertion of Roman ideals once the Romans themselves had gone. Their appeals to the Romans to return are the cackles of men 'huddling like frightened chickens beneath the comforting wings of their parents'. And Badon Hill, the final, for a time effective victory of the mysterious Arthur (Gildas himself mentions no names) had been 'almost the last slaughter wrought by us on that scum of the earth', the Saxons. Now the Saxon blaze had spread 'until it licked the western ocean with its fierce red tongue'.

By the time at which he wrote, the middle sixth century, things were, if anything, worse. What was left of the Britons' territory was the bulk of Wales and Cornwall, divided into five kingdoms and ruled by kings as deviously evil as Gildas' prose is stylistically convoluted. They squabbled among themselves instead of facing the common enemy, and Maelgwn king of Gwynedd, the northern part of Wales, having once turned to God and gone into a monastery, had left it to become the most treacherous devil's disciple of them all. He had put his own wife away, and taken the wife of another man for his own, and he had fought and killed without scruple. His distinction, however, was to have ultimately imposed some kind of unity over the British kingdoms, which was quickly swept away after his death through yellow plague. The whole of the British Isles were divided into countless petty kingdoms by now, but the British, Irish and Scots portions were the doomed ones. Their sporadic attempts at union—efforts of the Irish High Kings, and Maelgwn's vicious sword—never lasted. The world outside, though a permanent threat to them, was never important enough in their minds to merit a joint effort.

Brendan's visit was shortly before Gildas parted, finally and in dudgeon, for Brittany. It appears not to have been sullied by the current fiascos. There was a customary exchange of miracles, Gildas knowing by divine insight that Brendan, whom he refers to as a second Peter the Apostle, was due to arrive, and Brendan, temporarily at a loss when confronted with a Greek missal from which to read the mass, contriving to master the language in the minute or two he had available. His Irish understanding of animals was also called into play, for there had been recently a vast invasion of wild beasts in the area. At Gildas' request he went into the neighbouring wilds, followed by a mounted band of sceptical locals, and found the beasts' lair. They were lying asleep in the midday sun. Disturbed, the dam roared loudly and rushed towards the spectators. In the pandemonium that followed only Brendan, who had had—as he told friends—to cope with many worse events, kept calm. He approached the dam and addressed her: 'Follow us now gently, with all your cubs.' To the amazement of onlookers, and the reassurance of readers, the beast obeyed: and on the saint's command did no harm to any human any more.

His powers of eviction were highly reckoned in those days. Other stories tell of his banishing insects and disease from towns. Pests, from fleas to boars, were one of the social problems of the day. So also was the yellow plague from which Maelgwn died. There were epidemics of it throughout this period, carrying off large numbers of the population in the islands and on the continent. It recurred about twice a century, and neither saints nor kings were immune. In Byzantium in 540, a plague had grown till it was carrying off ten thousand people a day. It reappeared in 558 and quickly spread to Italy and Gaul. Always trade and missions were active to spread it to other parts of Europe and beyond. In 543 it seized Ireland, and some decimated monasteries were closed for all time. It was a vital factor in many of the definitive events of the day and played an insidious part in the crumbling of the Roman order.

A further contact was made with St David, but little is known of the Welsh patron saint, though his monastery at Menevia on the Pembroke coast has grown to the dimensions of a cathedral. David is said to have been the son of a nun, offshoot of a princely rape, and to have run his community on strict lines. As he is also said to have been on a pilgrimage to Jerusalem (just possible), to have been consecrated archbishop there, and to have owned a third part of Ireland, most of the gossip loses validity. The legends about him serve mainly to show the strong contact between Ireland and the west coast of Britain, making the Welsh marches a more important national boundary than the Irish Sea.

At last Brendan returns home. By this time—it is in the late sixties of the sixth century—he is over eighty, and approaching death. He goes to Annaghdown, where his sister Brig still runs the nunnery he founded for her, and calmly anticipates his end. Out walking one day, his companions are buffeted by a bitterly cold snowstorm, and when they complain that hell itself could be no worse than their present icy condition, the saint takes the opportunity to give a first-hand account of that place and of his meeting with Judas. It was presumably not the only time the old man awed his audience with reminiscence. He also played the role of peacemaker in an incident which shows that the martial habits of the country had not disappeared under the new religion's influence. The men of Munster made war on the people of Connaught, presumably for the usual reasons of adding to their cattle and their lands. The fact that there is no confirming mention of this raid in other sources than the lives of the saint means, if anything, that this sort of campaign was commonplace, rather than that it did not take place. Brendan was called on by the king of Connaught to dissuade the invaders. He tried, and failed; but was gratified to see, as a result of God's intervention, the intruders wandering round and round in untactical circles, until they saw they were winning nothing, and went away.

He may have been a little crotchety in old age. One story tells that he could not abide the sound of music, and had two balls of wax always beside him to plug his ears at the sound of any. Questioned about this by a precocious harpist he eventually explained that the horror of earthly music had been with him ever since the Archangel Michael, in the form of a bird, came and played him heavenly music for an hour as a greeting from God. It was a fine excuse from a man who liked the sound of the lapping of the lough's tides beside him, and the call of the gulls, and the watery echoes of his magical journey. He had an eye for situation. The view from the ruins of the convent that replaced his foundation is of the flat lake, amid flat country, but spattered with islands like an evening sky with feathery clouds. Crows fly above the crumbling stone and the vivid yellow of gorse. Behind the lake rise the hills of Connemara, gently rounded, and adding the blue of distance to the greens and browns of turf. It matches and surpasses the scenery of his other foundations. At Annaghdown, in the arms of his sister, he died in 577. On his instructions his body was taken for interment to Clonfert, where he was buried in the presence of many mourners. It was the end of an era of eccentric, irresponsible saints who had paved the way for men of more earthy achievement.

V

The Organisation-Abbot

Laws are made to fill a need, and the most complex codes are devised in times of approaching anarchy. Rome's law, her most lasting bequest to Europe, reached an apogee of subtlety as the empire declined to discord and disobedience. Napoleon's followed a period of national orgy. The Irish, who slotted most of life's ingredients into cerebral pigeon-holes with a rigid ingenuity, allowed themselves a life that was characteristically disorderly. Part of the essence of the regenerate Ireland was a tireless mental anarchy. This is most clearly seen in the acrobatics of imagination, the mazy curlicues of their thought-trails and their art, and the national expansion which was conditioned not by rule or precedent but by the tortuously driving impulse of their minds.

But the near and distant effects of sixth-century Ireland were not only achieved by a whimsical genius. There was, in sum, a happy synthesis of authority and anarchy, and if St Brendan's discipline over his monks recalls that of the old woman living in a shoe, there were others whose design was as ambitious and whose method of achieving it more consistent. St Columba was one of these. Despite the advantages of having a studious and infatuated biographer, he has come down the centuries as a cold hard man with his eye ever on the job. Even the most sentimental hagiographical stories about him fail to affect the impression of a purposeful man whose mistakes were seldom endearing human foibles, but the errors of a judgment that was set in rigid limits. St Columba was the prototype organisation-abbot. All the same, he is more important than most of his contemporaries, because he is the first historically vetted figure in the Celtic expansion. He brought the Irish Church to Scotland, and began a movement that was to have profound effects on the growth of English Christianity. Nevertheless the Church he knew and exported was different from Brendan's. Forty years lay between their births, and in that time the sown seed was growing fast.

An Irish individuality had already asserted itself on the organisation of the Church. Patrick, a Roman Briton whose Christianity had derived from the missionaries and bishops of Gaul, had tried to impose the orthodox imperial arrangement of bishops and dioceses. He failed because bishops need to sit in large towns and oversee the running of smaller villages through priests in their command. When monasticism came to Ireland by different routes it found a country that could already be described as lay-monastic. So it thrived. Abbeys and convents were founded throughout the country, and bishops, if they did not combine the office of abbot, were subordinate to the abbots on whose ground they lived. Bishops did not lift their heads for three hundred years, when Viking intruders began to build the country's first towns.

All this meant a change in the character of the Church in its first hundred years. Patrick's writings scarcely mention monasteries at all, though their existence in his day is not doubted. By the sixth century we find Columba deliberately rejecting the chance of promotion to the office of bishop, it had become so trivial. By his time abbeys skimmed the talent and wealth of the highest families. Monasteries were fulfilling their early ideals—they were becoming universities of religion, with Christ, a liberal chancellor, permitting the study of non-religious subjects. The number of monasteries existing towards the end of the sixth century must mean that a considerable proportion of the population of a few hundred thousand were having an advanced education, and they probably passed on a smattering to those who were not. Education had not the same importance that it has now—no country's economy depended on it. It made life richer in spirit, and perhaps thereby a little happier.

When the diocesan movement did take hold, much later on, efforts were made to change the history of this early period. The *Catalogue of the Saints of Ireland*,[1] a typical work of classification dating probably to the ninth century, describes three orders of saints. The first were Patrick and his contemporaries. They were all said to be bishops, very ardent and successful in their mission of converting, and summed up under the general head—'Most holy'. The second order were a grade below; they were 'Very holy', and they were meant to be under the faulty influence of Celtic missions from Wales—those of Gildas, David and Illtyd. This second order included most of the names mentioned so far in this book. The third was merely 'Holy', and included the hermits and ascetics who led lives of pious deprivation but showed little social sense of responsibility. The analysis is mostly wrong, in stress and chronology, and in the full account there is some conscious juggling with names to make the case plausible. What it shows clearly is the subsequent victory of the orthodox Roman school of Christianity in Ireland over the babblingly opinionated Celtic; and how far Ireland, in her isolation, had strayed from the Roman camp to warrant such refutation.

For by this time the Irish had cultivated marked foibles and eccentricities. Fertilised, but not conceived, by foreign missionaries, their spirit had bloomed differently from that of other nations. Columba's departure for Scotland is the beginning of a long confrontation between the two schools which we shall follow, on a wide territorial front, to its wistful resolution. All the same it is wrong to think of Irish religion being a unified whole. The south of the country had taken its character from Spain and Aquitaine—the last Celtic refuges on the Continent—and indirectly from the eccentric churches of Syria and Egypt. The north was based more on Rome through conscientious intermediaries like Patrick; but it had also felt the effects of native British Christianity, and was thus more of a breeding ground for British peculiarities like the heresy of Pelagius. In the seventh century, and for long after, popes were writing to the north urging the churches to tip out the Pelagian lees; and even long after, when the name became unfashionable, the strangely sensible doctrines of Pelagius were to be traced in the thinking of the churches in both these islands. Still, in the European scene, Ireland can be seen as a unified dissident. From its internal differences there emerges an entity. A characteristic that ties all Irish elements together is their refusal to be so tied in any formal lot. Cohesion was based on nonconformity; and while other generalities are plausible, they are modified always by this paradoxical one.

Most of the Irish differences were the results of Ireland's peculiar conversion: a peaceful mission and a gradual change. The pagan society that has already been glimpsed in these pages absorbed competently the message brought from abroad. It was thus able to maintain the bones of its old structure. The aristocracy of the days of Druids dispensed with the tree priests and gave its favours to the newcomers. So the Church became more than usually undemocratic. Most churches in their time have held the aristocracy in special affection, and the Gaelic Church did naturally, depending on it for land and money. After a generation a practice of mutual advantage was worked out. It became the custom for younger sons of ruling families to enter the local monastery, bringing with them a kind of ecclesiastical dowry, in return for which they would eventually rise to the office of abbot. It was not so much simony as a divine right of kingly families. Once under a family's appointment, the abbacy would stay that way, sometimes for as much as five hundred years. From this local patronising there developed a more ambitious empire-building. Monasteries founded, or ostensibly shown to have been founded, by the same man were grouped in unions of which the most influential abbot became a minor primate.

Columba himself was, as abbot, a product of this system. During training he became the favourite in each case of his current abbot, and sometimes made his colleagues jealous. A tale is told of his student days at Clonard which, while its moral falls flatly on modern ears, points to the sycophancy which took hold not only of his abbots but of his subsequent biographers. Another student, Ciaran, was one day grumbling about some privilege of Columba until an angel interrupted him. He had no right to complain, said the angel, laying before him an axe, a plane and a drill. All he had sacrificed to God were these paltry tools, for he was the son of a carpenter. Columba had given up a sceptre.

But perhaps the most illuminating trait of the Irish Church—

for it helps explain its faults, its high successes, and its subsequent history—was one which, again because of its isolation, it held to a larger degree than others. It was a distinct belief in itself as the chosen race. The phenomenon is still apparent, but in early times it went much deeper. The Holy Spirit had without doubt descended on the westerly isle.

'A chief leader in faith and piety throughout most of the world was this holy Brendan', begins the Irish life of St Brendan, and goes on to make him an eclectic amalgam of Abraham, David, Solomon, Moses, Jerome, Augustine, Origen, St John, Matthew, Paul, Peter and John the Baptist. Columba is given similar distinction by his biographer: 'Let this miracle of power, in raising the dead, be attributed to our Columba, in common with the prophets Elijah and Elisha; and a like share of honour with the apostles Peter and Paul and John.' Throughout the copious material of the Lives similar comparisons are scattered, and apostolic or Messianic qualities are attributed to even the most obscure abbots. So Columba is made to turn water into wine for the celebration of the Eucharist. In later times scribes were to select the 'Twelve Apostles of Ireland', including Columba, Patrick and Brendan, the two Finnians and Ciaran of Clonmacnois. And Columba chose twelve monks to accompany him to Scotland. As we read on we find more ambitious parallels being drawn. There are the circumstances of Brendan's birth: the light in the sky above the humble cottage in which he was born, the response of cows and the gift of calves, the arrival next morning of a local chief (and in some versions of three chiefs) are all obviously traced to the nativity of Christ. (Curiously, the three biblical Magi are first named individually—Caspar, Melchior and Balthasar—in an Irish text of the sixth century, and the names, which sound very apocryphal, suggest the same indiscriminate pleasure in exotic words that has been noticed in the *Hisperica Famina*. Further, the number of Magi is not given in the Bible. It remained for the Irish, with their passion for the triad, to found the tradition.)

Columba's birth is preceded by a heavenly annunciation!

The chosen race

An angel tells his mother 'You will bear a son . . . of such grace that he, as though one of the prophets of God, shall be counted in their number.' Descriptions of St Ita, Brendan's foster-mother, similarly evoke often the Virgin Mary, and a moving poem is attributed to her which speaks of her joy at fondling the infant Jesus on her knee. The whole cult of Mary, a third-century Christian development, probably found its way to Ireland from the East and from there was appropriated as other traditions were. Columba in one poem claims the presence of the Virgin hourly at the graveyard in Iona. A later poet, Blathmac, consoled the Virgin on the death of her son—'Come to me that I may keen with you your very dear one.'[2] Identification of Mary with the cause of Ireland appears in all the literature, but it is seldom explicit. If it were more so it would have become a heresy. As it was, the Irish coasted on a narrow plane that was more mystical than heretical. Mary was certainly in the mind of Brigid's biographers, but there is never any overt identification. In the same way it is impossible to read the Irish life of Brendan, or the remnants about St Ita, without being aware of a heavy symbolism related to the Virgin and her son; yet on a second reading it seems quite easy to explain everything away in purely Irish terms. When it came to the notice of the orthodox missions from Rome, this ambiguity was to prove infuriating.

There are other Irish claims to a favoured position in God's eyes. So many that they have prompted a modern critic to ask, in the style of Belloc's 'How odd of God to choose the Jews'—

> How did God fail
> To choose the Gael?[3]

One is the matter of banishing snakes. Folklore in modern Malta and Crete preserves the tradition that St Paul outlawed snakes from the two islands. The Irish, in turn, made St Patrick do the same for their country, for snakes have always been associated with the Devil. The legend was so successful that the meticulous Bede reported 'although often brought over from Britain, as soon as the ship nears land, [snakes] breathe its scented air and die'.⁴ A similar spell was told of Columba in Iona. Privilege was even to extend through to the end of the world. Irishmen on the Day of Judgment were to appear not before Christ, but Patrick; and Ireland would be spared the final horrors of Doomsday by a gentle wave inundating it a week before.

Moreover, there is a recurring similarity between the actions and words of Irish pilgrims and missionaries and those of the Old and New Testaments. Patrick and other early saints contending with the powers of the Druids go through the same kind of dramatic and palpable trials of strength as did the biblical prophets. And like the prophets they always win, and the protests of the Druids, like those of the priests of Baal, are shown as empty and powerless.

Resent it as they might, the Irish did not, and could never, invent an apostle to give the country a direct link with Christ. For all that, it is interesting to notice that the only apostolic claims of the British Isles were recorded at the Irish foundation of Glastonbury in Somerset. Here, soon after the settlement of Irish monks in the eighth century, the peculiar legend of a visit by Joseph of Arimathea grew up, and there was a nice subtlety in the choice of a figure who, playing little part in the life of Christ, was still the last to possess his body. And here also, and in the Celtic regions to the west, were framed the nationally pleasing fables of visits, not only by Peter and Paul, but by Christ himself in boyhood.

These traits and many others—the plagiarising of biographical details from the desert fathers, the picture in the Book of Kells of the Temple of Jerusalem which appears as a typical Irish beehive oratory—are the conscious appropriations of the properties of the Holy Land. They were certainly enough to arouse suspicion and animosity among the more wary and disciplined Christians of continental Europe. But Ireland's individuality went far deeper than conscious pillaging. It was present in the art and poetry of the time, and in the idealism that was not always justified. And it was very obvious and consequential in two connected realms of Christian activity. These were the development of the monastic idea and philosophy, and in the beginnings of the missionary movement.

In every aspect of organised Christianity in Ireland comes the same cry, of despair at past failings and of resolve to improve and be worthy of God. Along with the thirst for knowledge, the scrupulous copying of manuscripts in the monasteries, there was growing up a physical attempt to resolve the weakness of human nature. The recording of this attempt, in the rules and penitentials of the various abbeys, was one of the most important and lasting characteristics of the Irish Church. We have seen it in its beginning. By now the aims and disciplines of Irish monks were more mature and better formulated. These too were to be a cause of annoyance to those whose standards were not set so high.

That the resolves often failed is obvious from the refinement of the codes. Penance and sanction are sometimes too much for frail humans to bear, and not all the Irish were as tough as Brendan or Columbanus. But there was a comfort in the system because it seemed a viable one—most paper systems do. In the same way the Church confessors were an outlet and a foundation of hope. 'A man without a soul-friend is like a body without its head,' said St Comgall. To the confusion, and resentment, of foreigners, it was the system, not the practice, that became famous. The Irish were looked on as a race of enduring heroes, because it was thought they lived up to the standards they set themselves. Those standards may have been as remote from real life as the ambitious motto of a declining family. But they created an aura, and gave the Irish a special position in men's minds.

Not that there was apathy or lack of energy in the efforts of many to approximate to Christian ideals. The rules persisted for centuries, not as unattainable ideals, but as a practical target for earthly life. 'The martyrs were often consummated', wrote Athanasius, 'in a battle that lasted only for a moment; but the monastic institute obtains a martyrdom by means of a daily struggle.' The Irish knew that final rewards must come through exertion. With them the stress was more on discipline, the correction of backsliding, than on pain for its own morbid sake; but as all men slide back, discipline had a fearsome place. At the extreme lay the only means of saving a soul condemned to hell—three hundred and sixty-five recitals of the Lord's Prayer, a like number of genuflections, and a like number of blows of the scourge every day for a year, with a fast every month. In the intermediary stages are some choice witnesses of the ingenious legislator. Penances include a night spent in water and on nettles, or a night—this, as a voluntary penance, recurs in the saints' lives—passed in an open tomb with a dead body. Sexual crimes are met with sexual deprivation—'If any layman has defiled a vowed virgin and she has lost her crown and he has begotten a child of her, let such a layman do penance for three years. In the first year he shall go on an allowance of bread and water and unarmed and shall not have intercourse with his wife, and for two years he shall abstain from wine and meat and shall not have intercourse with his wife.'[5] But if there is no child—here is the basis of all grumbles at all bureaucrats—the penance is halved.

It can never be known how far the rules remained theory, and how much other Christian nations resented the paperwork, or the actual higher sanctity, of the Irish. Part at least of the rigour of the laws may have been the expressions of no more than a release that in other circumstances created the twists and spirals of the Books of Kells and Armagh. There is reason to think the Irish took themselves at times too seriously. As has been suggested, laws are made for the lawless. There is no need for them in heaven.

That all the Irish saints were not paragons, like failed and far-flung ambassadors with a hollow 'Excellency' for prefix, is constantly obvious. The priggishness of sanctity has been seen often on these pages and will be met again. And how silly, and unfair and conceited and narrow and pettish and fractious the holy men could be is constantly seen in readings of the actual lives. The saving grace of many biographers is that instead of omitting the failings of their subjects they describe them and then justify, leaving us—and perhaps in a wry way they meant us to—to discard the palliative. But there is one fault, or it may be part of the syndrome of devotion, that goes deeper than all those venial

sins. It includes, in its span, spiritual sloth and doubt and torpor
and tiredness and melancholy, and it is named, from the Greek,
accidie. Partly it is the reaction after fervour, the need of the body
and mind to achieve a balance. It is a phase familiar now as much
as then, and to layman as much as clerics, but churchmen have
fretted about it more than others and formulated its character.
John Cassian defined it but it is in his description of the symptoms
—like an Irish poet rejecting the general for the particular—that it
comes over most vividly. The sufferer 'gazes about him uneasily
this way and that and sighs that none of the brethren come to see
him, and keeps going in and out of his cell, and gazes up at the sun
very often as if it did not set quickly enough. . . . He supposes that
no remedy can be found for such an attack except in visiting
one or other of the brethren. . . . Then the same malady suggests
that visits are honourable and necessary duties, and should be
paid to the brethren'.

Accidie is behind many of those little glosses found on later
manuscripts, the marginal notes that stray whimsically from the
meat of the matter. Bede talks of the errant attentions, almost the
laziness, of some Irish monks who later were to wander as though
absorbed while English monks sowed and harvested the crop;
till Colman, their abbot, separated the two races and made each
fend for themselves. Accidie is the obverse side of the coin
of asceticism, a balancing fecklessness and something more. That
it was not a general complaint is seen in the mounting enthusiasm
of the exiles for the sake of God, that vast band who militantly
illustrate the other aspect of Celtic individuality. But accidie and
enthusiasm went together in the Irish framework. They formed
part of the paradox. For as long as it survived, the early Irish
Church owed its existence to a process as disorderly and inexor-
able as the spread, by wind and gravity, of thistle seeds across the
acres of temperate regions.

*   *   *   *

These qualities came together in the expansion of the Irish race
to places abroad. But in the origin of this movement none is more

apparent than the conviction that they were singled out as a chosen, special people. 'Get thee out of thy country, and from thy kindred, and from thy father's house, unto a land that I will show thee', said God to Abraham; and the Irish took it as a direct injunction to themselves. 'Every one that hath forsaken houses, or brethren, or sisters, or father, or mother, or wife, or children, or lands, for my name's sake, shall receive an hundredfold, and shall inherit everlasting life', said Christ to Peter, and the Irish took the message to their hearts. It was the perfect justification for their restlessness. Moreover Christ's life on earth was clearly seen as a sacrificial pilgrimage from heaven. If Ireland was good to live in, the more reason to leave it. It is hard to analyse clearly their motives, and no one word or phrase—pilgrimage, mission, voyage of discovery—covers all the cases, or all the aspirations. When they were young, the novices liked to travel from monastery to monastery instead of settling for all their training at one; continentals were more fixed. Then there were hermits who went out to seek God, for God's sake or their own but not for the sake of other men, in the woods and fields and on the sea. In neither of these is the missionary impulse even detectable. Yet there were missionaries too, who wanted involvement in the lives of others, and the others had to be not of their own kind. And there were pilgrims who again for their own sake went to sanctified places, Gaul or Rome or the Holy Land; as early as 333 a Gaul from Bordeaux had been to Palestine and written a guide to the journey, a sort of timetable of the stages, and his example had become a fashion in the sixth century.

Going into the unknown had a long and awesome tradition in Ireland. Forcible exile in a boat without sail or oar was an old and severe civil punishment. Around Britain many of the islands that were colonised by hermits had been penal settlements in Roman times, the Scilly Isles among them; and the inheritance added a taste of martyrdom. The basic desire was to renounce all for God, as it had been the desire of the Middle Eastern hermits. But as time passed it became obvious to those who travelled that there were more material aims to achieve in travel. Contact with Britain in the mid-sixth century revealed that that island was in a religious plight, invaded and dominated by the heathen, and disorganised in resistance. It was at this time that the young Irish Church, convinced of its own position, its own special preferment in God's eyes, began to realise its mission and that the first trickle of missionaries began to leave the country.

Even so, the first consideration in all the journeys was the literal obeying of Christ's injunction, to go forth with no intention—apostolic, devotional—but solely to lead the perfect life. Even Columba left Ireland, according to his biographer Adamnan, to be simply an exile for Christ, not an apostle among the tribes of north Britain. The Parker Anglo-Saxon Chronicle records the arrival of three Irishmen on the coast of Cornwall. Their boat was a light curragh, and they had set out wanting 'to go into exile for the love of God, they cared not whither'. Cormac, a friend of Columba, set out time and again to find 'a desert place in the ocean'. It was Irishmen like him—Brendan among them—who founded the bleak settlements that remain crumbled and deserted in the Orkneys, outer Hebrides, Faeroes and Iceland. Like the inhabitants of Skellig Michael they eked a precarious existence from fishing and taking birds' eggs. Unlike the Skellig monks, they had little chance of ever finding their way back to the mainland.

A curious fatalism underlies this surrender to the elements. It undoubtedly goes back to pagan times, for it gives to the elements themselves almost divine power; but still it survived under the mantle of Christianity and has even been met with among the western Irish within the last twenty years. Everyone was thought to be spiritually tied to three—it would be three—lumps of earth, the three sods of fate. The first was that on which he was born, the sod of birth. Second was that on which he died. And the third marked the place of his burial. In Christian times the burial sod was held to be the predestined site of a man's resurrection on the Last Day. There was little need then to worry on long journeys over land or sea. The traveller could only be interred where he had to be.

The Old Irish Life of Columba describes him as classifying three kinds of pilgrim. First was the man who left his home in body but not spirit, and thereby earned no merit. A poet put the matter succinctly and revelled in his paradox:

> To go to Rome
> Is much of trouble, little of profit:
> The King whom thou seekest there,
> Unless thou bring Him with thee, thou wilt not find.[6]

Second is the would-be traveller prevented by bodily weakness from taking off. He is a pilgrim by desire, and his spirit is right. Third comes the real pilgrim who leaves bodily and in will. He is the perfect pilgrim, of whom Columba himself can be taken as an example. Perfection is not always present. But as usual practice does not entirely conform with the rule.

Columba was born in 521, at a time when Justinian, through his lordly general Belisarius, was regaining eastern influence over the western Mediterranean, and a little before Benedict of Nursia travelled the sixty miles from his hermitage to Monte Cassino— the longest journey he ever took—to found the most powerful monastic order of the early Middle Ages. Gartan, in the east of Donegal, was a far cry from such developments. But Columba, who was born there in sight of the most dramatic loughs and hills of the Irish scene, was not born into a sequestered family. He was a direct descendant of a king, the pirate prowler Niall of the Nine Hostages, and his mother was herself daughter of a king. His ancestry put him in line for kingship, for the successor when a vacancy fell was chosen not on direct descent but from among the male descendants of a former king. Columba was eligible on this count, and his ambitions and talents would almost certainly have secured his election had he not felt obliged to serve exclusively his own conception of God.

In the retrospective eyes of Adamnan, Columba's biographer, sanctity accompanied the infant into the world. His arrival had been prophesied by saints of an early age—in phrases that echo the Messianic ring—and nothing seems to have pleased him so much in boyhood as sitting alone reading the psalms. Colum was the name of his baptism—in Latin Columba, the dove. He was also given the Irish name for fox, but this was dropped later. Instead Colum was lengthened to Columcille, 'Colum of the church', by which name he is still often known. Adamnan quotes the frequent use of dove-metaphors by Christ, always signifying the good and peaceful. He also refers to its being a mystical symbol of the Holy Spirit, and as with Brendan, as with many others, the Messianic parallel was drawn, the suspicion of heresy that no opponent of Ireland could ever be quite specific about. After such a perfect start, Adamnan leads him on to a perfect apprenticeship: 'Devoted even from boyhood to the Christian novitiate and the study of philosophy, preserving by God's favour integrity of body and purity of soul, he showed himself, though placed on earth, ready for the life of heaven; for he was angelic in aspect, refined in speech, holy in work, excellent in ability, great in counsel.'[7] One looks in vain for accounts of setbacks or defects, mastery of which would earn him so much more favour in our eyes. There were none recorded. He was a paragon; and consequently his errors, when they appear comparatively late in life, seem gross, and arouse a reaction that is not tempered by sympathy. It is hard on him, for the biographer ought to be blamed. As it is, we sit ready to pounce on Columba's first transgression.

He started on the best education available in the country, and seems to have spent longest at the monastery of Finnian of Clonard, where he learned his Latin, his scriptures, his history of Ireland, and the art of poetry. The tending of their own language was another mark of the Irish. They wrote the best poetry of the dark centuries, because they wrote in the language of their ancestors. At Clonard, the best of the Irish universities at the time and producer of many of the great missionaries, Columba was something of a pet boy. He brought with him bigger fees than others—everyone had to provide a cow for his sustenance and money for books—and was given special treatment by Finnian as a result. The sin here is an intolerable smugness. Put up your hut near the door of the chapel, he was told by Finnian, presumably as a privilege. The hut appeared some yards away. Columba explained; divine foresight had told him the chapel's door would move. And of course it did, by some act of God. All was not ease —the harsh discipline of Clonard has been referred to before—but it was easier for Columba than others. Hence the story of the angel and the carpenter's tools, and hence perhaps the wilfulness that was certainly to benefit Ireland's cause in the years to come.

Out of the jumble of fact and fable that comprises our sources for this period we sort out generally the likely and put it down as true. It is the safest rule; but sometimes there occurs a story so eccentric and unlikely that a basic truth seems the only reason for its being recorded. One such surrounds Columba's promotion to priest. When he was well qualified, Finnian decided to promote the novice to the rank of bishop. The status, as we have seen, did not carry the same prestige as that of abbot, for the abbot was absolute master of monastic, and so parochial affairs. But bishops were necessary to perform certain statutory functions (and so maintain the outward forms of the conventional church) and it would suit Finnian to have a dependent but well-connected young friend in the position.

Columba was sent to a neighbouring bishop for consecration. The bishop was in a field, removed apparently from ecclesiastical matters. He made a mistake and went through the ordination ceremony for a priest. Columba took the event as a sign that God had no use for him as bishop, and refused consecration for the rest of his life.

His tour of monasteries continued. He studied under the other Finnian at Moville. We have already seen this Finnian working through a dubious Christian apprenticeship at Candida Casa, the monastery founded by Ninian in Galloway in Scotland. He conveyed to Columba a picture of myriad pagan souls ripe for conversion in Scotland, a prospect that could have considerable impact on a single-minded young monk; though it was twenty years before the impact was to bear fruit. He went on to Glasnevin, now a suburb of Dublin, but his stay was cut short by an outbreak of the ubiquitous yellow fever. Mobi, the abbot, died of it. Columba returned to Derry to start his apostolic work.

Relations gave him a grant of land on which to found his first church. It was beside Lough Foyle, and a few miles from the old hill-fortress of Aileach, where Queen Maeve had held her sinister court and where now his own line, the northern branch of O'Neills, ruled over the surrounding kingdom. Though he spent the next few years travelling far from home in Ireland, and then left his country almost for ever, this part, where he had been born, remained always his most vivid memory. His poems hark back to his boyhood there with a delicate and unclogged nostalgia. But before everything he was a man of action, and Derry did not hold him long. How many of the monasteries attributed to him were in fact his own foundations is difficult to say. His name, like those of the other principal saints, occurs all over the country in association with wells, ruined churches, and some oratories or prayer-houses. Many of these are only indirectly his work, having their real links with his pupils and successors, and being subsequently joined in federations with a common rule. It is as though all Benedictine monasteries were to be attributed to the stay-at-home Benedict. From Swords on the east to Aran, bleak and windswept beyond the west coast, and from Tory Island in the north to Durrow in Meath his evangelising is claimed. 'A hundred churches which the wave frequents is the number of churches he has on the margin of the sea', says the Old Irish Life. He is said also during this period to have visited Tours in Gaul, whose founder Martin had always had particular reverence in Ireland. And probably he paid his first visits to western Scotland in this time, for the Irish colony of Dalriada, present day Argyll, had been established for over half a century.

Bede, who has sparse but good words for Columba, mentions only Durrow among his Irish foundations—'a noble monastery in Ireland known in the Scots [Irish] language as Dearmach, the Field of Oaks, because of the oak forest in which it stands'. Derry was on an oak-topped hill as well, and it is interesting that such sites, given a special sanctity by the Druids, should appear favourite scenes of the Christians too. 'Crowded full of heaven's angels is every leaf of the oaks of Derry.' The church was built off the usual east–west axis, to avoid chopping down the trees. The sound of an axe in the woods frightened him more than thoughts of death and hell. Durrow, like another foundation of the saint, Kells, is best known now for the book associated with it. Till recently it was thought that the saint himself had produced both books, but research has shown them to date from a later time. His interest in books was, however, intense, and was to have dramatic consequences.

Out of the cast of hagiography in which he is set, Columba emerges still as a man of greater stature than any of his typecast predecessors. He was tall and handsome and his voice was melodious and extraordinarily powerful. It was raised, when he sang in church, 'in an incomparable manner, and was heard at a distance sometimes of four furlongs, sometimes even of eight', yet in a miraculous way it did not too much bother those around him. Once, to overcome the influence of a pagan Pictish king's advisers, he raised his voice to the likeness of a peal of thunder and frightened them all into submission. He had deep resources of good sense, and used it rather pompously but always without hesitation and to good effect—a sort of borough Solomon. Doubtless many of the miracle stories arose from this speedy application of his practical intuition. He was strict with himself and with others, but did not put his rule above common humanity; at times he unbent his law, when a visitor called, when somebody was sick, and his heart was customarily soft where animals—nice animals—were concerned. But he did not hesitate to call down the wrath of the Lord on a menacing boar.

Best of all he comes over through the poems to which his name is attached. Some are in Irish, some Latin. Latin, as the language of continental Christianity, had high prestige, but no pressure had yet been felt to forsake the vernacular. When later the rims of influence of the two churches touched, the Celtic and the Roman, Irish was attacked as boorish and ungodly by men deserving Coleridge's stricture on Shakespeare-critics—those 'who ar-

raigned the eagle because it had not the dimensions of a swan'.
Only a hundred years after Columba his biographer Adamnan
deprecated Irish in favour of Latin, and Bede gave it short shrift.
Happily it never yielded. Columba made good use of it, for his
early training had brought him to the dwindling ranks of the old
bardic order. And later on, when he had settled on Iona, he was to
return once to his own country for a conference in which that
order, which offended some Christians by its devotion to old
values, was saved by his intervention.

He was always exploding about something, and his ensuing
repentance would swing him to the upper reaches of sanctity. The
most unforgivable—though also the most dubious—outburst of
his life was the immediate cause of his departure for Iona. The
episode is wrapped in doubt, but from various aspects it seems
that an action of Columba's was more or less responsible for a
disastrous battle in which three thousand men were killed.
(Nothing is to be taken literally; throughout the literature of the
period three thousand is one of the few large numbers mentioned.
It was the product of the three of the Trinity three times multiplied by ten—which, being the sum of one, two, three and four,
was, according to Augustine, the perfect number. So, three
thousand studied at the big monasteries, three thousand died in
battle; three thousand means a big number, big enough to be
uncountable, and in this case is quite bad enough without being
specific.)

Before describing the rival theories it should be pointed out
that still many monasteries were pettish places, and not as removed
as they might have been from lay mores. Kings may have perpetually quarrelled and rustled and pilfered, but the monasteries
were not far behind in irascibility. Monks were not excluded from
military service till the ninth century, and remained so devoted to
their martial experience that inter-monastic skirmishes were as
common as competitive sports among their modern successors.
Hundreds are recorded as being slaughtered in some of these
battles, and tenants and servants were all summoned to take part.
These were rough, if apostolic, days.

The first theory behind the battle of Culdreihmne, which took place in 561, illuminates—perhaps mythically—the great love of books and scholarship. Columba went once to stay with St Finnian of Moville. Finnian possessed the only copy in Ireland of St Jerome's Vulgate, the best Latin version of the Bible; and Columba, knowing that contemporary ethics were against him, retired to the library every evening to copy the book in secret. One evening he was surprised by his host, who claimed the copy as his own, and being refused took the case to the High King of Ireland, Diormid. There is nothing surprising about the heat generated by this issue. Books were still rare and of a value that surpassed their content, though that itself was venerated. Monks often travelled far into Gaul, even to Rome itself, to collect them; and a note in the flyleaf of a Syrian volume of the period—there would be far more books in Syria than in Ireland—reads strikingly: 'Whoso shall seek this book to read it . . . and shall not return it to its owners, may he inherit the halter of Judas for ever.' Books also had, as objects, some magical qualities, probably first attributed by the Druids, to whom containers of knowledge were the sources of the mystic and most elevated elements in life. Several stories are recorded of Columba's own writings being preserved unscathed after being accidentally dropped in water or fire.

So the case was heard. Diormid found in favour of Finnian—not surprising in the light of Columba's furtiveness—and gave a picturesque verdict: 'To every cow her calf, to every book its copy.' At which Columba decided on war and roused up the O'Neills to avenge him on the High King. But there is a more sober account, a likelier cause of battle, if not the only one, and more in tune with Columba's piety. He gave shelter to a man involved in some political squabble and trying to escape the wrath of Diormid; but the king sent a party to capture the man, who was then executed in spite of the monk's sanctuary. Again the same result—a battle between the O'Neills and Diormid under the slopes of Ben Bulben in Sligo—and again the three thousand deaths and the worsting of Diormid and the power of Tara. In view of the enormity of the revenge the churches of the region took action against Columba and excommunicated him. So much, and only that, is admitted among the adulations of Adamnan—excommunication 'on a charge of offences that were trivial and very pardonable'. He goes on to say that, in the light of certain witnesses' evidence of visions of fire and columns of angels, the charge was immediately withdrawn. But he admits that something culpable was done, and the other stories are extraordinary enough to be near the truth. Whatever the cause, Columba felt he had done wrong, and set himself a penance of perpetual exile. Or was set the penance, as one account has it, by St Molaisse, who told him to undertake the conversion of as many souls as were killed in the battle.

There is a third explanation, perhaps the truest in fact though the others provide insight. Diormid, it is said, was anti-clerical. He certainly came to grips with other priests than Columba. And somehow the line-up at Culdreihmne represented the last stand of paganism against the not so new religion. So the battle begins a new and happier age, and Columba—for those who would have it so—emerges untarnished at the end.

Dalriada, the Irish foothold on Scotland, was an obvious direction for a northern Irish missionary to turn. Irishmen had been there half a century or more, and they were surrounded by more or less pagan Picts. Dalriada was across a narrow channel; from some of the western islands Ireland was still visible. Faced with exile, Columba is vulnerable and human again. He intends never to return, though he does so when the need is great. 'It is the parting of a soul and body', says a later biographer, 'for a man to leave his kindred and his country and go from them to strange, distant lands, in exile and perpetual pilgrimage.' Columba sighs 'The great cry of the people of Derry has broken my heart in four.' He collects twelve companions—the apostolic figure—and prepares to embark from Howth, a humped headland just to the north of Dublin. The moment is remembered by him in a poem of great beauty that, coming soon after a battle fought on such a trivial pretext, supports Chesterton's verdict that:

The great Gaels of Ireland
Were the men whom God made mad;
For all their wars were merry,
And all their songs were sad.

It is another paradox of the enigmatic Irishmen, and not entirely without meaning today. Columba wrote:

Delightful to be on the Hill of Howth
Before going over the white-haired sea:
The dashing of the wave against its face,
The bareness of its shores and of its border. . . .
Great is the speed of my coracle,
And its stern turned upon Derry:
Grievous is my errand over the main,
Travelling to Alba of the beetling brows. . . .

And there is a simple stanza echoing the lament of St Patrick when he travelled in the opposite direction, and left his kinsmen behind:

There is a grey eye
That will look back upon Erin:
It shall never see again
The men of Erin nor her women.[8]

Columba was forty-one, and he was starting the life for which he is remembered.

VI

Iona and Lindisfarne

Till long after the time of the Norman Conquest the word Scot referred to an inhabitant of Ireland or his descendant. Brian Boru, the best known king of Irish history, signed himself Emperor of the Scots—*Imperator Scottorum*, in grandiose imitation of Charlemagne. The source of the word Scot seems to be an Irish verb meaning to plunder, and dates to the time—the fourth and fifth centuries—when piracy was the main intercourse between the Irish and their neighbours. Hence the Romans referred to Ireland, in the later stages of occupation, as Scotia. A hundred years after the Roman departure colonists had succeeded the pirate bands. There were Irish settlements in north and south Wales and in the western extremities of Scotland. Just as the latter took its name from the old Ulster kingdom of Dalriada, so the colonists preserved the name by which the Romans knew them in Ireland. They were the Scots, and their language, Gaelic, began gradually to replace the widespread (and related Celtic) tongue of the Picts in the north of the country. In time the English kingdom of Northumbria made inroads on the Lowlands, and replaced the vernacular language with English. So was set the pattern that remained fairly static till Culloden and the displacements of the eighteenth century: Gaelic was the language of north Scotland, the Highlands, and English that of the Lowlands. The time of Columba and his successors saw the emergence of this pattern.

How Christian Scotland was when Columba arrived has been a matter of scholastic and patriotic debate for nearly a hundred years. The scholars of Ireland and Scotland, negligent of their— admittedly dilute—blood ties, have reserved for each other a pungent and competitive rancour. The Irish make the gift of Christianity to Scotland almost exclusively the work of Columba and his companions. The penmen of Edinburgh claim he simply took credit for a job that was more or less done by the Pict Ninian two centuries before his time. Some light has been shed by one of those ingenious deductions that must lift the life of the fustiest antiquarians far above the plain of ink and dust and print that is their chosen medium.

The trail goes back to Bede, who briefly reported that Ninian was responsible for converting the southern Picts and Columba for the northern, dividing their areas by what he calls a line of 'steep and rugged mountains'. These have usually been identified as the Grampian range, which rises north of Glasgow and stretches north-east towards Scotland's angular shoulder. The division, though not belittling Ninian's efforts, gave the credit for greater achievement to Columba, and was much in favour with the Irish. Then somebody noticed Bede's sources. They included the only world atlas of the day—that of Ptolemy, who had collated some faulty information about Scotland's orientation and twisted it over to the right, making true west north, and true east south. Corrected, Columba's area is pushed to the west, not of the Grampians, but of Drum Albyn. And his personal achievement is seen to be less than suspected.

But even such revelations are dubious in a sea of doubt. However well or badly he compares with Ninian, Columba's arrival was at a time when previous attempts at evangelisation had lost their impetus. Part of the reason for this was the conglomeration of races in the country, each speaking its own language and therefore maintaining more hostile attitudes to one another than in Ireland. In the north of the country, roughly above the line of the Antonine Wall between the Firths of Forth and Clyde, were the Picts—a Celtic race linked by antique ties to the Irish Gaels, but quite differentiated after a separation of at least five hundred years. South of this line were British tribes, notably the Votadini, who had been more or less amenable to and influenced by Roman rule. Their link was with Wales, for both peoples had been pushed back by the Germanic invasions from their heritage in the English Midlands. (The name Wales derives from a

Teutonic word, Walas, meaning strangers—and the term at this period covered an area which stretched north beyond Cumberland to the Lowlands.) There were some smaller remnants of Pictish communities in the south-west of Scotland, west of the Solway Firth in Galloway. Besides these native groups, a large number of Irish had settled present-day Argyll, and founded the kingdom of Dalriada; and at the same time Angles of the kingdom of Bernicia—Northumberland—were pressing into and beyond the Border district.

Ninian had belonged to the old British inhabitants of Galloway, and went on his mission soon after the year 400. His father is said to have been a Christian king, and he himself went to Rome for his education and was there consecrated bishop. On his way back he called on Martin of Tours, the idol of early monastics, and was lent stonemasons by the saintly man to build a new foundation on his return to Whithorn in Galloway. The materials of contemporary buildings were not often as durable as stone—mostly wattle and daub with timber beams giving skeleton support. The new monastery, because of its architectural distinction, was named the White House, Candida Casa. During and after Ninian's time it expanded, won a distant reputation, and counted Finnian of Moville and other Irish pioneers among its pupils. It was the northernmost branch of Welsh influence on Ireland, before the current was reversed and the Irish streamed back to the larger island to retrieve its people for their creed.

Dedications of churches to Ninian run all the way up the east coast of Scotland, and more up the centre, along the line of the Great Glen that broadens in its northern sector into Loch Ness. Dedications are not enough in themselves—St George for sure never came to England—but other traditions help to suggest that Ninian and his companions made Christian inroads among the Picts of the north. According to Bede the Picts long before the arrival of Columba had 'left the error of idolatry for the true faith, through the preaching of Ninian, a most reverend Bishop and holy man of the nation of the Britons, who had been regularly instructed at Rome in the faith and mysteries of the truth'.[1]

Iona and Lindisfarne

But there had been a patent relapse. Archaeological evidence shows as much, negatively, by a gap of cultural remains between the Ninian period and Columba's time. St Patrick's plaintive letter to Coroticus, when he discovers the massacre wrought by Coroticus' men on a newly converted Irish community in Ulster, hits out at those British Christians who have turned against God in conscious knowledge of their mortal sin. Coroticus was a British prince in the region of Strathclyde. It is apparent that, however bold and pioneering the first wave of Scots missionaries had been, a second front was needed within a hundred years. It came, some stories have it, around the year 550 in the person of St Finbarr, a dynamic Irishman with a reputation that survives in Cork and Scottish place-names like Barra and Kilbarr. He crossed the Irish sea on horseback and proselytised in the western isles and Argyll. At his death the sun itself kept the wake, not setting for fifteen days. Others, more mundane, crossed in boats, for there was constant contact between the two countries. One was Caranoc, who built a church in Galloway round a coloured altar that dropped from heaven. In 560, a short while before Columba allegedly copied Finnian's library book, the Irish community in Argyll was invaded by the Picts from the north under their king Brude, and defeated. Brude and his people were by now diehard pagan. When Columba arrived and looked beyond the confines of the small harassed Irish settlement, he had to face the prospect of work in virgin territory.

In the channel dividing Ireland from Scotland there is no spot from which land is not visible on a fine day. Columba had sworn to turn his back on his native country and as he approached the skein of islands that forms the southern Hebrides he would anchor and climb to the top of the highest hill and look back and, seeing Ireland, sail on. At length he came to Iona, and landed in the rocky bay on the south of the island. To his own satisfaction, he was away from the spell of his ancestors. Iona, with cliffs rising to three hundred feet in the south, slopes down to a bumpy plain in the north. It is dwarfed by the surrounding terrain, the stark jagged hills of Mull and the mainland which are a sheer contrast

124

to the round soft fells of Ireland. The colour is different too, not the brown and green and yellow of gorse, but blue and mauve, cut by angular shadows. There is more darkness, and in Columba's time the dark obstinate clefts and ravines hid the swarthy souls of pagans.

But Iona was friendly and so, as he knew, was the land around it, ruled by Conall, a distant cousin of his, who granted him the land for a monastery. The land was already sacred, first turned to spiritual purpose in an age long before the arrival of Christianity, and reconsecrated to the Christian God perhaps by Ninian or Finbarr or one of the many missionary soldiers whose names have been lost. So Columba and his twelve apostolic companions settled there, and made themselves liked by the population. Three miles by one and a half, Iona could cater for their simple wants. The monks grew barley and cut twigs from the trees— sometimes to the locals' annoyance—to build their wattle huts. If the locals protested, the aid of God was invoked, and a bulky store of grain would suddenly appear to compensate for losses. The stone buildings whose remains have recently been excavated were not built till Adamnan's time or later. But wooden structures were strong enough, especially when fortified with oak beams towed from the mainland by twelve coracles at full sail. There was a large central church, the centre point of their lives, and a small private chapel; and a guest house, important here as in Ireland for the reception of many wandering abbots and hermits, and always supplied with water for washing the feet of new arrivals. There was a barn and other farm buildings, a kiln for drying the harvest, a mill for grinding corn. All these buildings have left traces for archaeologists, as has the hut in which Columba himself slept, with the bare rock for mattress and a stone for a pillow.

There was a busy routine. All the monks, Columba included, took part in the work of the farm; and when he was preoccupied he was still with the workers in spirit. Once, when they were being overworked by a senior brother in the fields, he felt their burden from afar, and his concern caused the brother to repent and declare a holiday. And another time when the harvest work was getting on top of them they all began to feel something strange—'a fragrant smell, of marvellous sweetness, as of all flowers combined into one; and also a heat as of fire, not painful, but in some manner pleasant; and in addition a kind of inspired joyousness of heart, strange and incomparable, which in a moment miraculously revives me, and so greatly gladdens me that all grief and all labour are forgotten'. And it turned out that Columba, dismayed at their late return from the fields, had sent out his spirit to meet them and lighten their return.

The life of intellect and spirit was not sacrificed to bread-winning. There were no concessions made in the necessity of prayer, which occupied the whole of Saturday night and Sunday, besides the normal daily devotions and recitals of psalms. On Wednesdays and Fridays the monks fasted till evening, and every day the same during Lent. The same iron wills that maintained this programme had to bend for long hours to the clerical needs of a monastery—copying out manuscripts, correcting and emending, and writing commentaries on the texts. Two books that survive—the Cathach, or psalter of St Columba, and the Book of Kells, have been supposed to date to this time and island, though the Kells book (which is said to have been removed to Ireland after the Viking invasions) seems to reflect later and more developed styles of design than those of the sixth century.

Part of the importance of guests was the way in which they enhanced the knowledge and intellectual life of these simple retreats. In Adamnan's time, a hundred years later (but this sort of thing would not be new), a Gallic bishop called Arculf was driven off course when returning to the north of France from a pilgrimage to the Holy Land. This old salt's narrative went on for days, for Adamnan took notes and wrote a work of three books on it, *De Locis Sanctis*. But an account of the birthplace of Christ and all the scenes of his and the apostles' lives would certainly have kept his audience awake as long as he was prepared to speak. There were other books to read to expand horizons—the lives of the Desert Fathers, prime movers of the ascetic life,

Josephus' history of the Jewish Wars, and learned works and instructions in the Christian life by Latin commentators.

Columba set the example and ruled firmly, and at times became unbearably smug. A monk had once copied out a psalter and another offered to read it through for mistakes. The abbot gave his permission, but pointed out that only one letter *i* would be found missing in the whole work. It turned out as he said, but must have made the corrector wish his prophetic gift had gone a little farther.

When the monastery had been organised it was time to press out, into the mountainous lands of the Picts, and the islands of the sea. As at home, the sea was of first importance, as a means of travel and no less as a source of fish, important in a diet that allowed little meat. There were several harbours round the island, and boats—of several sizes carrying between one and thirty men—were skilfully used by any of the community. It has been calculated that a good light boat with a favourable wind behind it could cover nearly ninety miles a day, though exposing its occupants to utmost danger. Indeed one monk, Cormac, a restless adventurer, was once driven north for fourteen days against his will and the efforts of his mariners and 'far exceeded the bounds of human travel'. (He was looking, like so many of his companions, for 'a desert in the sea'.) In Arctic regions they were surrounded by 'loathsome and exceedingly dangerous small creatures covering the sea, such as had never been seen before that time . . . about the size of frogs, very injurious by reason of their stings, but they did not fly, they swam'. Their stings nearly pierced the outer skin covering of the boat, and Cormac was very alarmed, though the winds changed in time to preserve them from a watery grave, and they lived to tell the tale. What the frog-like swimmers were nobody knows for sure. Some say mosquitoes, mentally bloated by imagination like the salmon of modern Irish fishermen: others—more credible—say jellyfish.

But the sea movement, that was shortly to colonise the outer Hebrides, the Shetlands and Orkneys and Iceland, was not yet in full spate. Once the Iona settlement was established Columba turned inland, with the aim of converting the Picts under King Brude. Brude's capital was near Inverness, and the mission involved a long and dangerous journey along the Great Glen that divides the north-west Highlands from the Grampians—beyond what Bede calls 'the spine of Britain'. One of the difficulties was language, which Columba and his companions had been studying since their arrival two years before, but still required two Picts in the party as interpreters. The Picts, as conquerors of the Irish a few years before, were not sympathetic to a mission from the vanquished. Adamnan tells many stories of conversions among them, sometimes with divine intercession and sometimes by the power of Columba's persuasion; but what he cannot be expected to record—and does not—is the scale of failure among a people whose minds were generally made up for them by their king. Brude himself was to determine the spiritual future of his people, and it was to him that Columba journeyed as directly as he could. The situation is reminiscent of Livingstone's travels, for a character was shared by the unknown brooding landscape and the imperious totalitarian rulers that both missionaries had to face.

There was a notable distraction on the way. If Columba's time and setting were more aerial and whimsical than Livingstone's, so was his discovery. Approaching the royal city he had to cross Loch Ness, and at one point came across a group of peasants burying a man recently 'seized and most savagely bitten by a water beast'.

'When the blessed man heard this, he ordered notwithstanding that one of his companions should swim out and bring back to him, by sailing, a boat that stood on the opposite bank. Hearing this order of the holy and memorable man, Lugne mocu-Min obeyed without delay, and putting off his clothes, excepting his tunic, plunged into the water. But the monster, whose appetite had earlier been not so much sated as whetted for prey, lurked in the depth of the river. Feeling the water above disturbed by Lugne's swimming, it suddenly swam up

to the surface, and with gaping mouth and with great roaring
rushed towards the man swimming in the middle of the stream.
While all that were there, barbarians and even the brothers,
were struck down with extreme terror, the blessed man, who
was watching, raised his holy hand and drew the saving sign
of the cross in the empty air; and then, invoking the name of
God, he commanded the savage beast, and said: "You will go
no further. Do not touch the man; turn backward speedily."
Then, hearing this command of the saint, the beast, as if
pulled back with ropes, fled terrified in swift retreat . . .'

and has infuriated posterity by his continued reticence.

Adamnan and the other, anonymous, biographer tell of trials
of strength surrounding Brude's conversion. The spirit of the
Old Testament is very near when we learn of Columba's approach
to the Inverness palace. Brude, with an open mind but swayed by
his Druidic foster-father, bolted and barred the gates to the new
arrivals to determine their power. There is nothing subtle about
the saint's reaction as he makes the sign of the cross, knocks and
watches the giant doors fall back of their own accord; and we
wish, as we wish in so many of these accounts, for a response less
obvious, more clever, and—since we are sceptical of miracles—
more convincing. Still, Brude was convinced. He was 'much
alarmed, and left the house, and went to meet the blessed man
with reverence; and addressed him very pleasantly, with words of
peace. And from that day onwards, throughout the rest of his
life, that ruler greatly honoured the holy and venerable man, as
was fitting, with high esteem'.

Broichan, the foster-father, did not succumb. He was a
magician, a fairy-tale character given irretrievably to the powers
of darkness. He sent his cronies to drown the noise of a mass
being celebrated by Columba in the forecourt of the palace; and
was only thwarted by the saint raising his unusual voice, with the
power of the trumpet and the volume of thunder, so that it could
be heard in all the hills and valleys around to turn the Picts
there to God. This sort of miracle happened only rarely, not

always, the writer explains. When the missionaries were due to return the pitiful Broichan, typecast to failure, threatened a wind on the loch that would prevent their sailing. Sure enough a mist and a stormy adverse wind met the sailing party. 'It is not surprising', Adamnan remarks, 'that with God's permission these things can be done at times by the art of demons, so that even winds and waves can be roused to violence.' Soon afterwards, however—'to the astonishment of all'—the winds abated, and gentle breezes filled out the sails to take the travellers in the direction they chose. Nothing went wrong, Columba made no error or misjudgment, and it is impossible to disagree with Adamnan's summing up: 'Let the reader reflect how great and of what nature was the venerable man, in whom almighty God made manifest to the heathen people the glory of his name through those signs of miraculous power described above.' Yet, underneath the miracles and bravado, there must have been something more solid and valuable for the saint to make the impression he undoubtedly did.

Certainly the religion had much to offer, even though we can only see the real advantages through the dazzling beams of the miraculous. It brought the offer of an after-life. It brought, as Livingstone brought to Africans, the lessons of a riper civilisation; for more of the technical knowledge of Rome had crossed to Ireland than had penetrated the fastnesses of the Highlands. There was medical knowledge and improved agricultural methods, and above all a satisfying, though exacting routine for life in a small community. However near or far the message of Christianity seemed to the new converts, it gave an edge and new point to life. If it was only a fad it did this, and it was more than a fad. Perhaps most persuasively it opened up a complete new world of storytelling; a corpus of tales that had a new point, more enhancing than the traditional praise of ancestors. These people were being unsettled by a positive kind of education, a knowledge that made them want more knowledge, and an ethic that made them want to get up and change things. It brought a change of tide, and the waves, joined with those of the Irish, began to float across the mainland of Britain till they met a similar, but ominously different wave approaching from the south.

Columba's party had grown when he returned to Iona, and now the consolidating process began: ordination of young novices, their departure for settlements in Scotland, and the maintenance of communication between all the daughter foundations and Iona. There are tales of saints everywhere in Scotland at this period; and over them all Iona, though without a bishop, retained her authority. Unlike the Irish Church, fragmented into a thousand monasteries that governed themselves, the Scottish recognised the supremacy of Iona and its abbot held the power of a primate over the whole hierarchy of Scotland.

To his other talents Columba added that of being a shrewd politician. In the hierarchy he was no more than a priest, yet in influence he was stronger than a metropolitan bishop. And he showed the extent of his influence, when, on the death of Columba's kinsman Conall, king of Dalriada, he was asked to crown the new king (who sat, for the ceremony, on what many claim was the Stone of Scone, now in Westminster Abbey). Moreover, despite the nastiness surrounding his departure from Ireland, he had not been forgotten there. He kept in touch— messengers were continually coming and going across the straits —with his foundations in his country, Durrow, Kells, Derry and others; and his advice was often sought across the sea on matters of spiritual and social importance. Then in 575, against the vows that some accounts attribute to him, he returned to Ireland for a congress of special importance. Such meetings were called every few years by the High King for the discussion of common interests. This was the Convention of Drumceat, and the main issues at stake were the power of the Ulster Dalriadans over their Scottish colony, and the social position of the order of bards in Ireland—a class whose wit and brains gave annoyance to many, and whose satire had brought a demand for their complete suppression.

Columba was personally involved in both issues, and he went to see the verdicts favoured his favourites. Whether by returning he broke his earlier vow is debatable. There is a smack of special pleading in the account of him covering his eyes throughout his stay to avoid betraying his pledge. Another story, that tells of his fastening clods of Scottish turf to his shoes to avoid the charge of treading again on Irish soil, only shows that some biographers were prepared to fog the issue with quibbles. As a poet, trained in poetry by a senior member of the bardic order, Gemman, Columba pleaded that the faults of arrogance and conceit could, and in the event of acquittal would, be washed away. His position in Church and family won him the day and the order was spared. In all probability there was another cause, the fact that he was a leading Christian. Most higher ranks in the land had by now been won to the new religion, and the monks had taken over many of the functions of poets. Irish culture was now predominantly Christian culture, and among the poets, with their veneration for the past and their conservative hierarchy, the greatest resistance to Christianity would have been articulated. Nothing could have supported them more effectively than the arguments of a leading cleric, and Columba's intercession had the desired effect.

He succeeded too on the other matter. There was time enough, for the Convention went on well over a year, and all matters of common dispute were discussed during it. In this second issue the people of his own Scottish colony were chafing at the tribute imposed upon them by their Irish overlords, far away and irrelevant in Ireland. It was absentee landlordism, and not the familiar way round. True to form, Columba won his case and gained home rule for the Scots. He took the chance at the same time of visiting Durrow and some other connected foundations, and his reputation spread as a result of the miraculous cures he made among the diseased and crippled who came to Drumceat to observe. Venerated already, he returned to Iona with added laurels to spend the last ten or so years of his life in Iona.

If his career has seemed cold and priggish, it may be partly because of the strangely cautious methods of biography at the time. Even so, some human rays have come down the ages. He became deeply attached to some of his monks, and they to him.

Columba the arbiter

There is a touching account of the death of the first of his original companions, Brito, as he lay in his hut waiting for the last moment. Columba could not bear to watch and went outside solemnly preoccupied. After a while he looked up and his expression changed to one of content. At the moment the monk died he saw angels and devils contending for possession of the spirit, and soon the angels carried him off to the 'joys of the heavenly country'. When a seal-poacher was brought before him for judgment he told the man to be open and honest; if he was hungry he should come and ask directly for supplies. And he sent him away with some sheep to keep him going.

Another incident showed a rare psychological insight. A husband came to him, complaining that his wife, dutiful in all other ways, refused to share his bed. The saint impressed on the wife the necessity for obedience. 'Two shall be in one flesh', he quoted from the marriage service, but she only replied 'I am ready to perform all things whatsoever that you may enjoin on me, however burdensome: save one thing, that you do not constrain me to sleep in one bed with Lugne.' She would, she said, prefer to go into a nunnery. Acutely, Columba kept her thinking on this point, and remained in meditation with the couple all day. Next morning he took up her offer. 'Are you ready to leave for a nunnery?' She did not know what had happened, she said: 'In this past night—how I know not—my heart has changed in me from hate to love.' So that, as Adamnan relates, 'from that day until the day of her death, that wife's affections were indissolubly set in love of her husband'.

He is not always so sensible, or so kind. There is the familiar peevishness, the quick revenge for a fault that seems venial. A priest, much loved and otherwise without fault, drove ostentatiously about the countryside in a chariot; and seeing him the saint prophesied nemesis, poverty, begging and death by choking on beef. And so it came about. Others die by fire, sword and at the hands of rivals, fates foretold with a certain relish. Yet there is more mercy and kindness for every example of vindictiveness. It is the typecast Irish mind, not confined to that epoch,

133

generous and mean, straight and wily, good and bad; a character
to baffle and exasperate. The time was approaching when the
character was to confront a people most vulnerable to the paradox, most prone to exasperation, the wall against which the Irish
spirit must bump and bruise like a butterfly and drop. But not
quite yet.

For an Irishman of his time, Columba was unusually insensitive
to animals. Instead of converting or reasoning with them when
they stand in his way, he calls on the Lord to strike them dead.
Yet there is a tenderness to those animals that wish him well, and
two of the stories told are among the tenderest in Irish literature.
One day on Iona he calls a monk: 'On the third day from this that
dawns you must watch in the western part of this island, sitting
above the sea-shore; for after the ninth hour of the day a guest
will arrive from the northern region of Ireland, very tired and
weary, a crane that has been tossed by winds through long
circuits of the air. And with its strength almost exhausted it
will fall near you and lie upon this shore. You will take heed to
lift it tenderly and carry it to the house nearby; and having taken
it in as a guest there you will wait upon it for three days and
nights, and feed it with anxious care. And afterwards, at the end
of three days, revived and not wishing to be longer in pilgrimage
with us, it will return with fully recovered strength to the sweet
district of Ireland from which it first came.' The brother did as
he was told; the crane flew in and dropped to the shore; he
picked it up, took it to the guest house, fed it and left it resting
while he went to report to Columba. 'God bless you, my son,
because you have tended well the pilgrim guest.' And after three
days, refreshed and satisfied, the crane 'rose from the ground and
flew to a height; and then, after studying the way for a while in
the air, crossed the expanse of ocean, and in calm weather took
its way back to Ireland, in a straight line of flight'.

Of such stories are the surviving lives of St Columba composed.
A thread of fact is woven into the warp of fiction, and the
make-believe is there to remind us of the nature of the Irish, an
airborne, aspirant nature that allows us sometimes to suspend

disbelief willingly. It is necessary, if we are to understand them at all, for they themselves believed themselves without question. Adamnan, living a hundred years after the saint, always invoked reliable witnesses at first or second hand for the incidents he related; and he was credited by most scholars as one of a handful of important chroniclers of his time in Europe. Yet he never doubted. True, he was writing in a tradition that put above most other considerations the creation of native Irish apostles; so that Columba was born in circumstances that remind of Solomon, he banished venomous snakes from Iona like Paul or Patrick, he multiplied loaves and fishes like Christ, and after his death he visited living men to tell them of things to come. But the accounts are no less credible to him for the element that we would call tendentious. It was the reality that they gave to things called unreal that made the Irish what they were, a race who made enemies among the mundane because they were so far from mundane themselves.

Columba had founded the abbey and community that was to be a rallying point for religion in Scotland throughout the centuries that followed. 'That man', wrote Dr Johnson, 'is little to be envied, whose patriotism would not gain force upon the plain of Marathon, or whose piety would not grow warmer among the ruins of Iona.' And nowadays a new abbey has risen to try to revive the faded message of Christianity. The saint also set up the dynasty that was to rule first Dalriada, then Scotland, for over five hundred years. However superficially, he had converted the Picts of the north, who had heard the gospel once, from Ninian, taken it in, and then by degrees forgotten it. He had lived the life of the organisation-abbot, more materially successful than most of his countrymen, harder, colder, stricter, but still part of this extraordinary bloom of a century. His name carried far, 'not only', according to Adamnan, 'throughout our Ireland, and throughout Britain, the greatest of all the islands of the whole world; but as far as three-cornered Spain, and Gaul, and Italy situated beyond the Pennine Alps; also the Roman city itself, which is the chief of all cities'. But for Adamnan—because of the way he tells it—the most moving tribute was of quite a different kind.

Columba, approaching eighty, was making for the monastery from the barn. Half way along he sat down. 'And while the saint sat there, resting for a little while, being weary with age, behold, a white horse came to him, the obedient servant who was accustomed to carry the milk vessels between the pasture and the monastery. It went to the saint, and strange to tell put its head in his bosom, inspired, as I believe, by God, before whom every living creature has understanding, with such perception of things as the Creator himself has decreed; and knowing that its master would presently depart from it, and that it should see him no more, it began to mourn, and like a human being to let tears fall freely on the lap of the saint, and, foaming much, to weep aloud.

'When he saw this, the attendant began to drive away the weeping mourner; but the saint forbade him, saying: "Let him that loves us pour out the tears of most bitter grief here in my bosom. See, man though you are, and having a rational soul, you could by no means know anything of my departure except what I myself have even now disclosed to you. But to this brute and unreasoning animal the Creator has, in what way he would, revealed clearly that its master is going to depart from it." Thus speaking, he blessed his servant and horse, as it turned sadly away from him.' Shortly after, he died at the altar of the church. It was the year 597.

*　　*　　*　　*

In the same year, St Augustine arrived at Canterbury, sent by Gregory the Great to bring the race of Angles within the Christian orbit. 'Non Angli sed Angeli'. In his persistent punning Gregory showed an unconscious sympathy with the Irish, who delighted in word-play. They called him the Goldenmouth. But he was also, in Bede's view, the real apostle of England, having while in command over all the affairs of Christendom given special attention to the salvation of the English through his chosen missionary. The point can, sadly, be pushed farther. Had Gregory been free from cosmopolitan claims, and come himself to the northern island, the Church in England would have been better founded. The acrid dispute that followed Augustine's officiousness would never have been.

England as it stood at the end of the sixth century was one of the few almost totally pagan countries of Europe, for the new invaders had brought Woden and Thor to replace the bud of Christianity that they cut. But it is never stated that the Angles and Saxons brought over women with them. If they did not, some traditions of Christianity would have lived on among them, suppressed but responsive to encouragement. Still, after Arthur, ancient British morals had declined. Even the churchmen, according to Gildas' gloomy annals, had warped the spirit of their law, preferring 'fasting to love, vigils to righteousness, their own invention to harmony, a little particular clause to the full doctrine of the Church, austerity to humility, and, last of all, man to God'. [2] And the Saxons and Angles would quickly have sent these old relics reeling to the safety of Welsh mountains and the remote sanctity of the west country.

For a time Rome showed no interest in reclaiming the land she had lost. There was too much on her plate. Even as late as the 550's Justinian's campaign to assert his authority on the western Mediterranean—the Gothic War—had kept the papal city more deprived and beleaguered than during the worst excesses of the barbarian raids, worse even than Attila's coup. But the second half of the century saw the emergence of two men whose interests and pursuits were neither defensive, nor confined to the parochial affairs of their city. First was Benedict, who founded a monastery, out of which was born one of the greatest orders of the Middle Ages. Second was Gregory, for his monastic ideas much in debt to the modest Benedict, and the first pope to realise the proselytising potential of the Roman Church. Before his time such missions as there were were accidental almost—Christian soldiers sent to the frontier, Christian traders linking Cornwall, Ireland and

Mesopotamia and Athens through their commercial journeys. Gregory, inheriting an authority that had shrunk for a century and more, decided to restore and expand the old boundaries. If imperial soldiers were to police the frontiers of Britain and the Rhinelands no longer, then the ethic and moral of Christ would.

Gregory is a dynamic and likeable figure, leavening his charged brio with a disarming aptitude to burst into tears from emotion. Born in the year that Belisarius took Ravenna for the eastern empire, he inherited wealth and position in Rome, and after a promising education passed rapidly through the grades of the civil service, reaching the post of *praetor urbanus*—a senior magistrate—at the age of thirty-two. Then he renounced position and money, and retired to the monastic life. During this period he heard of the pagan condition of England, after noticing the immortalised Angles in a Roman slave-market. He set out himself to convert Britain but was called back to various offices. In Constantinople for three years he obtained a clear picture of the way in which the eastern capital was trying to run the Church; and came back—and was soon elected pope—realising that Roman eyes must look to the west and north, and that Rome must be the centre of a self-sufficient world. Concentrating his efforts on France, Germany and Britain he succeeded in shaping not only the Church, but the cohesiveness of western Europe. In a sense he initiated the Middle Ages. In doing so he came up against Ireland, which, always an independent country, was now having an unprecedented influence on European affairs, as we shall see. He had a great sympathy with individual Irishmen, and there were Irish streaks in his character. But the Irish Christian movement was not in the mainstream, and Gregory's agents had the task of channelling it, or damming it up where it could not affect their own ambitions.

In Rome one day Gregory saw the triumphal arch of the emperor Trajan and noticed a carved relief showing the emperor with an old woman. The scene represented was of Trajan going off to the wars and being stopped on the march by this woman, a widow imploring justice. Wait till I return, said Trajan. 'And if you never come back, who will help me?', grumbled the woman. And so he stopped and arranged that she should be looked after. Hearing the story Gregory wept profuse tears, then prayed and prayed in St Peter's till he knew Trajan's soul had passed to heaven.[3] Weeping and praying formed the lovable side of this stern genius. They were not qualities shared by his emissary to England, Augustine of Canterbury, who arrived in Kent in 597, and was to build the first Benedictine mission station outside Italy.

There were still some Christian remnants among the country population, and more recently the king of Kent, Ethelbert, had married a Christian princess from Gaul. Augustine's success —the conversion of Ethelbert within a year of his arrival—was not due to his own persuasion alone. But it led quickly to more successes, and though these hint more of temporal occupation— the counting of heads as they tumble for God—they laid a basis for the establishment in Britain, if not of the kingdom of heaven, at least of the solidity of medieval Roman authority.

Augustine might have been expected to seek allies in those Britons who preserved their sequestered version of Christianity, the Irish, the Welsh, and scattered communities that remained on the east of the island. This he seemed determined not to do. Straight pagans require straight conversion. Approximate Christians require subtle persuasion, the balancing of nuance, and care not to bruise a fragile pride. Augustine lacked the qualities for the second task. He lacked a number of amiable qualities, and Gregory after a while, in his devout correspondence with the missionary, appears to have noticed the lack. He is forever having to answer Augustine's finicky questions, apparently asked more to ingratiate himself than to ascertain the truth.[4] Can two brothers marry two sisters, when there is no blood tie between the families? Why do customs vary in different churches? May an expectant mother be baptised? Gregory's answers are full of general principle, urging common sense over casuistry, and occasional showing impatience with the obsequious tone of the queries: 'Holy scripture, with which you are certainly well acquainted, offers us guidance in this . . .'. 'The punishment must depend on the circumstances . . .'. 'We give you no authority over the bishops of Gaul . . .'. 'Brother, you are familiar with the usage of the Roman Church, in which you were brought up . . .'. 'Why should an expectant mother not be baptised?' From time to time Gregory must have regretted his appointment.

The influence of the Irish Church was well established in Wales and parts of northern England and the areas of Scotland travelled by Columba. As Augustine's activities spread, a clash of some sort became imminent. Ireland, always respectful to Rome, had never recognised its authority as unquestionable. The Kent mission was here to assert and extend that same authority, and the first sparks came at a meeting between Augustine and the British bishops somewhere near the Welsh border. Understandably, the British were suspicious, for they were facing a Church that not only had divergent claims from their own, but came linked hand in glove with the Saxons, their recent godless conquerors. For them it was a degrading situation and they were not prepared to make initial concessions. Bede, whose sympathies and loyalty are both with the Romans, tells of the meeting in a detached way that leaves one appreciating the British point of view. On the way to the council the British clerics visit an old hermit to ask how much they should be prepared to forsake of their old traditions, and are advised to follow Augustine to the letter if he is genuine. But how are they to know? 'If Augustine is meek and lowly of heart, it shows that he bears the yoke of Christ himself, and offers it to you. But if he is haughty and unbending, then he is not of God, and you should not listen to him.' The test, he says, is to be on their arrival, in seeing whether Augustine stands up to welcome them, or sits aloof.

The prelate failed to stand. There followed an acrimonious exchange. The British must accept the Roman timing of Easter, the Roman method of administering baptism, and the responsibility of preaching to the Saxon. And if they do not, threatened Augustine, death will be their punishment. The British left huffily; and in time, as Bede points out sanctimoniously, Augustine's threats were carried out. At the Battle of Chester in 616, King Ethelfrith of Bernicia routed and destroyed the massed armies of the Welsh princes.[5]

By blood and tradition the Welsh and British were closely associated with the Irish in Ireland and Scotland. But as yet there had been no direct clash between the Irish and the new missionaries. It was not to come for half a century. During that time Augustine's successors consolidated their influence over lowland Britain and pushed it northwards to the kingdom of Bernicia, modern Northumberland. With the lessons of an empire behind them they built their foundations solidly. They made sure that Anglo-Saxon kings, still feeling their way precariously into their new authority, came to depend on their own political skill and diplomacy; they made the kings rely on Church contacts to carry on intercourse with Gaul and countries beyond. And above all they used their knowledge of legal theory to frame new civil laws, and so codify the state's dependence on themselves.

At the same time the mission stations founded by Columba multiplied and began to extend not only into the country of the Picts but south towards the border country. Their supervisors were not such masters of statecraft as their southern rivals. Their laws were too particularised for the strange complexities of Irish society to be of use to a pioneer civilisation. Their foreign contacts were few, based not on an organised diplomatic network but on the chance and erratic wanderings of restless Irish monks like Columbanus. But they could win loyalty and friends, perhaps more lastingly than others, by qualities that had little to do with influence and hierarchy. Using the methods and spirit that Columba had provided, Iona began to reach out and south until it came, like the Roman mission before, to Northumbria.

Northumbria had already been won to Christianity by the south long before the Irish mission arrived. In 626 its king, Edwin, had been converted by Augustine's disciple Paulinus in a more convincing way than royal conversions were usually effected. He had dithered and argued while his Christian wife—a daughter of the Christian king of Kent—added her prayers, and earnest debates went on between his advisers. It was at one of these arguments that a royal counsellor put the problem in a form that carried no more logical conviction than any other, but won the day by the way it was expressed. Imagine a dinner in winter, he tells the king; all the thanes and ministers sitting round in the warm congenial atmosphere. And imagine a sparrow that flies in from the winds and rains outside, flits through the hall and straightway out the other side, into the winter and the unknown. Life itself is like that span in a sparrow's flight, a moment of glitter; and if anything gives us more idea of the existence outside, before and after earthly life, it is worth our attention.[6]

Edwin was won, and backed a mission to spread the message to his people. Bede paints a clear picture of the mission in progress, Paulinus travelling the countryside, preaching and baptising the large crowds who came out to hear him. A few years later, in 633, Edwin was killed in battle against an alliance of Saxon and British kings, Penda of Mercia and Cadwallon of Wales. In the devastation that followed Paulinus retired to Kent with the Christian remnants of the Northumbrian court, and the first phase of conversion was at an end. Edwin had originally come in contact with Christian ideas twenty years before, when the vagaries and squabbles of new dynasties had forced him into exile in the south. At the same time another Northumbrian prince had gone north for refuge. This was Oswald, and during all that time he had lived on Iona with the hospitable Irish monks, learning with stable conviction the laws and spirit of the Christian faith.

Cadwallon's victory over Edwin brought Oswald for the first time out of exile, to claim the kingdom that was rightly his. As he prepared for battle with the intruder, the image of Columba came to fortify him, and next day his small army routed the vast forces of Cadwallon and killed the plundering king on the Field of Heaven, near Hexham in Northumberland. The Kingdom was Christian again, but this time it was Irish-Christian. As soon as he was established at his rocky fortress of Bamburgh, overlooking the North Sea, Oswald sent to Iona for a bishop and monks to settle the area and consolidate the Christian religion there. A bishop arrived, but quickly returned to Iona to report that the obstinate and barbarous nature of the English prevented him from teaching them a thing. The episode is appetising; it not only repeats a theme of initial missions being necessary failures before a second succeeds (Palladius before Patrick, Augustine before Paulinus, and John the Baptist's menacings before the arrival of Christ); but suggests some of the real tensions between Irish and Roman-English that in official reports are hidden under official and specious pretexts. But Bede does not dwell on the matter. A second bishop was chosen, Aidan. 'It seems to me', he says to his predecessor, 'that you were too harsh with your ignorant hearers, and forgot the Apostle's doctrine to give them first the milk of simpler doctrine. . . .' So he set off to Oswald's court. 'Time was to show', says Bede, 'that Aidan was remarkable not only for discretion, but for many other virtues as well.'[7]

Aidan is the last of the great founders of the Irish spiritual empire on English soil. There were to be many more Irish, and they distinguished themselves and spread Irish ways and beliefs much farther than Northumbria—to Somerset, East Anglia, even to Sussex; but they were individuals in a Church composed of mingled elements. Aidan, born in Ireland and trained at Iona, carried the traditions of his homeland with him and imposed them where he went. Bede writing about him felt confused; according to his Roman outlook Aidan erred on some fundamentals, yet he was patently a man on God's side and a man to whom God showed remarkable favours. It was very irking that with all this he should have cut his hair in an un-Roman way, and celebrated Easter on the wrong day. Perhaps Bede, who wrote nearly a hundred years after Aidan came to Oswald's court, did not really understand the issues that underlay skin-deep differences. More than once he is guilty of over-attention to details which blur his vision of the general spirit.

Lindisfarne, where Aidan chose to build his monastery, is on one of the bleakest stretches of the English coast. The land is flat and almost treeless for miles and in winter the northern light makes grass seem grey and the sea like torpid lead. The sea was aggressive, for it was always bringing godless invaders from Scandinavia and it brought the north wind too, direct across five hundred miles of flatness. In spite of this, Lindisfarne was an island, chosen—as the Irish had always chosen islands—because it was exposed and trying, and so putting its inhabitants full at the mercy of God. To the island Aidan brought the other harsh habits and disciplines that were characteristic of the Irish, the fasting and sanctions, the punishments for flowery show, the pursuit of simple solid virtues. Bede makes it clear that Aidan tolerated little compromise in asserting his idea of a Christian way of life. It was the mark of Irish monks, and eventually their harsh insistence alienated their following. The most important thing about Aidan, Bede claims, is the fact that the life he recommended to converts differed in nothing from the life led by himself and his monks.

He was very friendly with the king, for they had spent years together at Iona. Now Oswald would interpret for him on his missions, until Aidan mastered the new language. But in spite of royal favours he became neither a courtier nor a sycophant. Nothing would stop him telling noblemen that they had done something wrong, if they had; they generally took a harder telling-off than the peasantry. Gifts that came his way—and many did—went straight to the poor, and under his régime the monks remained in poverty. Once Oswald's successor Oswin gave him a stout horse, equipped with harness and all the trappings, a rich gift and a sign of great honour. In a short while the horse was a beggar's, one whom Aidan had met with on the road. That evening at dinner the king asked gently why Aidan could not have given the beggar a poorer horse, more fit for his purposes. Aidan made a little speech to the effect that charity could not be qualitative, and sat down to dinner. The king thought for a while, warming his hands by the fire, then came over to Aidan, knelt at his feet, and asked to be forgiven. It was Aidan's turn to ponder now, and as the king sat down in brighter mood, the bishop wept. A monk asked him why. 'Because', he replied, 'I have never seen so humble a king.'[8]

Aidan and Lindisfarne

There is no portrait antedating Bede's of Aidan which shows a cleric to be so clearly concerned with the spiritual welfare of ordinary people. He travelled about on foot, covering hundreds of miles—relieved at times by the short-lived ownership of a horse—teaching ethics by example and cultural matters by talks and books. Nowhere outside Lindisfarne did the legacy of native Irish culture settle so lastingly, nor the mature Irish scholarship which was directed at the classics of Rome. Aldhelm, a Saxon of the early eighth century who received much of his education from Irish monks, described the thorough grounding in grammar, mathematics, physics and exegesis that was taught by them. Still there was no fear of contamination from Virgil and Horace and the old myths of Ireland, nor from apocryphal works of scripture which elsewhere were labelled heretical; so that this course of education was based far more widely than any to be had elsewhere in Britain, and even on the continent. And at the same time the daily routine of the monastery continued as it had in the metropolitan foundation of Iona. Prayers were recited, the psalms orated by heart, farmland cultivated to provide essentials for monks and such lay neighbours as were in need. Converted landowners showered gifts on the mission—money, furnishings and land. Still in the effusion of its youth, the Irish Church was repeating on foreign soil the success it had enjoyed in the homeland, at Bangor, Clonmacnois, Clonfert, Moville, Clonard, Kildare, Glendalough. Churches were built all over the north of England, the original foundations of Jarrow, Monkwearmouth, Melrose, Durham, Ripon, Whitby and many smaller houses dating to this period. Yet it was not a time of peace. Oswald himself was killed in battle with Penda, pagan king of Mercia—the northern midlands—in 642. His kingdom of Northumbria was split in two, as it had formerly been, the old state of Deira passing to Oswald's brother Oswin. Nine years later Oswin too was killed, treacherously, by his neighbouring king who proceeded to re-unite Northumbria. The new ruler, confusingly, was called Oswy; and though crime brought him to power he mellowed in later years and gained a reputation for piety and wisdom.

Aidan died within a few days of Oswin's murder. By that time the monastery was well established, well enough to survive all the commotions that were taking place around it. Finan succeeded Aidan, and drove the missionary movement south into the Midlands. Scholarship and devotion flourished. Within fifty years the monastery was to produce an illuminated gospel which ranks with that of Kells in the care and beauty which outshine most other contemporary productions in Europe. Aidan's church, two wattle generations from the churches of Ireland, had itself bred many more in the north of England and even farther south. For a time it seemed that the Christianity of the whole island might bear the stamp of the Irish.

But beyond the gaping paganism of the midlands, Augustine's successors had spread their influence surely. Kent, East Anglia and latest Wessex had come over to the religion and acknowledged the primacy of Canterbury, which meant the direct authority of Rome, not the happy token respect for the Holy City that the Irish in their remoteness and preoccupation never failed to maintain. With care and efficiency the Kentish missionaries were reaching north again to win back provinces lost in a generation of dynastic warfare between Anglo-Saxon kings. In a few more years two Christian missions would meet, each deriving doctrine and spirit from precisely the same source, each teaching the same basic dogmas, sharing ritual, ethic and God; and each capable of the bitterest mutual spite. Till now the contact between the two principals had been incidental only, both in Ireland and Britain. One Irishman, however, had already lived and died on the Continent, fearlessly thundering his convictions at all who could hear, castigating queens, threatening kings, taming bears, repudiating the pope himself. His life is not part of the confrontation that had been building up on British soil for half a century. But it carries that feud on to the broad sweep of Europe, where isolated battles were being fought, jealousy aroused, and the fight for supremacy between system and intuition continued.

VII

France

'The patron saint of those who seek to construct a united Europe':
the words were from M. Robert Schumann, principal designer of
the concept of modern European unity.[1] The saint he nominated
as Europe's patron was Columbanus, a contemporary and near-
namesake of the first abbot of Iona, and another extraordinary
missile from the extraordinary Irish power-house. Christopher
Dawson, a giant among historians of the Dark Ages, called him
'perhaps the most dynamic personality the Celtic church produced'.[2] The last pope but two committed himself further. 'The
more experts study the most obscure problems of the Middle
Ages,' wrote Pius XI, 'the clearer it becomes that the renaissance
of Christian learning in France, Germany and Italy is due to the
work and zeal of St Columban.' There is a chapel in his honour at
St Peter's, and he has a statue in the National Shrine of the
Immaculate Conception in Washington. The Irish do him justice
on November 23, his feast day, and he is certainly the best docu-
mented historically of all his contemporary saints. To the English
he is less than a name. It may be because one Colum seems very
much like another, and there were hundreds of them at the time,
including Columba. The different Latin terminations were added
arbitrarily by enthusiasts determined to preserve the reputations
of the two greatest.

It has been seen that for the most part the Irish men of God
were no kid-glove saints, in spite of the efforts of subsequent
biographers pious with the fashion of their times. Columbanus'
first biographer, though he never met him, collected his materials
within a few years of his death, and happily did little white-
washing.[3] Deference to the man, and miraculous occurrences, are
thickly present, but bad appears along with good. In the sketch
of his early life we are given little indication of a heart that later

embraced any class, any nationality, on criteria that would have pleased Christ himself. As a boy, Columbanus appears to have been headstrong and painfully priggish.

Before he was born in 543, in the usual way and with untimely pride, the saint's mother saw the sun rising from her bosom in a dream, and filling the world with light. She watched him grow to exceptional grace and distinction, and was doubtless rather proud of the way he snubbed all the local girls. But she can hardly have been aware of the torment these multiple rejections caused the saint himself. For as the goodly biographer Jonas puts it, with a relish demanded by the matter, 'the old enemy aroused against him the lusts of lascivious maidens, especially of those whose fine figure and superficial beauty are wont to enkindle mad desires in the minds of wretched men'. Adolescence was clearly made wretched by sexual neurosis—and a united Europe may well be grateful for it—until the dichotomy of his desires was relieved by an old woman's monitions. 'Do you recall the wiles of Eve', she said, and recalled for him the wiles of Delilah, Bathsheba and the Queen of Sheba. 'Flee from corruption,' she cried. 'Away, away, forsake the path that leads to Hell's gates.' Her own sexual neurosis was obviously profound, but her words were good enough for Columbanus. He wrestled with his baser self and won, ran home with eyes ever to the front, collected essential belongings, knocked down his mother who pleaded at the door, jumped over her body and ran and ran till the fair maids of Leinster were safely behind him. The acrid Jerome would have approved. 'Depart,' he had advised the world, 'though your mother tear her hair and rend her garments, though your father lie flat upon the threshold of his house to stay your going, trample forth over him. Your only love and duty in this business is to be cruel.'

Jonas is very military in his metaphor. The shield of the gospel, the two-edged sword, and the menacing hostile lines of the old enemy are milestones throughout the saint's life. The trope is apt, for while Columbanus mellowed in maturity he never lost the directness of his earlier years. If kindness seems wanting in his youth, it can at least be argued that the tree shall be known by its fruit. When literal obedience to a creed, an obstinate characteristic of the Celtic Church, was joined to an understanding of people and experience of suffering, it made a man far more able to evoke sympathy, both from his contemporaries and posterity.

Flight led Columbanus to the monastery of Sinell, a graduate of Comgall's monastery at Bangor. From here on his education was typical of the aspirant missionary. He studied the psalms till he knew them by heart, and possibly wrote a commentary on them, using sources considered heretical by the orthodox church. Whatever reached Ireland that smacked of the esoteric was eagerly devoured. There was little appreciation of the specious and casuistical rifts in Mediterranean churches. Had Ireland's contact with Rome been more regulated, had her holy imports been carefully censored, her missionaries might never have stood out as they did on the continent. As it was they were distinguished by the peculiarity of their dogmas, and so given the publicity needed to spread the kernel of their message.

Sinell's monastery was by Lough Erne, in north-west Ireland towards Sligo. Trained in the roots of his religion, Columbanus passed east to Bangor, by now one of the foremost establishments in the country. His education was certainly a thorough one, for his later writings show him well grounded not only in Christian works, but in the style of the greatest Latin pagans. And here he came in contact with the greatest brains and characters of the country, possibly with Brendan and Columba themselves. He also decided to leave the country as a missionary—the old woman had advocated it—and was careful to note the running and administration of the monastery which became a basis of his various continental foundations. Then, equipped with knowledge and sanctity, he set off for lands unknown to him. 'My desire', he wrote later, 'was to visit the heathens, and that the gospel be preached to them by us.' His abbot reluctantly gave leave for the mission, for he had grown fond of him. He also provided twelve companions—the Messianic touches still recur—and a boat. So Columbanus sailed south; and although many Irish had been there before him he is the first shown by documents to have reached the coast of France.

It was about the year 591 that he arrived at the north coast of Brittany, so that if the date given for his birth is correct he was now well into his forties. Little is known of the first half of his life. From his activities in France it appears that before his arrival he had developed a great power of command and a skilful diplomacy that sometimes masqueraded under disingenuous bluffness. He had call for all these skills and more in the country of his adoption.

Nearly a hundred years before this time, Clovis had entered the Catholic Church and united Gaul under one leadership. His conversion had probably been nominal, and at all events the Christianity he imposed on his people was by now cracked by widespread relapses to paganism. His conquests too had not long outlived him. Although the Frankish territories remained in the Merovingian family, that family was so split by dynastic quarrels, divided patrimonies, external powers and personal feuds that they might have been separate clans kept apart by congenital mutual hostility. There were by now three basic divisions of the land. Neustria was the north-western portion, excluding Brittany, which had been colonised by Celtic fugitives from Britain; Austrasia lay to the east of Neustria, spreading well into what is now Germany, for Clovis had decisively subjugated the Allemanni of that area; while Burgundy covered what is now basically Switzerland with parts of France and Austria added. Even in their inherited parcels the Frankish kings did not have undisputed power. Their trouble was that of their medieval successors, who ruled in name but had little or no material possessions. Actual rule was in the hands of local dukes and chieftains, who were sometimes promoted to the paramount position of Mayor of the Palace. A hundred years after Columbanus' time a mayor of Austrasia was to seize power and establish the Carolingian dynasty. For the time being, however, the grandsons and great-grandsons of Clovis were fighting out their squalid rivalries, at the same time destroying most vestiges of the unified civilisation that had been handed down to them.

The Irish movement to the Continent shared few of the characteristics of its host. Superficially the Irish were a Catholic mission coming to a people more orthodox than themselves. Clovis had bowed without demur to the pope—it helped him in campaigns against heretic Burgundians. His successors remained Roman Catholic, and so did their subjects and vassals. France was nominally Christian. But continental Christianity had become divorced from any of the clauses of the Sermon on the Mount. It was a tool for use against Arians and pagans, a hoisted standard, as empty of spiritual meaning as the blue and green labels of the Byzantine factions, who massacred each other for preferring one pretty colour to another. The real source for most actions was a greed for power and the partiality for ease and debauch which contact with the relics of Roman civilisation had awakened in the Franks.

What made things worse was the available means of getting power. Had the Frankish chieftains kept to traditional structures they might have achieved more stability. Their trouble was a half-hearted emulation of Roman ways. They knew of the old greatness of Roman emperors, with lands stretching from Syria to Gibraltar; and they knew of the present grandeur and power of the rulers at Constantinople. They took them as models. But they were without the funds and natural resources to achieve or maintain such power even on a small scale. Emperors shrewdly kept their coffers full and, when necessary, paid attractive sums to the troops on whom their power depended. The Franks were never rich, for by now the west was not rich. Instead of gold they had to pay land. Their own territories dwindled while underlings added to their estates. The only thing a king could do to expand his own territory was to conquer. Where he could he did—and here his adhesion to Roman or Arian Christianity was at its most useful—but after a hundred years the captured lands, passing from hand to hand, were divided, badly farmed, exhausted and of little value. There was a general running down of the state.

Not only counts and dukes benefited at the king's expense. The Church was there, carefully exploiting a fruitful situation. Earlier it had been useful to kings, for it taught them something of the Roman way of working territories, the way they all respected. Now, through the bishop of Rome, it formed a diplomatic link with Constantinople, to which the aura of empire had long since parted, especially since the Gothic conquest of Italy.

But if bishops were a beneficial bond with Emperor Maurice in the East, they were hardly what they should have been, links with God. Cleverer than lay counts, they enlarged their lands at a fast rate. They taught politics but learned rougher ways from their pupils. So the message of Christianity was heard less and less. At the same time, since the break-up of the western empire, international commerce had declined. Raw materials had to be found in the country, and no longer through the balanced systems of export and import. Consequently townsmen left their houses and moved out to the country, where Christianity had never grown strong roots. In Latin the word *paganus* meant simply countryman. Country people, slow to change, kept up the worship of Celtic or old Roman gods, long after Christianity became the empire's official creed. With this rural trend, the Church's influence sank even lower.

In practical terms all this meant that Clovis's domains had lost such discipline and unity as he imposed. The Church—generally on a subtler level than others—joined in the prevalent ethic of murder, robbery and sexual excesses. Gregory of Tours, a conscientious chronicler of the period, painted a sorry picture of the strife and disunity that were spread wide.[4] In his pages, cathedrals and churches lose their value as sanctuary when churchmen connive, for money, at the slaughter of fugitives within. Bishops side with kings and princes in their squabbles, change sides, change back, and grow fat on the commission. Bishops send out marauding parties who murder for loot or advancement, then lock up these agents to silence their evidence. A year after Columbanus arrived the bishopric of Paris was bought openly by a Syrian merchant, Eusebius, who looked on the cloth as a step up from commerce. A king, Guntram of Burgundy, was remembered for piety after his death, and a French historian has expressed the reason—'not more than two or three murders can be fastened on him'.

Culture, where it existed at all, was almost sterile. During intervals of comparative security, landowners loved to ape Roman ways, to talk of literature, have pictures painted, parade their knowledge in the concourse of hot baths. The dilettante bishop Fortunatus Venantius could even travel the country and write charming lyrics in honour of his hosts, about streams and vineyards and pleasant woods. But the poet's patrons were seldom more than slippered thugs, and in much of his poetry—though there are shining exceptions—Fortunatus was a very lightweight Horace. All over the west books and scholarship were disappearing. The great library at Alexandria had held six hundred thousand volumes at the turn of the millennium. Bede, it is reckoned, used less than two hundred. And Bede lived in Britain at its cultural zenith, long after the worst of it. Activities in France at Columbanus' time that marginally merit the label cultural were mean, tawdry, stilted and seldom original.

In this setting one brand of religion meant little more or less than another. They were all means to material grabbing. Nor was paganism qualitatively different. The real meaninglessness of the distinctions is seen in the curious hybrid of Christianity and paganism that developed in country districts. Old habits of sorcery and magic persisted in new clothes. The Christian God was worshipped along with sun and moon. Sacrifices were offered to the God of Isaiah, his statue ranged with pagan idols for added security. Menhirs erected to old deities became crosses sacred to Christian saints, while still retaining something of their old significance. Christian priests predicted the future from the entrails of birds and animals. Where the successors of Druids had picked texts for augury from old books of heathen Roman divination, they now put their pins to the Bible, trusting God to be like, but kinder than, their former protectors. That, after all, was the condition on which they had turned to him.

'On account of the negligence of bishops', moderately complains a later Latin biographer of Columbanus, 'the Christian religion had almost disappeared from the country.' Only one branch of the Church had quietly resisted the ethic of the day. The

monasteries, from some of which earlier missionaries had taken
Christianity to Ireland, persisted still, on sites founded by St
Martin of Tours, Honoratus of Lérins, Germanus of Auxerre
and others. But here too the spirit had gone awry. Asceticism
had taken ugly turnings. So Gregory reports a nun who after a
vision decides to be totally recluse; and other nuns stand by
chanting while she is walled up in a narrow apse, a small window
left for essentials, and 'there she now devotes her days to holy
reading and to prayer'. He tells too of the blessed Radegund,
venerated to this day, who starved herself for long periods,
stepped on ashes, cleaned her companions' shoes, bound her
skin with hot metal plates, wore iron chains, branded herself with
the sign of the cross, and singled out for her embrace a woman
suffering from leprosy.

Between the self-persecution of the paranoid, and the licence
of the buccaneer, there seemed no middle path.

Among all this, whatever the locals thought of the immigrant
Irishmen, they must certainly have been impressed. Into an
atmosphere of shift and deception walked bands of Irish with a
clear and unequivocal sense of purpose. That purpose had
nothing whatever to do with vendettas or luxury or making money
or winning territory; little with emaciating themselves into
scrawny and impotent worshippers of a far-removed god.
Worship came first, but good worship presupposed good health.
They revived long-term farming methods on the land they took
over. With the product they fed themselves, gave free provisions
to the needy, and sold the rest for money to expand their activities.
They were healthy in mind as much as body and gave no precedence to material things. They showed how to order things
for the best in circumstances which were far from good. And in
their dealings with people they showed little fear or favour to
rich or poor; though some, other things being equal, to the latter,
their need being greater.

To a country that was sick for want of principle or criterion,
the sight of a file of these cloaked figures with their satchels of
willow osiers was a welcome one, tiny as their eruptions might

be. Their reputations went before them, they were talked about by villagers, chiefs and kings, and it was not long before they received royal invitations.

Kings, however, should always be suspect patrons of the Church. There is, for them, an attraction in alliance with heaven sometimes greater than earthly liaisons. In return for their support, however, they often demand what is not compatible with the Church's commission. Columbanus found an attractive welcome at various courts, and decided that it was best for integrity to keep at his distance. His first invitation came from Chlotar of Neustria, which he turned down in order to penetrate the country farther. Then Childebert II, who now ruled over the combined kingdoms of Burgundy and Austrasia—the whole of the eastern part of France—asked him to stay.

The dominant personality in this court was that of Brunhild, the king's mother. Twenty years earlier she and her sister Galswintha, princesses of the refined Visigothic court in Spain, had married, to cement an alliance, the kings of Neustria and Austrasia. These two kings, heirs to separate parts of Clovis' kingdom, developed a fierce mutual hatred and rivalry, which their wives soon adopted. Shortly after the marriage Galswintha was found strangled at the Neustrian court. Then Brunhild's husband was murdered after a victory over his brother—poisoned, it was thought, by agents of his brother's mistress. Brunhild was taken prisoner by the Neustrians, but managed to escape and from then on waged a fierce campaign of intrigue against the western court. As regent of the eastern Franks she was in a powerful position, and the official accession of her son, when he came of age, made little difference to her power. On the contrary, Burgundy was added to the kingdom at about the same time and her power was doubled. Even Childebert's death in 595 made little difference. Her grandsons were brought up under her direction, and it was many years before they were able to resist her. Her methods changed little with the years. Murder, poison, arson were her favourites; they were tidier than war.

At the time of Columbanus' arrival Brunhild was still acting as regent for her son. Little troupes of missionaries were hardly likely to disrupt her designs, and she was happy enough when her son, who had heard and marvelled at the Irishman's preaching, invited him to settle in his territory: especially since Columbanus had refused an offer to settle in Neustria. So Columbanus moved to a remote part of the kingdom, the mountain district of the Vosges, in Alsace, and settled with his followers, now grown numerous by the willing recruits who flocked to him from all over France.

The spot he chose was Anegrates, now Annegray, set in the middle of a wilderness of rock and scrub. There was a castle whose stones were used for the new buildings, originally put up two hundred years before by Romans to repel the same raiders who now ruled the country. Wolves and bears roamed in the district, and what people there were were Suevians, a border tribe still pagan and fierce, relics of a larger group that had moved on to Spain. It was a land to appeal to the Irish monks—hard and uninviting, the battered vestiges of old power, a waste. But within a few months they were forced to move on, not by the terrain, but because with growing armies of godly recruits it was imperative to find more space.

In this place and at this time asceticism was a welcome medicine. The rule at Luxeuil, where the community now moved, was strict, quite as strict as in the home monasteries from which Columbanus derived his rule. He comes down through his own writings as no more prepared to make concessions than Columba or Aidan. Abbots had always to be wary lest their monks were merely fugitives from the turmoil of the outside world, come in search of a cultured respite. Many failed, and their houses grew lax and dilettante and lost all purpose. Columbanus made sure by an almost inhumane discipline that his own neophytes found no escape or retirement, and yet he did not want for recruits.

Luxeuil was only eight miles away from Annegray, and the territory was as bleak. It had, however, in its time been a Roman spa, so that water ran freely—warm from some springs—and the buildings that remained were more spacious for the six hundred monks who were now with him. The rule of the monastery was a superstructure on the harsh deprivations caused by nature. There was little food—in the early days nearly everyone starved when for nine days there was no meat or fish, and frost killed most of the herbs. Bears and wolves were as hungry as men, and sometimes carted them off for a meal. In addition the Suevians were, to begin with, totally hostile. The early efforts of the farming brothers were perpetually frustrated by raids and pilfering. But they persisted, and when times improved—for correct husbandry began to pay off, and the locals came to respect their new neighbours—it was time for the full application of the rule of the monastery.

A story was passed around to illustrate the obedience Columbanus commanded. A monk of Luxeuil was drawing herbal beer from a barrel into a jar when Columbanus called him. Thinking of nothing else he ran to the call. On his return the beer, which had not been stopped, had piled itself in a column above the jar, and he was able to remove the beer in a solid body and place it in other jars without waste. Such was the promptness the abbot's call demanded.

It is plain that Columbanus was strict from several instances in Jonas' account. If anything he went to excess, reproving and punishing monks for things that were beyond their control, or for doing things the way that anyone without special insight would do them. Some monks, sent to bring all the fish they could find, brought back three and left two dead in the water. But Columbanus had not specified dead or alive; all they could find, were his instructions. So they must climb down the steep descent to the pool and bring back the bodies they assumed would be useless. During the harvest it was found that several monks were reporting sick and staying in the cells. Reflecting that it was the period of hardest manual work Columbanus ordered those he considered malingerers to get up and thresh the grain. Those who did not he condemned to a year's illness.

It is possible to see in the miracles which surrounded him some rational wiliness. There is a smack of strong practicality that runs

France

through all his writings and the writings about him. His dicta are short, but not ingenuous. 'He tramples on the world who tramples on himself.' 'Don't be afraid to disagree if need be, but agree about the truth.' 'Be hard among pleasant things, but gentle amid harsh things.' 'Love good people, but be rough with the dishonest.' 'Obey superiors, lead juniors, and equal your equals.' He was a literal, devoted, impatient man, full of maddening foibles and irrepressible energy—a combination of qualities that produce error and inconsistency. It may be partly for that reason that he appealed to local Suevians, for the best teachers are seldom faultless.

These Suevians lived in small family-groups, extracting what living they could from soil without any of the benefits of agricultural methods. Their pittance was subsidised by plunder from travellers crossing the Vosges by the local pass, but this was no steady source and petered out in winter. The Irish arrived, converted a ruin into a village run on Christian lines, and did not even bother to fortify their precincts. Here was a far steadier source of income, which the Suevians were quick to exploit. As the Irish stayed, contact became closer, but to start with it could not have brought any understanding. Nothing was farther from the old Teutonic pantheon and ethic than the pacifist doctrines of Christianity. There were no Christian war-cries, no gods to appease with sacrifice or the spoils of battle; only a young man who gave himself up to execution, a spirit linked with a dove that was so tenuous as to be incomprehensible, and a shadowy father figure who at first sight had attractively thundery characteristics but was soon exposed as a true and timid father of his son. Barbarians to the south had already managed to swallow a brand of Christianity by identifying Christ with a kind of Germanic demigod, and Arianism had swept those races which came in direct contact with the Eastern Empire. But they had need of Christianity down there—it was almost a condition for being taken seriously in the political field—while here, in the Alsatian backwoods, no such considerations weighed. The creed was taken for what it was, and found inadequate and inexplicable.

As time passed other things than doctrine began to modify Suevian opinion. The Irish produced good crops, and became men to appeal to, to depend on, to respect and to imitate. Increasingly young men of the tribes went across to the religion, and they served their purpose in educating their fathers. Moreover the monks within the monastery appeared to combine health and apparent happiness with complete rejection of all forms of aggression. They were not weaklings; their daily routine was the toughest any man could keep to consistently all his life. So new meanings were read into a religion that seemed at first perverse. For almost the first time on the continent, Christianity began to appeal to peasants and countrymen. This was something that had only been achieved in the east before, for Christ's particular appeal had been to the men of fields and villages.

It was of course originally to the East that the community life owed its existence. The modifications it underwent in Ireland have been seen already. Here in France it again changed to meet an altered situation. Under the lead of a man who never compromised it went as near to communism as a hierarchical society can. For principle, fervour and conformity, and for the sharing of all things as common property, the accounts of it sometimes read like modern Chinese manifestoes. The day's main exertions were divided between prayer and farm work, in which everyone took part, including Columbanus himself. After the first year, when the ground had been cleared of stones, sown, and harvested, the routines were spread over wider areas, for the numbers of the monastery continually expanded. But husbandry took second place to spiritual nourishment, and the reaping of that was vigorous enough. 'As guests of the world, let us not get entangled with earthly desires', Columbanus wrote in a sermon; and he persistently reminded his followers of the unimportance of this life compared with the next. This life was only a preparation. 'Think on death. Then shall pleasure and jest, lust and luxury, have fallen silent; then shall the body lie rotting in the clay.' The best medium of preparation lay in prayer and the scriptures. So, as in Ireland, the monks recited their psalms daily—never

less than forty-eight in the summer, and never more than ninety-
nine in the winter.

The Rule itself, drawn up by Columbanus, has survived. In
summary it is a model for asceticism, not the killing privations
of some hermits of the east, but as hard as any sane body can
undergo for long. There had to be complete and undoubting
obedience to senior monks, and silence all the time except on those
occasions when emergency or the needs of service or routine
demanded it. There was fasting twice a week, and on other days
the diet consisted mainly of grain, roots, leaves, bark, berries and
small hard apples. There were times for confession, and an
explicit *penitential* was drawn up listing fit punishments for each
crime. Since the harbouring of a crime was considered as an equal
offence to committing it, confessions were frequent, sometimes
before each meal of the day and before bedtime. They were held
in private, between the transgressor and senior priest, whereas
throughout the rest of Christendom they were proclaimed in
public.

In France, even more than in Ireland, the self-imposed morti-
fications of zealots have to be seen against a background that was
not gentle. There had been war in western Europe for two
hundred years, and it was the sort of war in which ordinary
people are held to be rabble, useful in the early stages for loot
and rape and later not even for these things. There was the same
rotting of value and principle that took place in the Thirty Years'
War. Armies themselves were despised by their employers who
generally ceased to be their employers when an opponent offered
a better price. Goth had fought against Goth, and Frank against
Frank, according as they were recruited by this or that general.
Though the arts of siege, both attack and defence, were matured
during the period, the main danger to those locked in a city
always came from their fellows, ready to sell the place and open
the gates for the fortune that was easily promised and seldom
provided. War bred plague too. Large towns were reduced by a
third of their population when it struck; and it struck often,
because in these conditions people had to take to eating rats and

horses which were often diseased. If as was usual their water supplies had been cut off, the plague spread like fire in dry bush.

So life was devalued. There was no security, no hope of better things, and no relish in the present. When men became cheap, morals became cheap too. All the horrors that intensify the passion of Greek tragedy became commonplace now. Sons betrayed or killed fathers, wives murdered husbands. Chiefs tortured underlings for information or sport. A chief's wife was forced by her husband to drink wine from a goblet that was her father's skull. And when old pagan Romans, nostalgic for the days of empire, nodded regretfully at the decline of the times, the barbarians reminded them of the doings in arenas, beasts and men killed for the bloodlust of hysterical crowds, and the licit tortures of the Roman code. The times were born of savagery and they wallowed in new savagery. In the context, Columbanus' regulations and sanctions seem less harsh. They are not gentle, but they are distinguished by two things; an impartiality to all men, and the consistency of their cause—the improvement of human souls, the provision of a better chance of entering heaven. If they are stricter in immediate practice than the contemporary rule of St Benedict, there is no trace of vindictiveness, and nothing is prolonged. The Benedictines allowed imprisonment, which would have been unthinkable to the Irish, while Benedict would have been horrified—his successors were—at the severity of punishments that Irish monks underwent for light wrongs.

Austerity is the real keynote of Columbanus' code; a literal return to the practice of Galilee. 'He who says he believes in Christ ought to walk as Christ walked, poor and humble and always preaching truth despite persecution by men.' Because of the fallibility of men, it is necessary to draft some basic rules of behaviour, though men cannot all be treated in the same way. 'All advice', he writes to a colleague, 'is not suitable for all, since natures are diverse.' Everything that can be naturally derived from a simple acceptance of Christianity is good; rules come only second, to fill the gaps in intuitive understanding. 'First of all we are taught to love God with the whole heart and the whole mind and the whole strength, and our neighbour as ourselves; next come our works.' Monks obviously have special obligations of silence, diet, chastity and attention to the liturgy, and above all obedience. Obedience is first clause of mortification, in which it is the monk's duty 'not to disagree in mind, not to speak as one pleases, not to go anywhere with entire freedom.' Attention to all these principles is the manifestation of the good life. But for those who need it there is guidance on details.

Penitentials were a characteristic of the Irish, and later generations were to condemn them as too strict, too solid and unbending. They were partly a corollary of that Irish love of classification, a kind of provision against future mental doubts by laying in stores of advice early. Taken alone, Columbanus' clauses make sadistic reading. Six strokes for the monk who has not waited for grace at the table, or responded with Amen at the end of it: six for him who speaks during a meal, unless the needs of another man have prompted the utterance; ten blows for the man who cuts the table with his knife. The monk who bites the chalice at Communion is liable to six blows for his sacrilege, he who giggles during holy office takes the same, unless he giggles aloud, when the penalty is doubled. There is a special fast for the glutton found in the kitchen after the last evening service. Penalties increase for more serious offences, particularly those of disobedience and lying. Fifty strokes for telling idle gossip that could harm someone else, and fifty for contradicting another monk.

There are times when the legislation becomes whimsically complicated. 'He who has replied to a brother on his pointing something out, "It is not as you say", except for seniors speaking honestly to juniors, with an imposition of silence or fifty strokes; only this may be allowed, that he should reply to a brother of equal standing, if there is something nearer the truth than what the other says, and he remembers it, "If you recollect rightly, my brother", and the other on hearing this does not repeat his assertion, but humbly says, "I trust that you remember better; I have erred in speech by my forgetfulness, and I am sorry that

I said ill."'" It is the perfectionist stranding himself on a rocky shore, far from the destination he deeply desires. Or the comedy of bureaucracy overreaching itself through the impractical medium of pen and parchment. 'Let brethren doing penance, however hard and dirty the work they do, not wash their heads except on the Lord's day, that is the eighth, but if not, on every fifteenth day; or certainly, on account of the growth of flowing locks let each employ the judgment of his senior in washing.' And at times there is blatant unfairness, as when 'he who through a cough has not sung well at the beginning of a psalm, it is ordained to correct with six strokes'. But these and others are the grotesque anomalies bound to develop in a general state of strain. The code was devised to persecute human weakness. In demanding, at times, the impossible, it became impossibly complicated. But there is no relenting in the ascetic spirit that created it. 'Let a man who is tired go to his bed; and let him sleep as he walks to it, nor go until he is forced by sleep to go.'

All the same it was not an austerity that repelled. Suspicion among locals was replaced by curiosity and then by affection. Annegray had overflowed, now Luxeuil was bursting its walls. Another monastery was founded in the area at Fontanas, the modern Fountains, where abbey ruins still stand, and which continued as an active community from Columbanus' time to the French Revolution. Now the busy and irrepressible abbot travelled from abbey to abbey, and when he could not visit wrote letters full of advice about difficult individuals, and points of farming and worship, and he never relaxed his control. But still he gave time over to the solitary life. It was recorded of many of the most dynamic abbots that they longed to shed responsibilities and settle in cells where

> A hedge of trees surrounds me,
> A blackbird's lay sings to me

and that they succeeded, if not for permanent retirement, at least for long spans. This concern for nature, for little things, for a microcosm of the world, enabled them to take a longer view of the world when they were involved with it. It made them different—more understanding, warmer—from those whose pre-occupations were allowed to keep them always in the busy centre of things. To the countrymen round them this Irish love of solitude must have appeared one of the most peculiar perversions, and at the same time, to people who invested every manifestation of nature with numinous quality, the most disarming. But it was also one of the persistent eccentricities of the Irishmen that endeared them to other men, the obverse sign of the coin of harsh rules and penitentials.

Several stories were told to show Columbanus' empathy with the natural state. He would often walk far into the forest taking little notice of the beasts of prey that he knew lurked there. One day he climbed up to a cave, the opening of which was visible far down on the path. At the end of his journey he found a bear, that growled at his approach. He dismissed the bear, explaining that the cave would be far better used for the solitary worship of God. And the bear, convinced, ambled off into the woods. In spite of his ferocious aspect, the quickness at losing his temper, he was a great favourite, we are told, among all the smaller and more acceptable animals. Squirrels and birds would climb on his arms and shoulders and frisk about like puppies. He had the accustomed command over them. When his gloves disappeared one day he deduced the nature of the thief in the following way: 'There is no one here who would venture to touch anything without permission, except the bird which was sent out by Noah and did not return to the ark.' While the monks looked about them for the offending raven, Columbanus stood in aloof dignity. A raven shortly appeared, and flew down before him with the gloves in his beak; then 'humbly, in sight of all, awaited its punishment'. The holy man commanded it to go.

These tales, that went round with him, would certainly have impressed the locals, but it is doubtful whether he was in need of imaginative publicity. From the scattered personal details in Jonas' Life it emerges that Columbanus possessed an earthiness, a strength, and a devotion that would make him a popular figure among peasant people. There was nothing loftily ascetic or sanctimonious about him. When a monk half severed his finger with a blow from a sickle, the abbot cleaned the wound with his own saliva before applying a bandage. Miracles added a picturesque quality. There is an inspired beauty in the tale of him posting four monks at the corners of a field in which he was harvesting hurriedly, and so kept bright sunlight in the field while all around the storm clouds brought dark and drizzle. But it was his personality that first assured his success. A simple directness characterises all his writings. He fulminates against what he considers wrong, and praises without qualification what is right. There was no guile in him, though his brain was outstanding in the age. And it was his brain, his directness, and his popularity that brought on him the greatest struggle of his life. His ways had come to the ears of the French bishops, and the Frankish court. As time went by, neither of them found much pleasure in the accounts they heard of the immigrant missionary.

For the bishops there was, before other complications were raised, a certain indignity in having to accept an Irish monk as a privileged protégé of the crown. They knew nothing of Ireland, since up to that time the traffic had mainly been to Ireland; Burgundy, moreover, was the farthest province from the northern sea. In the whole of Gregory of Tours' chronicle England is mentioned only twice, and Ireland and Scotland not at all. At the time Columbanus' troubles began Augustine had only just arrived in Kent. While later it became socially desirable for Anglo-Saxon children to be educated in France, there was now little more contact than a meagre interchange of goods. For many years the British isles continued to be regarded as provincial by the French. But there were other things to add to the bishops' peevishness. The Irish brought with them their learning, their zeal, and military discipline allied with rowdy argumentativeness. They were able to show the strong side of Christian meekness where the bishops had indulged in moral decline. For them, the Irish were a threat.

On their side, the Irish made no concession to tact or expediency in their dealings with the bishops. Columbanus never gave in to any demands made of him. In his charity to the peasants and obstinacy to the hierarchy he became a kind of religious Robin Hood, and where he settled it seemed that the poor and meek were at last inheriting the earth. He was forever attacking moral decay in high places, and he wrote his attacks in letters which doubtless circulated and spread the resentment of him. A contemporary wrote of him: 'He hurled the fire of Christ wheresoever he could, without concerning himself with the blaze it caused.'[5] At first the blaze was intermittent, but the fire grew. Attacks came from higher places, until they could no longer be ignored, even by a king who had granted Columbanus his royal patronage.

The annoying freshness of the Irish is easily seen in comparing literary styles of the time. Columbanus himself was a scholar, and knew his Latin classics well. His style has more in common with writers of the Golden Age than with the current productions of continental writers. The Frenchman's Latin at that time was refined to obscurity, not the style of the Golden Age nor the Silver —the tinsel age, as someone has called it. It was full of sophistry and sterile reference. Even Gregory of Tours, for all the fascination of his subject, is made difficult to read by clots of archaism.

Perhaps the most irritating quality of the Irish was a spirit that carries sympathy to the French. There was an element of spiritual *nouveau-riche* in these immigrants. Not long before Ireland had been poor in spirit, going to sleep at the end of its heroic age. Now Irishmen were full of the wealth of a new religion that fitted them to perfection, and they splashed their new riches without restraint among those who were more used to them, and more reserved and cynical about their efficacy.

Again the Irish lose some support when the specific charges brought against them are tested alone. The controversy that was brewing centred around three main points, three widespread Irish irregularities. First was the matter of the power of bishops. Because the institution of the monastery fitted so well in the social structure of Ireland, bishops had never had great importance after Patrick's first attempt to build up dioceses. Bishops existed, since they were necessary to perform certain nominal tasks, especially the consecration of priests. But by now, among the Irish, they had sunk to the level of rubber-stamp priests. Columbanus always had one among his monks, but his powers never approached those of the abbot. Even outside a monastery the abbot was supreme in the monastic boundaries and over the lands dependent on them. This rule of the monk-priest seemed invidious to the French bishops who exercised control and jurisdiction according to current Roman practice, which still took the town as the central administrative unit. That was one cause of dissent.

The second was a technicality which had more than obvious repercussions. It was the Irish system of private penance. Public confession, and the consequent public branding of sinners put far more power in the hands of the priests. Where the real message of Christianity had disappeared from view, it thus became a useful weapon in politics and the general gaining of ends.

Finally came the old question of Easter. As in Northumbria, so in France, the Irish celebrated the Passion on days different from those around them. The Roman system had been fixed most recently according to a nineteen-year cycle, which was adopted in Rome in 525. The Irish still worked on an eighty-four-year cycle that before had been widely practised in the West. The recent ordinance had passed them by, and when confronted with it they could at least claim the merit of antique precedent.

As complaints began to circulate, Columbanus took the precaution of writing to the Pope, Gregory the Great. Easter had been chosen as the main pretext for battle, and the letter was in the main a defence of the Celtic system. He wrote expressing his loyalty to the tenant of Peter's throne, carrying his respects only a little short of obsequiousness. But he showed that he would allow no interference in the hallowed traditions of Irish practices. Their system of calculating the Easter date, he claimed, was the oldest, having passed through generations from the first decisions of apostolic days. It was the universal custom of his people and nothing would change it. He implored papal sanction for this authentic convention. The Pope did not reply directly, but put Columbanus under the protection of the abbot of the monastery at Lérins, a shrewd move which left the drama to be played out in the wings. For the Pope was by no means secure in his western jurisdiction. Gregory was carefully amassing power, and may have wanted to stamp out unconformity. There was no point in condemning the Irish, who were certainly doing good works, on a matter that did not compare for gravity with the general sickness of the French Church; but still less was there anything to be gained by supporting them openly.

Three years later a synod was held by the French bishops at Châlon-sur-Saône to discuss, among other things, the matter of Easter. Columbanus did not attend himself but wrote a long letter defending his ways and those of his countrymen. His grounds were not technical; he appealed rather that he be left to his practices, and that others continue in theirs, 'for these are our rules, the commands of the Lord and the apostles, in these our confidence is placed'. There is a quiet threat about the consequences of offending God, but the claim to universal Irish rightness is framed, as a balance, in an emotional plea. 'Take care, holy fathers, take care what you do to these poor and foreign old men in your midst.' Are the deaths in godliness of seventeen of his brother-monks to be outweighed by the 'dubious and modern way' of Roman practice?

The verdict, it seems, was cautious condemnation. Columbanus wrote again, to other individuals and synods, maintaining his firm line, and though little is known of specific reaction, it becomes obvious that the times were against him. For by now, after twelve years in the area which he had made his own, the bishops were at last finding a new ally. The position of the royal protégé was waning, and Brunhild reappears on the scene to harry the poor and foreign old men out of Burgundy and finally out of all France.

Childebert, the king of Burgundy and Austrasia, had died in 595. He was succeeded by his two sons, Theodebert II who ruled Austrasia, and Theodoric II who ruled Burgundy. Theodoric became king at twenty, a docile and impressionable young man who inherited his father's respect for the Irish. He often visited

Luxeuil, and Columbanus became fond of him. He would not, however, allow affection to stand in the way of principle. At twenty Theodoric already had four children by four separate mistresses. Columbanus' sincerity in politics and personal dealings would be called a lack of discretion in others. He advised the king to stop living loosely and take a wife. Lust, if it were to exist at all, must have the sanctioned restraints. So the king negotiated with the Visigoth court of Spain—a country undisturbed by the recent wars and far ahead of other barbarian states in civilisation—and the princess Ermenburga, daughter of its king, was duly despatched to be his bride.

Till now Brunhild, Theodoric's Machiavellian grandmother, had lived with his brother at the Austrasian court. But her intrigues earned her the enmity of king and nobles alike and at last, around the turn of the century, she was expelled and came unrepentant to Theodoric's palace. Her first purpose, as always, was to insinuate herself into a position of power. As main rival she saw the Visigoth Ermenburga, and behind her arrival she quickly sensed the dangerous influence of Columbanus. She grafted her spite on to Theodoric, and within a year the princess had been returned to Spain, though her dowry stayed. Theodoric went back to his mistresses. Now Brunhild turned to tackle Columbanus, and one day at the palace she asked his blessing on two of the illegitimate children of the king. The abbot flared up. 'Know that these boys will never bear the royal sceptre, for they were begotten in sin.' Brunhild was succeeding. Her grandson would hardly countenance the abuse of all his kin. As Columbanus rampaged, an Old Testament prophet in a nest of royal depravity, she suckled the fruits of her policy. She intrigued with the bishops, and their campaign against Irish irregularities stepped up. She put the monks of Luxeuil under house arrest and prohibited all subjects from helping them or communicating with them.

One day Theodoric called on Columbanus. He wanted to see the whole monastery, he said, for he had heard there were rooms not usually shown to guests. Was this not discrimination against the laity? The abbot refused entry to his private rooms and chapels; they were sacred places reserved for monks alone. Theodoric stepped forward. Columbanus swore an oath; if he passed inside, the kingdom and whole royal family would be destroyed. To his horror, says Jonas the biographer, the king found himself standing already in a private room. He stepped back hastily and withdrew.

But it was the last straw. Both sides threatened and swore. 'You hope to win a crown of martyrdom through me,' said Theodoric, 'but I have better ways.' Within a few days, in the year 612, soldiers arrived to eject the monks. Jonas prolongs the expulsion, and talks of the soldiers being divinely blinded, wandering helplessly while the monks chuckled beside them. But in the end they submitted, when they learned the soldiers themselves would be punished for failure. All the monks agreed to depart, but even then the royal command frustrated their wishes. Only the Irish must go, said the order. Old friends took leave of each other, and for months afterwards, as he and his countrymen travelled along the rivers of France, Columbanus wrote solicitous letters from his misery: 'Because I know your heart I have mentioned only necessary duties, the irksome and difficult ones, preferring to check than induce tears ... it is no part of a brave soldier to lament in battle.'

Brunhild, in her battle, saw no reason to grieve. But her last years were heavy. A year or two after the Irish exodus, war broke out between the brothers Theodoric and Theodebert. The latter was defeated and Austrasia came into Burgundian dominion again. Theodebert himself was murdered by Brunhild. Then Theodoric died in a fire. Finally Chlotar II, king of the western province Neustria, arrived to resolve the situation. He defeated Brunhild's ragged forces, resumed the title King of all the Franks, then turned to his royal captive. Brunhild—Jonas is as vivid in such descriptions as he is in recounting the conquest of lust—'Brunhild he had placed first on a camel in mockery and so exhibited to all her enemies round about; then she was bound to the tails of wild horses and thus perished wretchedly.' She had still contrived to outlive three generations of her own progeny.

VIII

The Path to Rome

The journey was long and sad and arduous. The abbot was approaching seventy, ejected from what he hoped was his last settlement. He did not want to return to Ireland, or felt that it was his duty not to. But there was no resisting the detachment of troops which accompanied them through Besançon and the plains of Burgundy, over the Plateau de Langres and down to the north-eastern reaches of the Loire where they embarked on the boat that was to take them through to Nantes and the Atlantic. Nevers, Orleans, Tours. At Tours Columbanus wanted to pray at the tomb of St Martin, his spiritual ancestor. The officer said no, there was no stopping. But the boat wheeled round at his words, and forced him to comply. All that night Columbanus knelt at the tomb and prayed. Others were there, for it was a centre of pilgrimage. Next morning he took breakfast with the bishop. 'That dog Theodoric', he said, and recounted the list of his afflictions. Then he predicted the death of the king and went down to the boat.

Irascible Irishmen—*Scotti iracundi* was a familiar phrase. At the boat he learned the remnants of treasure they had brought with them were stolen. Back he went to the tomb of the saint, and 'complained that he had not watched by the relics of the saint in order that the latter should allow him and his followers to suffer loss'. Straightway the whereabouts of the thief was revealed to him. The goods were restored and the monks sailed on to the west.

At Nantes they were transferred by the guards to the ship that would take them back to their homeland. Columbanus wrote a last letter from French soil to his sequestered monks at Luxeuil. 'Hatred destroys men's peace; love kills their integrity.' Perhaps he himself loved: 'Honour Libranus and keep Waldalenus always, if he is there with the community, may God deal well with him, may he be humble. And embrace him for me.' Perhaps it was love that outweighed an old man's yearning for his native country. The ship creaked out from harbour and down the estuary. Then something happened—a trick, a vision, persuasion, a purse—and they were landed again before the ship put out to sea. Jonas has his own account and he may be right; that a storm arose and the boat wheeled and dipped till the captain dumped the Irishmen and took off immediately under cleared blue skies and running winds.

They had travelled five hundred miles across France. Now fresh spirits willed them to return. Chlotar II, the rising star of the Merovingians and king so far of Neustria only, asked the monks to stay, but it was no more than spiting his hated cousin of Austrasia. In three years he was to destroy him and reunite the domain of Clovis. Columbanus had predicted and was right. Columbanus stayed awhile, officiously putting to rights the laxities of the Neustrian court. Then with Chlotar's safe-passage he set off again to the mountainous hinterland that he had made his own. His aim now was to reach Rome, the seat of St Peter and centre of the church he believed he had loyally served.

At Metz on the Moselle he met Theodebert, again kindly for political hatred of his Burgundian cousin; and then passed through to the Rhine, sailed up it a hundred miles and after trekking round the coldly amenable country of modern Switzerland decided to rest at Bregenz on the eastern end of Lake Constance. This was the beginning of the Splügen Pass across the Alps. Theodebert owned the land, for a tongue of Austrasia here curled round and into the Alps, and he gave the band of monks land to build a new monastery. Winter was setting in—the winter of 612—and though Columbanus had his heart now on Italy he decided to remain. Again it was heathen country, where the Allemanni brewed beer to drink in their rites for the honour of Wotan. Still more forthright and indiscreet, less prissy and omniscient than the saints of other records, Columbanus shook the country with his evangelising footfall, burnt pagan shrines, smashed casks of beer so that the sacred liquid ran useless on the ground. His cathartic ravages brought him near to death some-times. 'Now there was an upheaval, cries of anger. The monks had to run away speedily. Columbanus, of a certain age, ran slower than the rest. The pagans caught him, threw him on the ground, and beat him with rods.' In time they left him, bruised but capable. He got up and cursed them roundly. 'Think on death; then shall the body lie rotting in the clay.'

Times were hard, but worse was to come. In his last year the treacherous Theodoric overcame his brother at the battle of Tolbiac. Switzerland was restored to Brunhild, not yet sacrificed to revenge, and her puppet grandson. Again the band had to move on, for they were exiles in any land of Theodoric's, and the final climb and descent over the Alps began. An old monk, Gall, had been with Columbanus through all the changes of fortune, right from the graduating days of Bangor. Now he was ill of quartan fever and felt he could not make the last journey. But the vagrant abbot's piety was not meek. Gall must come, said Columbanus, and as the weak man still refused he gave him a savage order, a penitence to endanger the welfare of his immortal soul. He was to say no more masses in Columbanus' own life-time. Gall stayed. He recovered and built the monastery that is still great and scholarly in the Swiss town and canton of St Gall. His body lies there now in its antique tomb, and there is a German phrase book in his own hand in the library.

Meanwhile those who could continue did so, Columbanus leading them over Septimer Col, a busy Alpine pass rising to 7,500 feet. Then finally Italy opened before them and they came down the beautiful passage past Lake Como and on to the plateau that stretches from Turin to Trieste, the plain of Lom-bardy. Lombardy had just acquired its name. In the middle of the sixth century a second wave of barbarian migration, with its source in the expansion of Germanic tribes beyond the Car-pathian mountains, had pushed each ethnic group a little farther to the west. Under its impact the Lombards pushed south into Italy, reached and breached the gates of Rome, then settled as the dominant tribe in the country with their capital at Pavia, near

Milan. Their king, Agilulf, had heard of Columbanus' approach and sanctioned his entry into the kingdom. Forty miles from the capital the old churchman and his tired companions set to building another monastery by the River Trebbia. Bobbio was a site where St Peter was supposed to have founded a church of his own. Nearby, and long before that, Hannibal had trounced the Romans. It was a position of great beauty, accessible to Rome; and while Agilulf welcomed the Irishmen, Chlotar of the Franks sent money to finance the building. Even so the old man did not rest. The administration of the building went on with his relentless instruction and the help of his flights of practical ideas. Outside the building there was a bigger challenge yet. The Lombards, though Christian, were of the Arian heresy. His fervour, and his sense of his own infallibility unimpaired, Columbanus straightway set out, in Jonas' words, 'to cut out and exterminate with the cauterising knife of the Scriptures' the perfidious doctrine of Arians.

During the chaos of the sixth century Italy had been the scene of the last effort of the Empire to regain its hold on the west. For thirty years Justinian, still titled Roman but ruling an empire that centred on Constantinople and looked more to Persia and the Middle East than to Rome, had carried on a futile war with the Ostrogoths who controlled Italy. In the end, in mid-century, he won technically, but in reality routed his own western ambitions. Within a few years the Lombards came down from the north and undid the precarious work of his generals. Only one institution gave any consistency to the period, and that was the Papacy, but it had neither the prestige nor the authority that it was to develop later. Before Gregory was elected its strength was ebbing fast, because it tried to appeal to the Goths without throwing over the patronage of Byzantium, and the two were irreconcilable. When the Lombards surged forward the eastern links were cut and from then on the papacy was to regard itself as an essentially western institution. It was still no better off. The Lombards held political power and they were Arians. They had no respect for Rome. 'Unspeakable Lombards', Gregory had called them; and hated them the more because they were richer than the remnants of Italians in the south, and bribed Catholics to go over to them with the promise of lighter taxes. That was at the turn of the century, fourteen years before the arrival of the Irish. And Gregory, while his tact and diplomacy laid the foundations of the later papal authority, watched gloomily while the Rome and Italy he knew declined and grew sick. 'Of this city', he lamented 'it is well said "The meat is boiled away and the bones in the midst thereof".'[1]

In Rome demoralisation gnawed the Christians. Byzantium was a useless patron, too remote, too preoccupied. The culture which emanated once from Rome was dead. Rivalry between Christian and pagan was only less violent than the Byzantine struggles of Blue and Green. As Rome and Ravenna sank farther, the last Italian heirs to the cities and magnificence of Augustus and Trajan, a creed of despair spread, along with the recurrent plagues that ravaged cities. People whispered of the millennium. Ideas of destruction and judgment seemed plausible and perversely attractive. In the tradition of mysticism monks over Italy ferreted through the works of Eusebius, Jerome and other Fathers, and came up with forced predictions of the imminent destruction of the world. 'The whole world is failing, is about to die . . . this is God's decree', Cyprian had written three centuries before. Gregory himself was convinced. Pestilence seemed a disguised mercy to him: 'There is solace in reflecting on the death that threatens us when we think of the way other men have died.' 'Rome is already empty and burning . . . already the pot itself is being consumed in which were first consumed the flesh and bones.'[2] Columbanus himself reflects the pessimism at times, but he responds to the misery and despair with characteristic force. The simple logic of the affair gives him hope. The world is evidently the vale of tears through which it is necessary to pass to reach the promised kingdom. So, instead of melting in the widespread resignation, he found an enemy to fight—an ark to build— and his attack was sanguine and positive. The enemy was Arianism, and the Lombards were Arian, and as usual Columbanus found, through his honesty, that he was biting the hand that fed him.

When Ulfilas the priest had edited the Bible that was to be the basis of Arian beliefs, he had omitted the Book of Kings on the principle that it contained too much warlike example. The heresy nevertheless appealed to the more aggressive barbarian tribes and spread among them till the split of Roman and barbarian was augmented by their respective identity with Catholic and Arian Christianity. It was this breach that Columbanus now set himself to heal. His method was his own. He thundered and argued, extolled the merits of Rome and the tradition of Peter and his own infallible instincts. He wrote to the Pope and the bishops, and his own monks took his message around the country-side. Christ, he persisted, was unequivocally Christ; not some Teutonic demigod. He preached at court, and soon the queen, Theodelinda, was agreeing with him, though not Agilulf. Columbanus was not satisfied. He rounded on Theodelinda and accused her of another, if lesser, heresy—of being partisan in the Three Chapters dispute that revived in the west the heresy of Mono-physitism. In the year that he was there he tried harder than anyone to restore the world to what he thought was gospel orthodoxy.

Either Agilulf was merciful and indulged the habits of this aged hell-fire preacher, or he was prevented by other distractions from turning his wrath on Columbanus as his last royal patron had. The monastery at Bobbio was allowed to grow in peace. Like Luxeuil's, its monks were cosmopolitan, for the abbot had no interest in men but as men, and being on the descent of an important pass Bobbio attracted large numbers of travellers who, given hospitality, stayed sometimes to become inmates. Again its reputation spread. Again the work of building continued with enthusiasm and the helping hand of God. When a mountain bear devoured one of the foundation's oxen, Columbanus com-manded the bear itself to take over its victim's functions, which of course it did with distinction. When the monks bowed under the crushing weight of a log till several dropped, Columbanus willed lightness into the log which promptly made itself easy for a few to carry. Well into his seventies, the old man had lost none of his pioneer's energy. And when, after the death of Brunhild and Theodoric, the victorious Chlotar invited him to return to Luxeuil, he refused. A new life was opening up for him in Italy. But he was weakening. Travel and disappointment, it seemed, would deprive him of the longevity of many of his compatriots.

He still kept up the full fervour of his intellectual life. Surviving Pope Gregory he proceeded to put his problems and convictions in dogmatic but humbly phrased letters to his successors. Only a few of his writings survive, but the little that comes down through fourteen centuries points to the abundance that existed once. He emerges more as an academic than a literary writer, and more an evangelist than an academic; but he displays the qualities of all three. There is a pathos in all his prose, a lightly spattered Irish melancholy; and there is a literary virtue, perhaps the only real literary virtue, in plain beliefs plainly expressed, added to the pathos of a sometimes misguided simplicity. Yet that is to undervalue him as a writer and a mind. His knowledge of and feeling for the humanist classics was far greater than that of most thinkers of his age. There are echoes of Virgil in his lines, and he loved Ovid and experimented in old age with Greek metres. His Latin boat song, composed for the journey up the Rhine, catches the power of muscular rhythm

> *Heia viri, nostrum reboans echo sonet heia. . . .*

A mystical prayer he wrote in Ireland gives a glimpse of the delicate and sensitive mind that underlay the bluff exterior: 'Lord, I covet those wounds. Happy is the soul so wounded by love, for it will seek the fountain, always drink, yet always thirst, for to drink here is to thirst the more.'

The bulk of his work is that of the disciplined abbot and assured missionary. In prompting Gregory to back the side of common sense, in reminding his relinquished subordinates of the ways he taught them and of their godly duties to each other and those outside the monastery, he is the tireless evangelist. He dramatises and emphasises and thunders out his own unequivocal convictions. Subtlety goes. He wants the bare truth, and the only colour he allows himself is a pun, appealing no doubt to Gregory, but jarring to prim and casuistical bishops. Issues have a right and a wrong side, and he is right and opponents wrong. To Gregory's successor, Boniface IV, he overreached himself, for he did not understand—he was factually wrong about—the complex controversy of the Three Chapters. Nevertheless he made an Irish impact on the papacy and on Italy, in spite of the size of his country and its remoteness from the patriarch's city. That he and his country did not make a greater impression is due to a fundamental difference between the papal Church and the Irish. The Irish wanted a kingdom of heaven and nothing else. Gregory and his successors were not blind to the importance of heaven but saw its attainment through earthly organisation. They wanted obedience, essential to the building of their spiritual empire and the conformity of a great church. Columbanus happily offered obedience, but it was the hazy obedience of his native land, based more on friendliness and respect that unquestioning execution of orders. Clockwork discipline was the ideal of his monasteries. But it ended in the confines of the monastic lands. Outside was a dialogue of equals, directed only by the sanctioned conventions of Christ's religion.

There was no reconciling of the general and the particular outlook. For Columbanus a man brought to Christianity was a man saved, and that was as good as anything else could be, for there was no quantitative comparison of salvation. But the papacy, because of its history and its position in Europe, had to take quantity into account, even though Gregory might have preferred things otherwise. The mark of the papacy was becoming the accumulation of power. Inevitably Rome's bishops had gained a predominance in the west. By the end of the third century the word 'papa' or pope was applied more than any other to Roman bishops, though it was not till the eleventh century that the title was exclusively Roman. Inevitably money and lands came into the bishop's care, through donations and legacies, so that papal territories were spread over the mainland, across the islands of the Mediterranean, and through parts of north Africa. Inevitably the virtual withdrawal of Byzantium from the western sphere had left the pope with temporal power and responsibility; and the split between East and West speeded the process by eliminating any rivalry or competition from Byzantium, Antioch and Jerusalem. The process could not be reversed. All over Europe the Church looked to Rome as an ally against the philistinism and paganism of newly established barbarian régimes. Gregory may have groaned under the weight of administration, and longed to be a monk and devote his time directly to his God. He may have cherished a deep affection for the Irish, and the two Celtic islands of the north. But it was not in his power—and his organising ability was too great—to indulge this affection in the personal way he wanted. When Columbanus wrote to him from the Vosges, it was Brunhild whom he had to consider first. Degenerate herself, she paid money and lip service to the Church, and that might have been the means of saving a million souls. Besides, she checked Jewish ambitions in her area—a valuable crusade, in papal eyes. So the Irishman's pleas had to be ignored. And in the northern lands themselves Gregory's concern could only be shown by the despatch of a typically papal mission, Augustine and his retinue. He had not lived to see it, but already after fifteen years the Canterbury foundation was pushing the Irish back to their own frontier and gradually stamping out the overt traces of their influence. In this respect the Irish represented the artisan trying to live alongside the technologist. His appeal remained, but could never again flourish with such universal importance as before.

Augustine's mission was Benedictine, and it was naturally to the Benedictines that Gregory's favour went. They were Italian, and he was to some extent their protector. When the Lombards sacked Monte Cassino, the Benedictine centre since the Order's foundation in 529, Gregory gave them a building on the Caelian Hill in Rome. It was from Rome that Augustine started off for Canterbury. Close to Gregory and obliged to him, the

Benedictines became a useful vehicle for his policies where before monasticism had always been too intense and extreme to be anything but a confusion and a nuisance. They were ultimately more practical than the Irish, and in noticing the differences between the two monastic practices it is possible to see some of the inherent weaknesses of the Irish system.

Where Brendan, Columba and Columbanus crossed seas and climbed mountains on pilgrimages that lasted years, Benedict of Nursia travelled scarcely more than a hundred miles in his lifetime. He and his movement were more moderate and more controlled than the Irish. 'Knowingly ignorant and wisely untutored', was Gregory's tribute to the Italian, and his disciples had little interest in culture or the preservation of old writings, poetry or art. Benedict's own state of perfection was *summa quies,* utter peace. Peace must come from a total acceptance, 'to wonder at nothing'. The secret of Benedictinism lay, to quote Newman's account, in 'having neither hope nor fear of anything below; in daily prayer, daily bread, and daily work, one day being just like another, except that it was one step nearer than the day before it to that Great Day which would swallow up all days, the day of everlasting rest'.[3] The age of martyrdom was over, and a level consistency would be the only stable ingredient of a febrile world. Life in the monastery was neither too strict nor too lax. The adequacy of diet was more than scant; two cooked dishes with fruit and vegetables, a pound of bread, or more for those on hard work, and a pint of wine a day throughout the year. Mattresses, blankets, quilts and pillows are allowed in the Rule for each monk's bed. Life took the middle course between the habits of sybarite and beggar.

The Irish were worlds apart. Their instinct was for the dramatic and the extreme. Benedict, according to Gregory, 'drew back his foot lest, entering too far in acquaintance with the world, he might have fallen into that dangerous and godless gulf'. The Irish lost tempers and risked lives, climbed mountains, interfered, found joy in nature and dejection in sin, took subtlety too far and were led by blatancy into error. They strained every nerve for perfection's sake and fell far shorter of paper perfection than those who knew a mean. But it was in them and it was them and it could not be otherwise. The Benedictines could only have found the Irish passion out of date and distasteful. Columbanus' disciplines trained men to be saints, Benedict's how to live soberly, farm well and die content. The age of saints, the Benedictine would argue, was long past. In a way that was true. The Irish brought the spirit of the early Church into an age that had seen it and watched it decay, for Ireland came late into the race. But the Irish did achieve a renaissance in the parts they colonised, and their contribution for some—some was enough—was incalculable. Perhaps theirs was an approach that burned itself up. When they had gone, the gentler nature of the Benedictines laid more lasting foundations. Latin organisation followed Celtic expansion. System followed inspiration. Possibly the sequence was as inevitable as middle age following idealistic, wrong-headed youth.

Not that the issue was so clearly stated then, nor so neatly resolved later. Celtic Christianity was transitory in only a specious sense. The humanity, and more tangible qualities of the Irish were remembered and imitated for hundreds of years. And Benedictinism became stronger only when it changed its nature from the concepts of its founder. Benedict's simple rule and aphorisms grew branches. Culture came to be valued, farming developed into more of a science, which had a prospering effect on the whole of medieval Europe. Nor was there ever an official confrontation between the two versions of monasticism. In Columbanus' time both still flourished, and neither showed obvious sign of decline. The advance of the Benedictines was steady and assured; that of the Irish erratic and floundering at times. But while in France both systems were soon to replace the old Gallic monasticism of St Martin of Tours, it was two centuries and more before the Benedictines were supplanting the Irish hold in that country.

But if the Irish Church prospered still, its individuals came and went. A year after his arrival in Italy, Columbanus died, on

November 23. Perhaps there went with him an energy that the Irish could never replace, though his name and lessons outlived those of most of his contemporaries. He had worked out the Irish drama on the Continent, and come across the same needs and enemies as his compatriots in Britain. That is why he is an essential part of the Irish expansion. And his character stands out more vividly than most as the prototype Irish evangelist, an apostle too late, a necessary anachronism.

He was big and bluff, dedicated to an ideal, and single-minded in pursuing it, immensely strong, stern and—ostensibly anyway —with a very literal mind. An ox with a soul and a call to God. In the manner of hagiographers it is tempting to compare his qualities—adding the span of generations since his time—with those of other good men and true, Dr Johnson, Livingstone, Robin Hood, Elijah, the impulsive Peter. Their kind is always present, yet rare enough. Giants whose subtlety is channelled, not into guile or sophistication, but into love, to make their love the greater. Giants with tenacity and the stamina to back it. Certainly Columbanus was one of the toughest of his race, of his age. He was the first of the great missionaries, for though Columba had crossed the sea he had gone to Irish territory. Like Columba, like Aidan, he was disposed to like kings, partly from native respect, partly for the good they could do. Like those two also he refused respect to abstract kingship if the man of flesh and blood was wanting in goodness. He clashed with Theodoric like Columba with Brude and Aidan with Oswin. The Irish appeared to have almost a knack of offending kings, natural perhaps with those whose hierarchy genuinely leads to God. At the same time his toughness appealed to the men among whom he chose to live, first, second or third generation settlers of barbarian tribes with still the blood of pioneers and horsemen in them. The Christianity they had adopted was earthy and raucous. That which they encountered in Europe was twisted with specious clerical nicety. What they found in Columbanus was a headstrong, obstinate variety that convinced because of its sincerity. He never doubted, regarding the Irish Church with some kind of apostolic infallibility. A buoyant optimism carried him through. 'Give the beggar some food,' he said once to his companions, 'and don't save anything for tomorrow.'

Yet with all this he was a scholar, one of the best in a poor age. Suggested throughout his writings is a view that, put forcibly, would have been heretical in his time but now seems palatable; that only good existed in the world, and anything else was not-good, the negation of good, but no positive quality in itself. It is there as an inference, but it shows the originality and scholarship of a mind that was partly in debt to Plato and that strengthened a streak of nonconformist common sense running through Irish clerics well into the Middle Ages, and exerting its greatest influence through the pen of John Scotus. A fine scholar and a fine poet. And not so obstinately right that he could not be loved by those around him. The primitive infallibility surrounding St Brendan is diluted in Columbanus. Smug at times, he still makes mistakes and acknowledges them. One of his companions, an original companion from Bangor, is dying at Luxeuil. Columbanus prays for his life, vehemently and with tears. But the monk is happy at the prospect, old and resigned. He tells Columbanus and mildly reproaches him. And the abbot is aware it was selfishness that prompted his prayers, and the fear of losing a friend. Shame comes over him and he prays only for the monk's immortal soul.

Because of his greatness he is, of all the leaders of Irish missions, the one whose character is least ornamented with miracles. They are there. Wounds heal, amputated limbs graft themselves back without scar, animals confess their faults, death is delayed at his intervention. Bears above all respond to his commands, but it is not only for that reason that his emblem is a bear. Apocryphal Messianic stories gather round him, justifications of the chosen race, so that at his prayers a house is filled with grain and he feeds five thousand; and at another time with two loaves and little beer he feeds sixty monks. But in general to Jonas is owed the least fanciful of saints' lives, and to Columbanus' character and eccentricities the fact that it could be written as it was.

His influence was wide and profound, and grew through its own momentum, not through any plan of campaign conceived by the saint. Bit by bit, though often only technically, Europe was reverting to Christianity. When Columbanus arrived in France only Ireland, France and Spain under the Visigoths were in any sense Christian countries. Within a hundred years of his death Britain and Germany were added to the list. Then the movement spread north and east, taking in Sweden, and by the end of the tenth century Norway and Russia. Among the central countries Columbanus' influence spread and gained a hold that was not easily supplanted. Particularly Germany, Switzerland, Austria and Alsace owe their first consciousness of the religion in large part to him and his compatriots, and still venerate him in their churches. But he did not, of course, leave these countries pious and God-fearing any more than he found them—as some would have it—charred and smoking and wrecked by barbarian inroads. A hundred years later the Anglo-Saxon Boniface could write of Germany to the pope of his time: 'Religion is trodden underfoot. Benefices are given to greedy laymen or unchaste and publican clerics. All their crimes do not prevent their attaining the priesthood; at last rising in rank as they increase in sin they become bishops. . . .'[4] The main effect of the Irish of the sixth century had been fleeting, literally vital to those who felt it, but not lasting, for no religious spirit can last long in unsullied originality.

The Irish mission was not planned or sustained consciously. The urge that drove them to leave their shores was in them in Ireland, not caused by the need of continentals. It was the recurring passion to leave all to find Christ, the obedience to biblical command, and the imitation of Abraham. But if chance and accident played their part in this mission the effect of Columbanus and his successors was a remarkably even distribution of Irish houses throughout the northern continental countries. It has been calculated that before the end of the seventh century there were ninety-four monasteries on the continent that owed their foundation directly or indirectly to Columbanus himself. On his various travels he had often enjoined penitents to found religious houses on their own account, and Jonas tells of a number of children, blessed by the abbot in infancy, who grew up to imitate his life in monasteries of their own founding. Luxeuil itself became supremely important, a kind of monastic metropolis of western Europe which sent out colonisers to found mission houses throughout France, Germany and Flanders. Some remained famous throughout the Middle Ages and are still famous today; St Vandrille, Solignac, Corbie, St Bertin, St Riquier, Péronne, Remiremont in France; Stavelot, Malmédy, Marmoutier in Belgium; St Gall and Disentis in Switzerland; St Martin's at Cologne, St Peter's at Ratisbon.

After a hundred, sometimes two hundred years, many of these went over to the Benedictine rule. In two councils of the mid-eighth century Carloman, Duke of Austrasia, ordered the standardisation of monastic procedure according to the Benedictine form. It was not universally followed. At times a kind of hybrid rule was used that brought together what the abbot considered was the best of both rules. And in many parts of France the Benedictine rule was neither understood nor much heard of till well into the ninth century. In the end Péronne was to be the only foundation which did not go over, and was known always as *Peronna Scottorum,* of the Irish. New waves of Irish were always reviving Irish habits. As late as the twelfth century in Germany Irish monasteries were founded at Würzburg, Nuremburg, Eichstadt, Vienna and Prague by newly arrived immigrants.

More besides the Benedictines competed with the Irish. The sixth-century expansion of Avars in the East was not the last of the rumblings that resulted in floodings of Europe by displaced barbarians. Seventeen years after Columbanus' death the new prophet of the East, Mohammed, died, and within months of his death the furious expansion of the Arabs began. They overran the Middle East and spread like fire along the north of Africa. Before the end of the century they had reached Damascus and Constantinople. In the opening years of the eighth century they crossed the sea from Morocco and occupied Spain. And soon after their raids into France brought them temporary possession of Aquitaine and plunder from all over the country. Among their spoils were some of the riches of Luxeuil, Annegray and Fontaines, all three of which lay in ruins at their departure. They rose again, this time to face the Nordic raids of the next century, and to survive again and live on to the present. But at each recurrence of war Christianity reeled at the blows. Power became more important, the power to resist armies and control fortunes. And, since neither of these had been Irish preoccupations, Irish influence could seldom expand through these turned-up times.

Besides, the list of foundations can give no true picture of the impact and work of individuals, many of whom left the monastic life in favour of solitary evangelising, or the pacific life of the hermit. The records of most will never be known. Some names have lived on in the Christian folk-lore of different countries. Fridolin is associated with Poitiers, and is said to have restored the church of its founder, St Hilary; and again to have built the first church in the south German town of Säckingen. Fiacra was a colourful figure who founded a hostel for Irish travellers in the Brie region, and eschewed, and encouraged those around him to eschew, women. Severe sanctions were set against women approaching his land, and many who did came to grievous ends. His unlikely associations are primarily with haemorrhoids, which prayers to him are said to cure, gardens, of which he is the French patron saint, and taxis, which in France were named after him. Deicolus was at one time a monk under Columbanus at Luxeuil, and at the abbot's departure he retired to solitude in the surrounding countryside. His habit of staying up all night in prayer aroused the suspicions of locals who concluded he was indulging in some vicious nightly orgy. He was suitably castrated. But his innocence being proved, too late, he was given a plot of land and lived in happy retirement for the rest of his days. He used to hang his cloak on a sunbeam, and people ask for his help to this day.

More historically attested is St Fursa, whose visions have earlier been mentioned, and who settled at Lagny on the Marne where with Irish bluster he condemned the vices of the royal court. His final settlement was at Péronne, which housed only Irishmen and acted as a kind of transit camp for those on their way to the mountains or Germany. St Frediano went farther, to Lucca in the Romagna. He is sometimes unreliably identified with Finnian of Moville, and is still venerated by the Italians. But myth has at most times got the better of fact. Renan, still popular in Brittany, brought back to life a baby murdered by her royal mother and the mother herself, stoned to death by an avenging crowd. St Kilian was murdered—or martyred as some have it— by the wife of a Duke who had been imprisoned when the Irishman told the Duke of her unchaste behaviour. The list is endless, and its benefits are seldom more than picturesque. But there was an undoubted Irish contribution at the end of the eighth century when Charlemagne called many Irishmen to Paris to enhance the reputation of his court. So high, at that time, was Irish scholarship and learning held.

Some habits the Irish left did not die out. Private confession, that originated perhaps at Bangor, spread across Europe superseding the old public disgrace. Penitentials, which almost certainly originated in Ireland, were accepted in many monasteries on the continent, both Irish and native, till the habit became too bureaucratic and inflexible. In the ninth century two separate councils condemned them, but they were not eliminated. In changed form and sometimes unrecognisably, they had a profound effect on the development of medieval church discipline. Mainly the Irish impact was felt by those with whom the Irish came directly in touch, for lives were enhanced by the direct example of a dedicated and unshakeable belief in God and Christ's ethic. Second to that was their impact on learning in general. At a time when culture hung in the balance the Irish preserved the old traditions, and spread them by their tireless copying of manuscripts. Not sharing the prejudices of continentals they kept alive pagan classics that would almost surely have been suppressed and forgotten without their care and industry. To some extent they were responsible for the modern languages of France, Spain and Italy. Without their skill in Latin, the language might have been less thoroughly preserved in these tongues. Long after Columbanus's time missions continued to bring hundreds of monks to the continent, and Ireland's fame went on drawing continental pupils and pilgrims.

A last comparison of Columbanus. He was the gad-fly that Socrates had been to a decadent Athens. His influence was felt in tiny enclaves of Irish religion but he became a pricking conscience of Europe. So he personified the Irish movement. Wherever they went the Irish retained their personality and stayed outside the mainstream. Many responded to their sincerity and fundamentalism and the slightly mystical aura that always surrounded them. But many were annoyed. Reforming outsiders always annoy. On the continent their fortunes were to vary till their direct influence melted slowly, leaving the ties between continent and Ireland that still exist and are stronger than any link between Britain and the continent. But in England their influence was more thorough, and their irritation proportionately greater. The time was coming when the gad-fly must be wiped out as a pest. The synod of Whitby was to be Ireland's draught of capital hemlock.

IX

Trial

In the year 605, while Columbanus followed his private path across Gaul, his reputation came through to the English at Kent. Archbishop Laurence, Augustine's successor, wrote to the Irish Church in Scotland: 'We have now, however, learned through Bishop Dagan on his visit to this island and through Abbot Columbanus in Gaul that the Scots [Irish] are no different to the Britons in their behaviour. For when Bishop Dagan visited us, he not only refused to eat with us, but even to take his meal in the same house as ourselves.'[1] Laurence had inherited some suspicions of Celts from Augustine, but he made a genuine effort to reconcile the British and English churches. Many were to do so after him. Nevertheless, for half a century, the independent, ingenuous and headstrong ways of the Irish vexed the Roman missions, maturing a will for requital. During that time only the politics and warfare of the newly-made state prevented a direct confrontation between the two groups.

From south and north the work of the two groups went on; Augustine, Laurence and their followers extending Roman Christianity as far as Northumbria; Mercian heathens displacing their settlements with slaughter and savagery; Aidan and the Irish reconverting that disputed territory, and holding the willing attentions of kings Oswald and Oswy. At the death of Aidan there was no apparent change. The Irish remained at Lindisfarne under, first, Finan, then Colman. They did not let up their expansive work; and soon individual Irish monks were working as far south as Suffolk, Sussex and Somerset. At the same time individual Englishmen, representatives of the Roman brand of Christianity, came north and sometimes reached high positions. During all those fifty years there was no outright breach. There were puffs of animosity, that must have been caused by brash rudeness or perhaps something more. But in the main the task was still to convert the heathen, who were myriad. No peasant population has ever been so flexible as to concur immediately with a king or chief who on a whim opts for some new creed. It was the job of the prelates to follow up and confirm a royal decision.

Not all the kings were as easily won as Oswald or Edwin. Mercia and East Anglia, in particular, came into and left the Christian fold with a suspicious volatility. Just before the Synod of Whitby in 664 the great ship burial of Sutton Hoo had taken place in Suffolk, with what must have been one of the greatest pagan ceremonies ever seen in a Nordic country. Northumbria itself had a strong pagan reaction in 633 after the death of Edwin, and the unfortunate bishop Paulinus had to flee with the queen to the Christian security of Kent and Rochester. Alliances, as on the continent, were dictated more by politics and material ambition than any concept of Christian fellowship (of course it would be hard to find any period of history to which this did not apply). To this extent proselytes of both Roman and Irish persuasion found common cause and worked side by side.

For nearly thirty years, up till the year 654, the greatest threat to Christian stability (and the greatest deterrent to Christian groups settling their differences) was Penda king of Mercia, the region of the English Midlands. He was probably the best general of his time, and used a skilful diplomacy to recruit to his side kings whom he scorned or feared to conquer. He was the great pagan menace, for his kingdom at its greatest extent stretched from the Wash to Wales, and from the Humber to the Bristol Avon, a square of brute strength forcing the kings of Kent and Northumbria into their humbler reserves. His forces had killed Oswald in 642 and led to the temporary estrangement of Aidan's mission. He had gained at the expense of the Kingdom of Wessex, at this time pushing forward to Somerset and the Devon peninsula. His victory in 634 had baulked the advance of Christianity in East Anglia by a rout of the Anglian forces there. Then at last in 654 Oswy, Aidan's second patron, crushed the Mercian forces at the battle of the River Winwaed. Penda himself was killed, and the

tide was with the Christians. For ten years there was pioneer
work to be done in the Midlands, where Woden and his retinue
were still worshipped. The work had not been completed when
the two streams of missionaries were again irritatingly close to
each other. Controversies began to flare up, small points of
ritual and doctrine were exaggerated into enmity. By the sixties
it was necessary for separate kingdoms to make a choice between
Celtic and Roman practices.

Oswy, in wise old age, saw the decision ahead of him. For him
the problem resolved into his mature affection for the Irish against
a temperamental approval of the efficient modernity of the
Romans. At Ripon, under its new abbot Wilfrid, he had seen this
at work and was impressed. In his dilemma he called a council.
Spokesmen for either side were to put their case to him and he
was to be sole judge. The future of the Northumbrian church,
and consequently the northern and Scottish churches, would
depend on his word. In 664, at Whitby on the Yorkshire coast,
counsel began to gather to put their respective cases.

The work of two hundred years was standing trial, and though
the effect of the verdict was not immediate, nor even dramatic, it
had repercussions throughout the history of these islands. Like
the trial of Ruskin for his libel of Whistler—'flinging a pot of
paint at the public's face'—or of Wilde for vice, the actual charge
was no more than a pretext. In the nineteenth century the cause
was new art. In the seventh it was something to do with the Irish
nature. Bede's account is the best of few sources, and it makes no
attempt to dig below the surface. Ostensibly the Irish stood trial
for a date and a tonsure. Underneath the patina it is largely for us
to find the reality.

In a sense this was the clash of two civilisations. Ireland stood
for a small federation of social groups, as inept at centralising as
they were biased against it. The English mission stood for the
Roman Church, an ecclesiastical empire that needed conformity
to function properly. Stemming from this basic difference, many
of the others took on larger proportions. It became a clash of
culture, of philosophy, of doctrine, of temperament. But the first

consideration is this social one. Rome was powerful, responsible, and saw her spiritual purpose in terms of material ambition. Ireland was small, divided, and saw her spiritual purpose without reference to anything else. She was a self-sufficient country with an urge to advertise her message. And while Rome could applaud her intentions and sincerity, she could not tolerate her excesses, or the anomalies of her practice. The rift was between an international system and a provincial.

What would certainly have surprised, and sometimes annoyed, observers of the Irish was the ingenuous way in which the latter persisted in their beliefs, in such a blithe manner that no guile could be pinned down. Given that Ireland had been isolated from the Roman empire during its supreme centuries, it was still strange that after two centuries of contact she should be happily impervious to continental developments. But it was true. In Ireland there had never been an issue between God and Caesar, for kings had been almost the first to accept Christianity. There had never been persecution or restrictions on Christians, and Columbanus could write honestly to the pope, 'Liberty was the tradition of my fathers, and among us in Ireland no person avails, but rather reason.' There had always been—has always been—a strong conservatism among them, the despair of those who want reforms necessary for bigger commitments. The Irish refused to see things in universal terms, and kept doggedly to tradition. They took the word of God more literally than others, and catered for the individual, which was easier for them, having as they did the heritage of the village and not the empire. Their isolation and self-sufficiency gave them a pride in the past and belief in their present. Their gratitude to Rome and Christendom for bringing them the creed is present always in their respect and general philanthropy; but it was essentially gratitude to their original converters. What had passed since in the councils of the world was of little interest to them. However much they absorbed and copied—liturgy and doctrine and symbols—they remained distinct, a church of individuals trying to do what was good and jibbing at the general acceptance of compromise.

From this divide came all the characteristics that marked them off from the Roman adherents. Irish discipline was austere, far harder than that which prevailed in most other churches, and still owed its inspiration to the rigid asceticism of the Middle East. Their attitude to ardours was that of the martyr; and love of martyrdom was often mentioned in Irish writings as a sacred quality. Their monasticism had spread healthily, and brought benefits to thousands of people beyond their shores. But it was in these practices—monasticism, asceticism and martyrdom—that they began to arouse rancour among the Romans. Ausonius had long before seen monasticism as the break-up of the classical world, for it put itself above normal social obligation. It is possible Patrick himself was sent to Ireland to try to quench the monastic movement and put diocesan organisation in its place. As early as the fourth century the fashion of becoming a hermit was seen as an escape from duty by the Romans. The Theodosian code had forbidden monks to go to the desert, regarding it as a way of escaping taxes. While to the Romans the spirit of martyrdom was out of date; Constantine had put an end to its need. In a way the Roman must have felt like a burdened adult jealously watching a child revelling in the formative, idealist years. But Rome was not all adult, nor Ireland all child. There were differences in character which would persist at any age.

Above all things was the simplicity of Irish aspirations. It was not an exclusive simplicity, for along with it went the devious complications of the Irish mind seen in some of their poetry and art. It was more a simplicity of character, while the other was the complex web of intellect. Ritual and liturgy in the Irish practice were both more simple than the Roman. So was their love of nature, and their delight in the little things of it. To the English, hills were abhorrent, and they were often compared with abhorrent things. The Irish regarded all natural things—mountains, bears, mice—as the creation of God, and praised them, or tacitly welcomed them, wherever they went. More important, they extended a similar fondness to men; and though they made exceptions they seemed in general to be better disposed to all fellows than the Canterbury school, which allowed priority, dignity and such considerations to overrule often its duty to neighbours. Irish simplicity extended too to their attitude to obstacles. Problems, basically, could be overcome. To think a thing was to do it, for that was what Christ had said. A story was told of Columbanus that, out walking one day, he started to wonder whether he would sooner be attacked by robbers or wild animals; animals, he decided, since they would not be thought to sin. And straightway a pack of wolves rushed at him and tore at his clothes. He remained calm and prayed and they soon went off abashed. The point of the story is in the teller's mind. It argues a directness and literalness that were an essential Irish characteristic. It links with all the precipitousness with which Irish monks rushed to obey God's command, to proselytise new countries, to sail out to the unknown where they would be under only God's protection. The Irish temper was less restrained and sophisticated than the Roman—and we are sophisticated spectators—but it still appeals to a deep and convinced urge within us.

Side by side with simplicity, a recurring paradox, went their taste for whimsy. It crops up everywhere, in their poetry, their animal stories, their playful humour, their doodles and diagrams. The writer of solid texts turns aside to compare his lot with that of Pangur Ban, his cat. The scholar of classic history or Bible evolves his exegesis into curious allegorical interpretation, or cryptograms with hidden banalities, or the outlandish and elastic extensions of the *Hisperica Famina*. He revels in puns and particularisms, the heavy wit of Goldenmouth Gregory or the poetic distillations of the saga writers. There is, and presumably was, nothing more irritating to outsiders than the esoteric indulgence of mature whimsy. It is interesting that this same quality should later have become a characteristic of the English, seen in any comparison of national literatures, and in the Englishman's devotion to the amateur state against the professional. And to remember that according to some historians the major part of the population of England was still Celtic, after all the immigrations of Teuton and Scandinavian conquerors.

Whimsy and pedantry

If a mature cultural coherence is beginning to emerge in the character of Irishmen, it can only be reinforced by considering their cultural background. Some of their particular features had roots in old Celtic Druidism which they had never cast off with the finality of revolution; and behind that, again in smooth descent, was the megalithic religion of western Europe in the only country that could claim to have learned from it. The high status of holy men and of learning in the monasteries derived from it. And from it came their assurance.

Learning and scholarship showed another characteristic of this tiny nation: their adventurousness. For their daring was not confined to physical tests. They were active and tireless intellectually, digging deep into their own pagan culture and rewriting it in a way that sometimes matches Homer, and exploring their new discovery of classical writing with the *praefervidum ingenium Scottorum* that was becoming their hall-mark. It was a very intense approach to learning. Little that they wrote is leisurely or contemplative, though that exists. They wrote the essentials, and when they used imagery, of which some of them were masters, it was clear and economical. There was, too, resentment from outside at the free use of their vernacular language. The Irish at this time developed their tongue far more than any other European race and much of their best literature was written in Gaelic. In a typically carefree way they never came to regard Latin with the same awe that others did, and yet they excelled in that too. And of course they sometimes went too far, parading as experts on matters of which they were ignorant, explaining in their commentaries the meanings of Greek and Hebrew words they did not understand, puffing themselves into civic grandeur—pedants with a facility for the matter in hand but no real understanding. In the Book of Armagh the Lord's Prayer is written in Greek letters, but the words they form are Latin.

It was geographically that their redoubtable assurance carried them farthest. Their love of the sea took them across it with the same vigour the Vikings had, and in all directions, and without the anarchic destruction of the northern men. Iceland, Greenland, all the countries of Europe, perhaps America—these were the ways they charted. It may have been the weakness of their wills and their inability to live up to their own Christian standards that put them under the command of a sparse nature, determined that the earth or the sea would discipline them where their own resolution had failed. Yet there is little evidence of that, for their missionary undertakings were successes, and they never failed to win the astonished respect of a neighbourhood. Did the antagonism rise from their success? Greater powers look tolerantly on the achievement of smaller till that achievement impinges on their own. Or kings may have grown wary of Irish popularity with their humbler subjects.

But the Irish were not angels. Their energy could blind them, and they became insensitive or smug or aggressive. They were at times intolerably self-satisfied. In every life of their saints occur those incidents drawn straight from gospel descriptions of Christ —the miracle births, the twelve followers, the feeding of large numbers from a basketful of provisions. The idea of the chosen race is always present. It was not peculiar to them; most countries have at one time or another selected an apostle, diverted his last journey to their own land and so assumed the kind of sanctity that Rome claimed from Peter's settling there. St James at Compostela, Joseph of Arimathea arriving at Glastonbury, the Virgin's sister and Mary Magdalene retiring as hermits in the Auvergne—these are prototype legends in the Christian myth of any country. But a fault does not have to be unique to aggravate others: and the Irish anyway took it farther than most. In their case, and for the purposes of the Whitby trial, it was augmented by the attitude to Rome that went with their convictions of sanctity. Like their Christianity, their ideas of the Pope dated from the time they had first heard of his existence, back in the fifth century or earlier, when his powers were at most those of a first among equals. Now, when he had grown in stature through his own campaigns, and saw the stability of Christianity through the expansion of his power and prestige, he resented the friendly consideration given him by the Irish.

They doffed their caps and passed on, making up their minds for themselves. There is no trace of any abbey in Ireland during these early centuries ever asking Rome for permission or guidance on any point. Indeed their delight with their new treasures often made them offer advice to him, affronting him with the unsubtle generosity of the *nouveau riche*.

More directly to precipitate the clash at Whitby comes the attitude of the Irish to the Anglo-Saxon, Roman-dominated Church: and the temptation of the English Church to confuse immigrant Irishmen with the native Celts of Britain, as they were often confused in English minds. Dagan's treatment of Laurence was only one recorded incident in a half-century of scorn. What annoyed the recently-arrived Anglo-Saxons, who were eager for learning and religion, was the way the native British ignored them. The British, displaced and decimated, felt no inclination to go among their new neighbours to help them find a place in heaven. And when the Roman representatives turned up in Wales the Welsh showed their determination by putting them through a forty-days' penance, scouring their plates after meals at which they refused to sit by them and prophesying their future with the Devil. Yet these are all British reactions, not Irish. Though Aidan's predecessor had reported to his fellows that the Anglo-Saxons of Northumbria were 'barbarous and obstinate', he is not shown to have expressed his feelings to their faces. Aidan himself and most of the Irish showed more than a willingness to work among the invaders. Bede grants his loveable nature and the virtue of his work, but condemns him with the other Irish. The impression of confusion with the native British, who shared many of the outward forms of the Irish, is a strong one.

Perhaps all these characteristics were at work on the minds of the Roman party. Some or all of them could have worked on them to produce a phobia of the Irish. But there were other reasons too, dimly suggested in the evidence at Whitby. They could have been real reasons, or exaggerations of small sores. They had to do with heresy, a traditional and major pretext for war throughout the Mediterranean countries, but little resorted to in the British

Isles. If Ireland's heresy were true, it was of the blackest sort.

To start with, the Irish followed what seemed to them common sense in preference to elaborate dogma. Pelagianism, which had often broken out in Ireland, was a rationalist heresy, denying original sin and the divinity of Christ as many fully sensible people do nowadays. There is no evidence that Pelagius' beliefs gained a firm hold on the leaders of the Irish Church at any time, but plenty to suggest that they followed their own reason in preference to anyone else's. It is impossible to attempt any deep study of the philosophy of the Irish, but as pointers two figures stand out at the beginning and end of the Irish golden age. Pelagius ushers it in, anathema to Rome. And John Scotus Erigena brightens its decline in the ninth century. Moreover it is known that Pelagianism was still being studied in Ireland at that time. In the intervening five hundred years there was a continuity of independent thinking.

John Scotus belonged in the Neo-Platonist stream. He believed in ideals, which in his case were characterised by God, and that evil did not exist in its own right but only as the absence of ideals, or good.[2] Evil, he claimed, is a privation of God, and it has its origin in freedom from God's control, in free will. Satan does not exist, nor did the Garden of Eden, which was an allegorical fantasy. John's outlook is a psychological one with strong religious ties. It was strongly disapproved of in his time and the Pope ordered his best work to be destroyed, a sentence it escaped. But his Neo-Platonism may have been common to the Irish (who may equally never have expressed it as a system), as it was common in the Middle East throughout the early centuries of Christianity. There are hints of it. There may never have been more than hints, but these would be enough to rouse suspicion in orthodox, and especially jealous, militants. More clearly they would have seen the Irish pursuit of apocryphal works, condemned time and again by popes, which nevertheless continued in favour in the Irish schools. They would have seen the unapologetic delight of the Irish in pre-Christian literature and traditions. The sagas, after all, were as un-Christian as the Old Testament. And the legend of St Brendan is in one reading a cameo heresy in itself.

The argument at Whitby revolves mainly round the dating of Easter, but in one curious passage the Irish abbot of Lindisfarne, Colman, claims that his system for dating the feast was handed down from St John. Little more is said of the matter, but it opens out a whole field of hypothesis. For St John has been the guiding spirit in a strange near-heresy that has existed all through the life of the Church. Connected early with his name was the mass of rumours that Christ had not in fact died on the Cross, his place being taken by Judas just before the crucifixion. More important was the speculation caused by the mysterious words that conclude St John's gospel. 'Lord,' said Peter to Jesus at the Ascension, 'and what shall this man do?' The man was John, the disciple whom Christ loved. Jesus replied 'If I will that he tarry till I come, what is that to thee?' It was a strange reply, and was soon filled with the deepest meanings. Peter had undoubtedly been given the commission of establishing Christ's church, but now eastern theologians began to read into these words the seed of another, inner church. They evolved a system round the words; the history of the world would ultimately be composed of three reigns. The first, that of God the Father, was the reign of the Old Testament and of fear. Second was that of the Son, placing his authority in Peter, the reign of the gospel. Third was to be the reign of the Holy Spirit and of love, with John the beloved apostle succeeding Peter. It added bite to the mystical predictions of millennia, resurrection and last judgment. It pleased the tortuous minds of sorcerer-theologians. And because Colman claimed John as authority for his Easter date, it was attributed to the Irish. There may have been no more reason than that.

That was not all. Another name was mentioned at the hearing, of far more sinister implications. Again it was a casual mention, dropped during the discussion of tonsure styles. The Irish style derived, said the Romans, from Simon Magus, arch-sorcerer of New Testament times, and founder, according to some, of the Gnostic heresy—so much a heresy as to be an inversion of the Christian order. From Simon Magus comes the word simony, but his attributed aims were far more serious. Though a baptised Christian he claimed to be a god himself, practised magic in Samaria and as far as Rome, where he clashed with St Peter, and later became the prototype for Faust in medieval legend and the darker theories of mysticism. Gnosticism may owe him nothing, though his name is often linked with it. It was essentially a continuation of sophisticated pagan lore under a Christian guise. It was queer, and involved the juggling with mysterious symbols, cryptograms, auguries and acrostics that inhabits a permanent nether-world of all western civilisations. It claimed salvation through knowledge, not faith, but the knowledge was so involved and convoluted that salvation was an esoteric privilege. In its more grotesque forms it made God the fount of evil and Satan the epitome of good. It was black magic, and it spread surely though surreptitiously throughout the western world.

The Irish were victims of association. Overt omissions in their practices were replaced, in the minds of enemies, by crimes, seditions and the workings of the devil. But these were not part of the indictment. Oswy was to judge on technical matters, apparently free from criminal implication. And these need a word of explanation.

The calculation of the date of Easter has always been a difficult matter. Alone of all Christian festivals—perhaps because it is the most important—it has been calculated not on the date of Christ's rising, but on the repetition of solar and lunar positions that prevailed at that time in the year 32. In an ideal calendar system the date and the day of the week would be one and the same. But the year is not an exact number of days—we still need leap years to correct our system—and the moon's phases are not in total harmony with the earth's course round the sun. Moreover, it has always been considered vital to commemorate the first day of the week as the day of Jesus's rising, though the Hebrew-Jewish week is yet another arbitrary element to complicate the issue. Successive brackets of seven days have no relevance to astronomic movements.

An early divergence among Jewish-Christian sects was to

celebrate Easter on the fourteenth day of the month Nisan, the first month of the Jewish year. In spite of attempts to label it so, this was not an Irish practice. The Irish always conformed to the Roman practice of holding the feast on Sunday. They had learned their system in the fifth century from Roman contacts, and held to it. Unfortunately, as with so many things, Rome had meanwhile changed its mind about which Sunday, and the Irish in their hundred years of isolation had not been told the news. In the middle of the fifth century the Romans had modified their system, calculated on an eighty-four-year cycle, to one of 532 years. Later they changed again to a cycle of nineteen years. The Irish meanwhile were happy with the first theory. Even when it caused confusion they stuck to the old way, resisting newfangled methods of mathematics and astronomy.

Tempers rose around the issue, especially when the two systems overlapped. At the Northumbrian court one year, Oswy, convert of the Irish, was celebrating Easter while his queen, trained by Kentish missionaries, was still enduring the weeds and fasting appropriate to Palm Sunday. A later English bishop wrote with feeling that those who employ the Celtic system were being 'sucked down and drowned in the whirlpool of Charybdis'.[3] Bede himself had reason to feel strongly. As a historian he had to reconcile incompatible dates from the two systems, and for all his skill he made mistakes. So he can add the weight of a cardinal sin to his summary of Aidan who was 'loved by all, even by those who differed from his opinion on Easter'.

The matter of the tonsure was a similar pretext, but even more a bureaucratic quibble concealing some bigger cause. The Irish shaved their heads from ear to ear over the top of the head, leaving their hair to grow at full length at the back. It could hardly have flattered their appearance, which may have been the reason they persisted. The Roman practice was to shave the top of the head leaving a circular fringe. It was originally the mark of a Roman slave, though later held to be a ghoulish commemoration of the crown of thorns. It was said wrongly to have originated with St Peter. Again the insidious associations grew. Some held the Celtic style a Druidic, and so pagan, practice. Others called it the way of Simon Magus, and the same English bishop could write to the Pictish king he was trying to convert 'If you seek the society of the blessed Peter, why do you imitate the tonsure of the man whom Peter cursed?'[4] He added a run-through of the conformist tonsures of Old Testament heroes, showing glittering precedent for his case.

There were other technical differences, of which the most important was the low status of bishops within the Celtic Church. The abbot was still dominant figure in their church, and the bishop, to whom all appeals were made in the Roman Church, was merely an abbot's underling. Where the Council of Arles had decreed a minimum of three, and if possible seven, bishops to take part in the consecration of a new bishop, the Irish were content with one. It was an untidy disobedience that rankled in the minds of Romans, trying to establish an ecclesiastical empire. Equally untidy were differences in the ritual of baptism, mass and ordination. It may have been, moreover, that Irish clergy were allowed to marry. Certainly marriage was practised in the Welsh Church till the twelfth century.

Some or all of these issues were present in the minds of those who assembled at Whitby. The scene chosen was a double monastery that housed both monks and nuns under the authority of the abbess Hilda, described by Wilfrid's biographer Eddius as 'a very wise woman, the best of comforters and counsellors in the whole province'.[5] Whitby rises sharply above the sea around a harbour on the Yorkshire coast and was known at the time as the Bay of the Beacon. The cells and chapels of the monastery were spread over a wide area, and its own farm extended far into the country. There was room to house many of the royal retinue within the monastery, as well as the clerics representing both sides of the case. Oswy came with his son, Alfred, who ruled the southern portion of Northumbria in his father's name. Alfred's sympathies lay with Rome, for he had patronised, and in turn learned from the impressive legalistic mind of Wilfrid. For the southern church came Agilbert, a Gaulish bishop of the

West Saxons, whose sole contribution to the issue was to excuse himself on account of language difficulties; Agatho his priest, Wilfrid, James the Deacon who had remained in the province through all its changes of fortune of thirty odd years; and Romanus, Queen Ethelberga's chaplain. Representing the Celtic cause were Colman the bishop of Lindisfarne and Aidan's second successor, his Irish advisers, and Chad, the future bishop of Lichfield and Mercia, who has come down as a humble kindly prelate who in the Irish manner travelled his large diocese on foot till his archbishop, hating inefficiency, ordered the use of a horse.

Wilfrid, the Roman spokesman, was a stormy figure. Born in Northumbria in 634 he had crammed his first thirty years with more experience than many twice his age. Early on, his biographer reports admiringly, he had 'none of the silly fads common to boys',[6] and it may be that as a result he lacked a sense of humour. Tense and tireless, he left home at the age of fourteen for dislike of his stepmother, and made for Oswy's court, where he found favour in the eyes of Queen Eanfled. He matured in Lindisfarne under Aidan, then took off for the continent in the hope of seeing Rome. He was welcomed at the Holy See, blessed by the Pope, and taught the current practices of the Church by solicitous archdeacons, including the method of computing the date of Easter. Afterwards he made for Lyons, where, on the outward journey, he had already formed a passionate attachment for the Archbishop. France, however, was still in the throes of dynastic wars and conspiracies. Directed by a virago in the mould of Brunhild, the dukes of Burgundy were now purging disloyal elements in the Church, and the time came for the archbishop of Lyons to be tried and executed. Wilfrid stood by him, delighting in the prospect of martyrdom, but when he was found to be English the order was given for his release. 'In his youth', writes Eddius with satisfaction, 'he was already worthy to be counted a confessor like St John the Evangelist, who sat unscathed in a cauldron of boiling oil and drank deadly poison without taking hurt.'

In England again he was welcomed by Alfred, and made abbot

of Ripon in 661. He gained the love and respect of all those put
under his care, but the bruises of youth seem to have left him with
a bitterness. The ups and downs of his later life support the theory,
for he was always offending those who at first were impressed by
him. From his behaviour at Whitby it is not hard to see what
impressed them. His tone was harsh, almost inquisitorial, and he
seems sometimes more eager to parade knowledge gained in
Rome and Gaul than to follow any dictates of Christian humility.

King Oswy sat on the throne provided, and earnestly and
judiciously explained the issue.[7] If he was trying to be a Solomon,
it was a worthy aim; and if his intentions were at last to seem a
little personal, there was no great harm in that either. All who
served the true God, he began, should observe one rule of life.
There should be no difference in the celebrating of the sacraments.
Before the synod were two conflicting traditions, and it was the
synod's task to determine which was truest. Their decision
was to be accepted by all. He asked Colman, the Irish bishop of
Lindisfarne, to explain first the Irish tradition.

Colman was later to establish himself as a shrewd arbiter in
national grudges. But his convictions brought him arduous
wanderings and hardship. Convinced and unshakeable, he gave
his defence plainly and briefly. The Easter customs he observed,
he said, were taught him by his superiors; not only they, but
all his forefathers, men certainly dear to God, had observed the
same customs. 'And lest anyone condemns and rejects them as
wrong, it is recorded that they owe their origin to the blessed
evangelist St John, the disciple especially loved by our Lord,
and all the churches over which he presided.' The king then called
on Agilbert to explain the origin and authority of the English
and Roman customs. Agilbert begged leave to propose Wilfrid
in his place. His English was shaky, and an interpreter would be
unable to present his case well.

Wilfrid was prepared, and started strongly, recalling his
personal experience of the practice in Rome itself. 'Our Easter
customs are those we have seen universally observed in Rome,
where the blessed apostles Peter and Paul lived, taught, suffered

and are buried. We have also seen the same customs generally
observed throughout Italy and Gaul when we travelled through
these countries for study and prayer.' The observance stretched
throughout the Mediterranean lands, Africa, Asia, Egypt, Greece.

His temper rose as he thought of it, and he concluded with a
politician's abuse: 'The only people who are stupid enough to
disagree with the whole world are these Scots and their obstinate
adherents the Picts and Britons, who inhabit only a portion of these
two islands in the remote ocean.' He had obviously learned to
orientate himself to Rome, for he had learned the Roman's scorn
for outlying provinces. 'God', Pope Boniface had written earlier
in a more indulgent Roman manner, 'has begun to warm to the
cold hearts of nations at the world's end.' Wilfrid too had learned
the law of apostolic supremacy—that discipline should radiate
out from Rome. That the circles of influence might reach the
edge and ripple in again was not, to him, a salutary thought.

Colman was composed. 'It is strange', he replied, 'that you
should call our customs stupid when they rest on the authority
of so great an apostle, who was considered worthy to lean on our
Lord's breast and whose great wisdom is acknowledged throughout the world.' But Colman was on weak ground. He had nothing
of his opponent's legalistic equipment, and had done little to
prepare his case, relying on straight exposition and the rightness
of his stand. He was wrong, and Wilfrid knew, and had the right
answers ready. 'Far be it from us', he retorted, 'to charge John
with foolishness.' Where John had tolerated reprobate observances it was because he wished to give no offence to men whose
acceptance of Christianity was new and precarious. But as soon
as he knew the facts of the Easter computation, and could
impose them without offence, he did so. 'And this is the custom of
all the successors of blessed John in Asia since his death, and is
also that of the world-wide church. . . . It is quite apparent to us,
Colman, that you follow neither the example of John, as you
imagine, nor that of Peter, whose tradition you deliberately
contradict. Your keeping of Easter agrees neither with the Law
nor with the Gospel.'

It is plain that Colman is at sea among Wilfrid's facts and tight-knit arguments. As the statistics and computations pour forth he must be relying more on the incomprehension of the judge than his own ability to counter them. Wilfrid invokes science and Peter and the Council of Nicea. He claims the rest of the world for his side. And he blinds with his sure grasp of the complexity of the subject: 'If the Lord's Day did not fall on the day following the fourteenth day of the moon, but on the sixteenth, seventeenth, or any other day up to the twenty-first, he [John] waited until that day, and on the Sabbath evening preceding it he began the observance of the Easter Festival.' Again Colman's answer is weak. He has no hope of directly answering the question. The best he can do is invoke those spirits of the dead, who, he thinks, might have been able to do it for him. 'Do you maintain', he says bravely, 'that Anatolius, a holy man highly spoken of in church history'—a pitiable description from a man in straits—'that Anatolius taught contrary to the Law and the Gospel, when he wrote that Easter should be kept between the fourteenth and twentieth days of the moon? Are we to believe that our most reverend Father Columba and his successors, men so dear to God, thought or acted contrary to Holy Scriptures when they followed this custom? The holiness of many of them is confirmed by heavenly signs, and their virtues by miracles; and having no doubt that they are Saints, I shall never cease to emulate their lives, customs and discipline.'

Wilfrid has at least provoked Colman's robuster self. It was appropriate to mention Columba who, like Aidan, was given anyway grudging appreciation by Celt and Angle alike. 'Whatever type of man he may have been', Bede wrote, 'we know for certain that he left successors distinguished for their purity of life, their love of God, and their loyalty to the monastic rule.' But Wilfrid has ready answers to both points. No Celtic trap can catch him, set as he is to win a victory for the expanding Church, unconsciously preparing for the holy empire of Charlemagne. If Augustine's arrival sixty years before had been the first Roman offensive, Whitby is the second, with Wilfrid in the van. 'It is well established', he concedes, 'that Anatolius was a most holy, learned and worthy man; but how can you claim his authority when you do not follow his directions? For he followed the correct rule about Easter, and observed a cycle of nineteen years.' Anatolius in fact did not, but neither Colman nor the quietly pensive king was to know. More technical data follow, more sand blown in the eyes of a discouraged opponent. Then Wilfrid comes to the second point. 'And with regard to your Father Columba and his followers, whose holiness you imitate and whose rules and customs you claim to have been supported by heavenly signs, I can only say that when many shall say to our Lord at the day of judgment: "Have we not prophesied in thy name, and cast out devils, and done many wonderful works?" the Lord will reply, "I never knew you".'

No charity, no giving an inch. Even Columba is criticised, whose name among his own people and others who met him or heard of him is without blemish. For Wilfrid the end justifies the means. Religious orders that have grown in more recent years have followed his example, the lesson of intellectual war, directing all weapons and tactics at a single object. He cannot even value the military usefulness of his opponents; for granted that the empire of papacy must grow as a centralised hierarchy, the Celts have held a dazzling place as a guerrilla forefront to the ordered masses. The speech continues. Columba is not finally condemned. 'I feel certain that if any Catholic adviser had come to them, they would readily have observed his guidance, since we know that they readily observed such of God's ordinances as they already knew. But you and your colleagues are most certainly guilty of sin if you reject the decrees of the Apostolic See and the universal Church. . . . For although your fathers were holy men, do you imagine that they, a few men in a corner of a remote island, are to be preferred before the universal Church of Christ throughout the world?'

More debate, more calumny. The last word is with Wilfrid, before the king speaks again. He quotes, with climactic conviction, the words of Christ: 'Thou art Peter, and upon this rock

Trial

I will build my Church, and the gates of hell shall not prevail against it, and to thee I will give the keys of my kingdom of heaven.' The simple words prevail more than long speeches, hard for any audience to understand. In some relief the king fixes on the quotation and resolves the issue round it. First he turns to Colman: 'Is it true, Colman, that these words were spoken to Peter by our Lord?'

'It is true, Your Majesty.'

'Can you show that a similar authority was given to your Columba?'

'No.'

The king addresses both spokesmen.

'Do you both agree that these words were indisputably addressed to Peter in the first place, and that our Lord gave him the keys of the kingdom of heaven.'

'We do.'

'Then, I tell you, Peter is guardian of the gates of heaven, and I shall not contradict him. I shall obey his commands in everything to the best of my knowledge and ability; otherwise, when I come to the gates of heaven, he who holds the key may not be willing to open them.'

Wilfrid and Colman alike might have been tempted to smile at the earnest words and their cautious reverence. But Colman would not have smiled for long. His cause was lost. In a little half-comic summing up the kindly king had quashed the independent aspirations of the Irish. This is not to overstate the case, though the context and conduct of the trial seem modest and restricted. The narrow issue of Easter held undertones of all the differences between Roman and Celt, and the Irish took it as such, and went away.

In the European context the immediate significance of Whitby was small enough. It was a victory on the periphery for Gregory's successors, trying with mixed results to continue his campaign of expansion and consolidation. The obstinacy of absolute governments in France and Germany were closer problems, and their efforts there meant more to them. But in England Whitby was a turning point, a necessary climax. It turned the scales in favour of Rome. From now on the city of Peter was to be the centre of civilisation and the arbiter of religion. Those 'few men in a corner of a remote island' were to wield their colossal and disproportionate influence now in infinitely diluted form. It was harsh payment. In their way the Irish had restored the faith in Britain and in large parts of the continent. Their dramatic, awesome reputations had spread far from the trails that individuals carved. And now they were reversed, banished for the felonies of tonsure and calendar by men who were newer to religion than they, and were ostentatiously proud of their acquisition. So, perhaps, had the Irish been as they wandered through France with scant respect for the traditions they met. But on the continent they could be aware of a sympathy and an acceptance, from peasant, king and even preoccupied Pope Gregory. In Britain they were beaten by the subtleties of dialectic, and nobody can calculate the loss to both parties.

X

After the Verdict

Almost immediately after the synod an epidemic of plague
that had taxed the Continent broke out in Britain and Ireland.
It must have killed thousands, for all the English bishops save
one were victims. The kings of Northumbria and Kent sent to the
Pope for help, asking also for a new Archbishop of Canterbury.
After an interval of five years Theodore of Tarsus arrived,
consecrated to the archbishopric by the Pope himself. He headed
the wave of administrators who followed up the victory of
Whitby and organised the Church in Britain in a Roman and
lasting manner. The year after Whitby Wilfrid was elevated to a
bishopric. He lived another forty-five years, spent in different
parts of Europe largely because of the antagonism he roused in
each place. Twice he was exiled from Northumbria for resisting
the orders of his superiors. But his achievement was great. He
founded many religious houses and churches all over the country.
He led a mission to Sussex and the Isle of Wight (almost cut off
from the rest of the country by the thick forests of the Andreds-
weald along the Downs) and was largely responsible for bringing
both areas into the Christian fold; though an Irish monastery,
that had been at Bosham some years already, had made some
impact. He taught the locals fishing, a food source they had
apparently not appreciated before, and founded a monastery at
Selsey Bill. 'The hostility of King Egfrid', says Bede, 'made
it impossible for him to return to his own province or diocese,
but nothing could deter him from preaching the Gospel.' He
also did effective missionary work in Frisia, having been blown
there when he hoped to sail for France; and there prepared the
way for his greater successor, Willibrord. When he died, he was
returning from Italy with papers from the Pope justifying all his
behaviour to the king and bishops of Northumbria.

King Oswy died only six years after the synod. His last pious hope was to recover from his illness and visit Rome and the holy places there and die among them, so complete had been his assumption of the Roman mantle. His verdict had had far-reaching effects on the country. Organisationally the land was parcelled into bishoprics; and minsters, built now of stone and not the Irishman's perishable wood, were the centre of each diocese. Later the parish system evolved. Authority and uniformity were maintained by regular synods and councils to discuss and rule on all issues of divergence. The monasteries developed a progressive system of education, and with kings and bishops in general agreement in a prosperous country, religion became the fashion. Kings collected relics and queens took the veil. The Benedictine order completely replaced the Irish, though not all the Irishmen of Northumbria departed. There were occasional lapses in the moral code, as when Egbert, King of Northumbria, gratuitously invaded Ireland in 684, and brutally harassed, in Bede's words, 'these inoffensive people who had always been so friendly to the English'. But the following year he invaded the Picts of Scotland and was himself killed. By and large these were gleaming years for the English. The great names of Benedict Biscop, Aldhelm, Theodore, and later Boniface and Alcuin dominate the cultural scene. Out from England went streams of missionaries to the still unconverted parts of the continent, and this less than a hundred years after Augustine had imported the creed. The inspiration and example of the Irish were a strong force, as they were too in the cultural revival of the period, but the new vigour was English.

The second half of the seventh century is sometimes called the Northumbrian renaissance, for no part of England has ever occupied a position of such European importance. The two traditions of Celtic Ireland and Benedictine Italy fused into a burst of cultural activity. The monasteries of Ripon, Wearmouth, Jarrow and Hexham benefited from Wilfrid's three and Benedict Biscop's six journeys to Rome, for the bishops brought back with them a proud knowledge of Roman artistic achievement. They brought also artisans capable of reproducing and adapting some of it. Music gained an importance the English had never given it before, as the monasteries absorbed and enhanced the basic themes of Gregorian chant. Art and architecture, on continental models, took leaps forward. Both Theodore and Hadrian were from the eastern Mediterranean and they introduced the higher level of culture maintained by the eastern Church and cities. With them came refugees from the onrush of Arabs, now sweeping westwards under the inspiration of Mohammed. Oriental influence was clear in most of the English art of the time, though in many cases it came through the agency of the Irish, whose contact with the East had been more thorough. Syrian motifs are seen in the decoration of books, manuscripts and jewellery, Roman prototypes are adapted to the building of great churches, and Irish themes are common in the carving of crosses, and in such monumental artistic works as the Lindisfarne Gospels.

Above all England began to excel in literature. Bede wrote the finest Latin of his age, not to be rivalled till the time of Charlemagne. His words are simple yet varied and seldom monotonous. Italian and French writers were sunk in verbosity and sophistry. Bede had a powerful story—it had never been told before—and he related it with a simple clarity. But in their vernacular tongue too the Anglo-Saxons outshone all their contemporaries save the Irish. *Beowulf*, with its evocative melancholy, was written down for the first time in the eighth century, Caedmon dictated his Christian lyrics, while Cynewulf wrote several of the Anglo-Saxon classics—*Elene, Juliana, Fates of the Apostles*. As late as the tenth century the English were the only race in Europe to possess the scriptures in their native tongue.

England hardly felt the impact of Whitby. She was too preoccupied, first with disease and dissension, then with an expanding range of religious, political and cultural activity. Sixty years after Bede's death there was a slowing down of this expansion when the Danish raids began. But in a sense the invasions, over a century, had a unifying effect, and the mixed tribes of Angle and Saxon cohered, as a single race, for a glorious period under the leadership of King Alfred. Unqualified welcome of Rome was not to last. Before many years were up breaches began to appear in the bland alliance. So they did in France, Spain and Italy. But there they could always be patched or fought to resolution, while in England the rift of disunity widened with the centuries. It is arguable that one cause of this was the wilfulness of the Irish Church, which lingered in England in spite of Whitby. Perhaps it became part of the identity of the English Church which was never to fall in line with Rome, even in its most submissive moods.

Bishop Colman went first to Iona after his defeat. He would not live with the pressures upon him, and he had learned to dislike the ascendant Wilfrid as much as he is said to have abhorred women. His successors at Lindisfarne were Irish but Romanisers. They were disapproved of by those loyal to their own traditions, but these did not stay to remind them of betrayal. When the business of Whitby is done, Bede gives space to a long nostalgic passage in which he recalls the virtues of the exiled Irishman. Colman's frugality was only realised, says Bede, when his successors arrived at Lindisfarne to find hardly any buildings apart from the church. Their only property had been cattle, and all who had visited the monastery, kings included, had been obliged to share the meagre table of the monks and then depart, unless they wanted to sleep in the open. 'For the sole concern of these teachers was to serve God, not the world; to satisfy the soul, not the belly.' Colman was loved by all who knew him, and his sermons attracted large crowds. Bede ends his tribute with open generosity: Colman and his monks 'were so free from the sin of avarice that none of them would accept lands or gifts for the building of monasteries unless expressly directed to do so by the secular authorities. This was the general practice for many years among the churches of Northumbria.' For Bede, writing fifty years later, the memory of Colman was a sweet one, even in the country that had turned him away.

From Iona Colman went back to Ireland, taking with him a group of Scots and Irish who had decided to stay with him. They all retired to the island of Inishbofin, off the west coast of Galway, and there built a monastery. It was not to be the undisturbed rest Colman had hoped for. The Irish grew perverse in their habits. They took no part in the work of harvesting, but expected to benefit during the winter from the exertions of their English fellows. There is probably more to the story, but we are not told. As a result, Colman secured a second strip of land on the mainland and gave it over to the English. It remained for more than a century in English hands, with new recruits drawn from the home country. And it rose to high status.

Bit by bit the Roman custom advanced through Scotland. Adamnan, Columba's biographer and abbot of Iona at the end of the seventh century, tried to have the Roman practices adopted by his subordinates, but failed. Twelve years after his death an Englishman, who had been trained as a monk in southern Ireland (where the Roman rule had long been observed), arrived at Iona and put his case strongly enough to win the community over. This is almost the climax of Bede's chronicle, if such a level work can be thought to have one. 'This seemed to happen by a wonderful dispensation of God's grace,' he writes, 'in order that the nation which had willingly and ungrudgingly laboured to communicate its own knowledge of God to the English nation might later, through the same English nation, arrive at a perfect way of life which they had not hitherto possessed.' It was not, however, the end of the struggle on English soil. Isolated communities were always being discovered clinging to the old and discredited ways. Wales did not come over till the middle of the eighth century. Devon and Cornwall were not won round for two hundred years after that.

Iona still had prosperous times ahead. It was looked on as a metropolitan bishopric after the change, and it preserved a powerful position in the ecclesiastical affairs of Ireland. Then at the turn of the eighth century, two hundred years after Columba's death, the Viking raids began. The buildings were plundered in 795 and again in 801. Five years later the pirates returned, sacked the restored buildings, loaded loot, and massacred sixty-eight monks on the strand on the south side of the island. It was only beginning centuries of troubled history for Iona: after the Danes, the Norwegians, and then reversion to the Scots, and embroilment with Scottish religious disputes till its almost total decline in the sixteenth century. For a while the Irish stayed, resisting each invasion, and hoping vainly for resultant peace. But the primacy of the Columban church had long before returned to Ireland, to the abbey of Kells, which Columba himself had founded.

Ireland herself after Whitby was far from spent, but the seeds of decline were already there. Decline is a relative thing, and it was partly the restoration of culture and civilisation in Britain and Gaul that blurred the memory of the Irish. But in some areas a spirit of waste and exhaustion took over the ebullient urge for expansion. That there was never any central authority in the Church had been an advantage at a time of spontaneous enthusiasm. Ultimately it caused the extinction of the old virtues. Standards relaxed in the seventh and eighth centuries. Abbeys grew richer, and came to depend more on their riches, and on the kings and chieftains who provided them. The system of inheriting abbacies grew up, and the inheritance itself was often preserved in royal families. Abbots assumed the habits of kings, touring the countryside to collect tithes as the king collected his own dues. Rivalry and competition grew, but not in a productive sense. There were battles between monasteries as they came to regard themselves as petty kingdoms. There is a record of a fight between Clonmacnois and Durrow in which two hundred monks lost their lives. And the incident was not isolated.

By Bede's time Ireland was more pitied than wondered at. Bede himself could write consolingly that the Irish were 'a harmless nation, ever most friendly to the English'. And later in the eighth century Alcuin wrote to the English at Mayo, the monastery founded by Colman through the lethargy of his own countrymen, 'Let your light shine among that barbarous nation like a star in the western skies.' The old missionaries and adventurers were forgotten, zeal was sunk in torpor and piety in avarice. In the minds of outsiders the Irish might have seemed a nation castrated, weak and unspirited, a harmless shadow of their former selves.

But as the inhabitants of Columba's Ireland had not all been saints, their successors were not uniformly sinners. Many fled from what they thought to be the satanic evil of the monasteries to the isolation of islands and remote countryside. The ascetic hermit tradition was never stronger. Even within the organised communities reform set in gradually. For a century the main issue was the Roman one, which affected the ethic of the Church hardly at all but reorganised it on diocesan lines and strengthened it, perhaps, for the deeper reforms of the next age. It is possible that much of the confusion around St Patrick is owed to the efforts of the Roman party. Patrick's two main biographies, written in the seventh century, are much at pains to show the antiquity of the episcopal tradition in the country, though this had patently never been strong. In bending the facts to their purpose, both Muirchu and Tirechan may have created a legend which fitted little with the facts of the real but obscure St Patrick. Whatever the case, the efforts of the reformers at last began to yield fruit. Towards the end of the eighth century a group known as the Culdees, or Friends of God, began to make their influence felt in the country. They revived the sternness of their forefathers, banished abuses, and gradually but with military thoroughness took over the running of the Church. Their interests were not cultural or artistic, but ascetic. Such writings as have come down from them are rules and records, not the creative imaginings of poetic minds, though the protection and efficiency of the Culdees at length enabled a remarkable revival to come about in these fields. Their discipline is characterised by the harshest rule in Church history; and there is reason to believe that its clauses—beatings, genuflexions, recitations by the hundred, spending nights on nettles, or beside dead bodies—were carried out with far more severity than the earlier ones.

Through their agency a cultural revival did come about. It was in the eighth century that the written tradition really began to spread, though there had been isolated manuscripts prepared before that time. Poetry and the recording of old tales got under way, the beginning of that great mass of written Irish literature (including the tale of St Brendan) which remains the greatest single achievement of the Irish, piteously neglected outside the country because Gaelic was never attended to. Art flourished too in this new age, and the craft of illuminating manuscripts was studied and imitated diligently all over the continent. Metal work of the Irish made little impact outside the country. Each nation was experimenting with its own ideas, and, though some basic techniques seem to have been shared, every country developed its own characteristics. All the same few of the continental artifacts that have come down can match the exquisite, restrained richness of the Ardagh Chalice or the Tara brooch. Peculiar also to Ireland were the proliferation of carved stone crosses, with their elaborate scenes from biblical history, the half-comic uniformity of biblical figures, their ingenuous expressions and gestures. Better known, because more striking and more portable, are the masterpieces of book-making of the time, the Book of Kells, the Book of Durrow and of Armagh, and the many works of Irish origin that ended up in continental monasteries.

For the movement of Irish to the Continent was one facet of Irish Christianity that never abated. Indeed it was itself an indirect cause of the decline in the mother country. It has always been a phenomenon of the Irish, that the young leave their country for anywhere as soon as they are through with their training, and sometimes before. Too often, it was the potential liveners of society who emigrated, taking their skills and talents and initiative to benefit other countries; and leaving behind them the conservative and phlegmatic. There was no break in the line of ascetics, taking their quirks and devotion to the remote and weathered corners of needy countries; like Baldred who in the middle of the eighth century sailed to Scotland, and finding the giant Bass Rock blocking the mouth of the Forth River, carried it to a safer place—its present position off the coast of East Lothian, and lived upon it as a hermit. But, more important, the steady exile of missionaries continued in the tradition of Gall and Columbanus, and the reputation they gained brought more and more continentals to the Irish monasteries to learn and train at the feet of the most famous masters.

The Irish abounded at the court of Charlemagne, some of them specially summoned by the king to enhance the quality of his court. There is a record of Charlemagne sending a sum of money to the monastery at Clonmacnois in token of its benefits to European learning. Irish names were found at all the leading centres of the Carolingian revival—Rheims, Cambrai, Soissons, Laon. Though even here they were not universally approved of. Upstarts, a Spanish scholar called them; men who could not carry learning lightly. But their prestige grew. And in the late ninth century a bishop of Auxerre was writing: 'Ireland, despite the dangers of the sea, is migrating almost en masse with her crowd of philosophers to our shores, and all the most learned doom themselves to voluntary exile to attend the bidding of Solomon the Wise.'[1] Solomon in this case was Charles the Bald, grandson of the great king and emperor of the West.

The tenth century saw them still scattered. When Maelbrighde, abbot of Armagh, died, he was 'the head of the purity of Ireland and the greater part of Europe'. No longer nationally distinguished, Irishmen were still working in England, forming a great part of the community at Glastonbury and other leading houses. And John Scotus had already redeemed the philosophic apathy of the ninth century, becoming, by his original mind and clear style, the one eminent, if to some invidious, philosopher of the centuries before Aquinas.

But Ireland herself, in spite of the militancy and efficiency of the reform that swept her, had lost her character before this under the impact of the Norse invasions. Then, not long after, the English disembarked on Irish soil. For a thousand years England played the Hyde in Ireland to her Jekyll in other affairs. The country became like a yard, untidily swept by the English. The Irish and the mountains were brushed to the periphery of north, south and west. The midlands and the east were left anglicised, flat and agricultural—in a word, the Pale. Celtic intuition and imagination were superseded by the pedant and bureaucracy. The fate of John Scotus is somehow a microcosm of the fortunes of his country. A genius, a philosopher in the line of Plato and the mould of Aquinas, his achievement was marred—in the eyes of Catholic doctrinaires—by logical slips and heretical conclusions. In the great age before, mistakes and backslidings had been part of the magic, an impetuous synthesis of good and bad, right and wrong, sublime and ridiculous. When it came about that men weighed and tested the Irish achievement by commonplace criteria, it mattered little if they found it wanting or adequate. The magic itself was gone.

Chronological Table

IRELAND	BRITAIN	EUROPE	AFRICA AND THE EAST
400 Cashel capital of Munster 405 Patrick slave in Mayo		400 Pelagius at Rome	
411 Patrick escapes	410 Romans leave	410 Vandals take Rome 418 Visigoths in Spain 419 d. Jerome	
	420 Start of Anglo-Saxon invasions 425 Vortigern king		
427 d. Niall of 9 Hostages 431 Mission of Palladius 432 Mission of Patrick	429 Mission of Germanus 432 d. Ninian	429 d. Honoratus of Lérins 430 d. Augustine of Hippo 435 d. Cassian	429 Vandals in Africa 433 Attila K. of Huns
	447 2nd mission of Germanus	447-51 Campaigns of Huns under Attila	
450 b. Brigid	450 b. Illtyd 453 Hengist settles in Kent 455 d. Vortigern	451 Attila killed 455 Vandals sack Rome	

Year	IRELAND	BRITAIN	EUROPE	AFRICA AND THE EAST
470	461 d. Patrick 463 Aillil Molt High King	470 fl. Ambrosius Aurelianus		
480	482 d. Aillil Molt 484 b. Brendan		480 b. Benedict of Nursia 481–511 Clovis K. of Franks	
490	c. 495 b. Finnian of Moville	490 B. Badonicus of Mons (?)	485 b. Cassiodonirus 493–526 Reign of Theodoric at Ravenna 496 Clovis baptised	
500		500 b. Gildas 503 Irish colony in Argyll		500 b. Belisarius
510	516 b. { Comgall of Bangor { Ciaran of Clonmacnois		507 Clovis takes Aquitaine 511 d. Clovis	
520	521 b. Columba 525 d. Brigid 527 d. Enda		526 d. Theodoric 529 Benedict founds Monte Cassino	527 Justinian Emperor
530	530 Finnian founds Clonard	530 (?) Death of Arthur 535 d. Illtyd	536 Belisarius takes Rome 539 Belisarius takes Ravenna	537 St Sophia built at Constantinople
540				

Chronological table

	IRELAND	BRITAIN	EUROPE	AFRICA AND THE EAST
540	543 b. Columbanus 545 Kevin founds Glendalough 548 Ciaran founds Clonmacnois		540 b. Gregory the Great	
550	550 d. { Ciaran { Finnian of Clonard 558 { Brendan founds Clonfert { Comgall founds Bangor	547 d. Maelgwn of Gwynedd	550 d. Benedict of Nursia	
560	561 Battle of Culdreihmne	560 David at Menevia		565 d. Justinian
570	574 Convention of Drumceat	565 Columba founds Iona 570 d. Gildas	567 France divided into three 568 Lombards in Italy	570 b. Mohammed
580	577 d. Brendan 579 d. Finnian of Moville		574 Sigebert killed 575–613 Regency of Brunhild 584 d. Cassiodorus	
590	591 Columbanus leaves Ireland		590 { Columbanus in Burgundy { Gregory the Great Pope 591 Columbanus in France 595 d. Childebert of Burgundy	
600	601 d. Comgall	597 { d. Columba { Augustine at Canterbury		

Chronological table

	IRELAND	BRITAIN	EUROPE	AFRICA AND THE EAST
610		601 Ethelbert of Kent converted 604 d. Augustine of Kent	604 d. Gregory the Great 612 Columbanus expelled from Burgundy	
620	618 d. Kevin 624 b. Adamnan	616 B. of Chester 626 Conversion of Northumbria 628 b. Benedict Biscop	615 d. Columbanus	622 Mohammedanism estab. at Medina
630		633 Edwin killed by Penda of Mercia 634 b. Cuthbert, b. Wilfrid 635 Aidan at Lindisfarne	629–39 Dagobert K. of All Franks	632 d. Mohammed 634 Arabs invade Palestine
640		642 Oswald killed by Penda		
650		650 Adamnan in Iona 651 d. Aidan 654 B. of River Winwaed; Penda killed		
660	665 { Great plague / Diormid High King	664 Synod of Whitby 665 Great plague 669 Theodore of Tarsus Bishop of Canterbury		
670		673 b. Bede		673 Arabs attack Constantinople

References

I. European Background

1. Helen Waddell. *The Desert Fathers.*
2. Op. cit., Preface.
3. Op. cit., The Sayings of the Fathers.
4. Harnack. *Expansion of Christianity.* Quoted in op. cit., Introduction.

II. Pagan Ireland

1. Kuno Meyer. *Ancient Irish Poetry.* Deirdre's Lament.
2. *Instructions of King Cormac.* Ed. and trs. by Kuno Meyer in Todd Lecture Series, Vol. XV. Dublin 1909.
3. From the Triads of Ireland. Trs. Kuno Meyer, in *Ancient Irish Poetry.*
4. J. B. Bury. *The Life of St Patrick.*
5. T. F. O'Rahilly. *The Two Patricks.*
6. D. A. Binchy. *Patrick and his Biographers.*
7. R. P. C. Hanson. *St Patrick, A British Missionary Bishop.* Nottingham Univ., 1966.
8. Letter to Coroticus. Newport White, *St Patrick, his writings and life.*
9. Tirechan. Life of St Patrick. In Whitley Stokes: *Tripartite Life of St Patrick.* London 1887.

III. The Awakening of Ireland

1. Whitley Stokes. *Lives of the Saints from the Book of Lismore.*
2. Op. cit.
3. Joseph O'Neill. *The Rule of Ailbe of Emly.* In *Eriu* III, 1907.
4. Kuno Meyer. *Ancient Irish Poetry.* Columcille the Scribe.
5. Eleanor Duckett. *Gateway to the Middle Ages: Monasticism.* Ludwig Bieler. *Ireland, Harbinger of the Middle Ages.*
6. Robert Graves. *The Greek Myths.* Introduction.
7. Trs. by Robin Flower. *The Irish Tradition.*
8. Trs. by Robin Flower. Op. cit.
9. Giraldus Cambrensis. *The Topography of Ireland.*
10. Trs. by Robin Flower. *The Irish Tradition.*
11. All quoted by Robert E. McNally. Old Ireland, Her Scribes and Scholars. In *Old Ireland.*
12. Trs. Kuno Meyer. *Ancient Irish Poetry.*
13. Op. cit.
14. Op. cit.
15. Bede. *History.* I. i.

References

16. Quoted by Robert McNally in loc. cit.
17. *Hisperica Famina.* Ed. Francis Jenkinson. Cambridge 1908.
18. W. P. Ker. *The Dark Ages.*
19. Trs. James Carney: The Impact of Christianity, in *Early Irish Society*, ed. Myles Dillon.
20. Entry in the *Martyrology of Donegal* (October 21).
21. Quoted in Diarmuid O Laoghaire. Old Ireland and her Spirituality. In *Old Ireland.*
22. Plummer. *Vitae Sanctorum Hiberniae.* ii. 260.
23. Whitley Stokes, op. cit.
24. Bede III. 19.
25. From Kuno Meyer and Alfred Nutt. *The Voyage of Bran.* London 1895.
26. Whitley Stokes, op. cit.

IV. THE SAILOR SAINT

1. The extracts in this chapter describing the journey of St Brendan are from Denis O'Donoghue: *Brendaniana*; and C. Plummer: *Lives of the Saints of Ireland.*
2. R. A. S. Macalister (trs.). *The Latin and Irish Lives of St Ciaran.* 1921.
3. Daphne D. C. Pochin Mould. *The Irish Saints.*
4. Op. cit.
5. O'Hanlon. *Lives of the Irish Saints.*
6. Anderson. *Adomnan's Life of Columba.*
7. Gildas. *De Excidio Britanniae Historia.*

V. THE ORGANISATION-ABBOT

1. A. W. Haddan and W. Stubbs. *Councils and Ecclesiastical Documents relating to Great Britain and Ireland* (1869–78).
2. James Carney. Old Ireland and her Poetry. In *Old Ireland.*
3. Op. cit.
4. Bede I. l.
5. Bieler. *Ireland, Harbinger of the Middle Ages.*
6. Quoted by Diarmuid O Laoghaire. In *Old Ireland.*
7. Extracts in this and the following chapter, unless otherwise specified, are from Anderson: *Adomnan's Life of Columba.*
8. Trs. by Kuno Meyer. *Ancient Irish Poetry.*

VI. IONA AND LINDISFARNE

1. Bede III. 4.
2. Gildas, op. cit.
3. *Life of Gregory by a Monk of Whitby* (*c.* 713). Ed. F. A. Gasquet. London 1904.
4. Bede I. 27 ff.
5. Bede II. 2.
6. Bede II. 13.
7. Bede III. 5.
8. Bede III. 14.

References

VII. FRANCE

1. Quoted in *Irish Monks of the Golden Age*. Ed. John Ryan. Dublin 1963.
2. Dawson. *Religion and the Rise of Western Culture*.
3. Extracts in this and the following chapter, unless otherwise specified, are from Jonas: *Life of Columbanus*; and E. S. Duckett: *Gateway to the Middle Ages*; and *Sancti Columbani Opera*.
4. Gregory of Tours. *History of the Franks*.
5. Quoted in Daniel-Rops. *The Church in the Dark Ages*.

VIII. THE PATH TO ROME

1. Dudden. *Gregory the Great*.
2. Op. cit.
3. Newman. *Historical Studies II*.
4. Dawson. *The Making of Europe*.

IX. TRIAL

1. Bede II. 4.
2. Bertrand Russell. *History of Western Philosophy*.
3. Bede V. 21.
4. Loc. cit.
5. Eddius. *Life of Wilfrid*.
6. Op. cit.
7. The rest of this chapter and much of the next is based on Bede's *History*, using Leo Sherley-Price's translation (Penguin Books).

X. AFTER THE VERDICT

1. Quoted in *Cambridge Ancient History*. III. Chap. 19.

Select Bibliography

EUROPEAN BACKGROUND

J. B. Bury. *History of the Later Roman Empire*. 2 vols. Macmillan, New York, 1923.

J. B. Bury. *The Invasion of Europe by the Barbarians*. Macmillan, New York, 1928.

Cambridge Medieval History. Vols. I–II. Cambridge University Press, 1911–13.

Christopher Dawson. *The Making of Europe*. World Publishing Co., New York, 1956.

Edward Gibbon (ed. J. B. Bury). *Decline and Fall of the Roman Empire*. Oxford University Press, New York, 1909.

W. P. Ker. *The Dark Ages*. Nelson, London, 1955.

M. L. W. Laistner. *Thought and Letters in Western Europe, A.D. 500–900*. Cornell University Press, Ithaca, N.Y., 1957.

F. Lot (trs. P. and M. Leon). *End of the Ancient World and Beginnings of the Middle Ages*. Knopf, New York, 1931.

H. St. L. B. Moss. *Birth of the Middle Ages*. Oxford University Press, New York, 1935.

T. G. E. Powell. *The Celts*. Praeger, New York, 1958.

Joseph Raftery. *The Celts*. Mercier Press, Dublin, 1964.

EUROPEAN RELIGION

Nora K. Chadwick. *The Druids*. Verry, Mystic, Conn., 1966.

Christopher Dawson. *Religion and the Rise of Western Culture*. Sheed and Ward, New York, 1950.

F. H. Dudden. *Gregory the Great*. 2 vols. Longmans, New York, 1905.

Dom Louis Gougaud (tr. Maud Joynt). *Christianity in Celtic Lands*. Sheed and Ward, New York, 1932.

T. Kendrick. *The Druids*. Methuen, London, 1924.

Helen Waddell. *The Wandering Scholars*. Doubleday, New York, 1955.

MIDDLE EAST

Robert Graves. *Count Belisarius*. Random House, New York, 1938.

Percy Neville Ure. *Justinian and His Age*. Penguin, Baltimore, Md., 1951.

Helen Waddell. *The Desert Fathers*. Holt, Chicago, 1934.

W. Montgomery Watt. *Muhammed, Prophet and Statesman*. Oxford University Press, New York, 1961.

IRISH BACKGROUND

Ludwig Bieler. *Ireland, Harbinger of the Middle Ages*. Oxford University Press, New York, 1963.

Select bibliography

Edmund Curtis. *A History of Ireland*. Barnes and Noble, New York, 1951.
H. Daniel-Rops (ed.). *The Miracle of Ireland*. Helicon Press, Baltimore, Md., 1959.
Máire and Liam de Paor. *Early Christian Ireland*. Praeger, New York, 1958.
Myles Dillon (ed.). *Early Irish History*. Three Candles, Dublin, 1954.
Giraldus Cambrensis (tr. John J. O'Meara). *Topography of Ireland*. Dundalgen Press, Dundalk, 1951.
P. W. Joyce. *A Social History of Ancient Ireland*. Longmans, New York, 1908.
James F. Kenney. *Sources of the Early History of Ireland*. Columbia University Press, New York, 1929.
Lord Killanin and Michael Duignan. *Shell Guide to Ireland*. Norton, New York, 1966.
Robert McNally (ed.). *Old Ireland*. Fordham University Press, New York, 1965.
Eoin MacNeill. *Phases of Irish History*. Gill, Dublin, 1919.
Eoin MacNeill. *Celtic Ireland*. Martin Lester, Dublin, 1921.
Sean O'Faolain. *The Irish*. Penguin, Baltimore, Md., 1947.
T. F. O'Rahilly. *Early Irish History and Mythology*. Institute for Advanced Studies, Dublin, 1964.
Sean P. O'Riordáin. *Antiquities of the Irish Countryside*. Methuen, London, 1953.

IRISH RELIGION

Nora K. Chadwick. *The Age of Saints in the Early Celtic Church*. Oxford University Press, New York, 1961.
Daphne D. C. Pochin Mould. *The Irish Saints*. Burns and Oates, London, 1964.
John O'Hanlon. *Lives of the Irish Saints*. 10 vols. Duffy, Dublin, 1875.
W. Alison Phillips (ed.). *History of the Church of Ireland*. Oxford University Press, New York, 1933.
C. Plummer (ed.). *Vitae Sanctorum Hiberniae*. 2 vols. Oxford University Press, New York, 1910.
C. Plummer (ed.). *Lives of the Irish Saints*. 2 vols. Oxford University Press, New York, 1922.
John Ryan. *Irish Monasticism*. Longmans, New York, 1931.
Whitley Stokes. *Lives of the Saints from the Book of Lismore*. Anecdota Oxoniensa, Medieval and Modern Series, part V. Oxford University Press, New York, 1890.

IRISH LITERATURE AND ART

James Carney (ed.). *Early Irish Poetry*. Mercier Press, Dublin, 1965.
Myles Dillon. *Early Irish Literature*. University of Chicago Press, 1948.
Myles Dillon. *The Cycles of the Kings*. University of Chicago Press, 1946.
Robin Flower. *The Irish Tradition*. Oxford University Press, New York, 1947.
Françoise Henry. *Irish Art in the Early Christian Period*. Cornell University Press, Ithaca, N.Y., 1965.

Select bibliography

Douglas Hyde. *Literary History of Ireland.* Scribner's, New York, 1889.
P. W. Joyce. *Old Celtic Romances.* Devin-Adair, New York, 1962.
Kuno Meyer. *Selections from Ancient Irish Poetry.* Constable, London, 1959.
Gerard Murphy. *Saga and Myth in Ancient Ireland.* Three Candles, Dublin, 1961.
James Stephens. *Deirdre.* Macmillan, New York, 1923.

BRITAIN

Anglo-Saxon Chronicle (A-text). Dutton, New York, 1953.
Bede (tr. Leo Sherley-Price). *History of the English Church and People.* Penguin, Baltimore, Md., 1955.
Peter Hunter Blair. *Introduction to Anglo-Saxon England.* Cambridge University Press, 1956.
Peter Hunter Blair. *Roman Britain and Early England, 55 B.C.–A.D. 871.* Nelson, Camden, N.J., 1963.
Nora K. Chadwick (ed.). *Studies in Early British History.* Cambridge University Press, 1954.
R. G. Collingwood and J. N. L. Myres. *Roman Britain and the English Settlements.* Oxford University Press, New York, 1936.
Eddius Stephanus (tr. J. F. Webb). *Life of Bishop Wilfrid* in *Lives of the Saints.* Penguin, Baltimore, Md., 1965.
Eleanor Shipley Duckett. *Gateway to the Middle Ages: France and Britain.* University of Michigan Press, Ann Arbor, 1938.
Gildas (ed. and tr. H. Williams). *Works.* Cymmrodorion Society, London, 1899.
J. E. Lloyd. *History of Wales.* 2 vols. Longmans, New York, 1939.
A. Hamilton Thompson (ed.). *Bede; His Life, Times and Writings.* Oxford University Press, New York, 1935.
A. H. Williams. *An Introduction to the History of Wales.* Oxford University Press, New York, 1941.
H. Williams. *Christianity in Early Britain.* Oxford University Press, New York, 1912.

PATRICK

D. A. Binchy. *Patrick and His Biographers,* in *Studia Hibernica,* 1962, No. 2. Dublin.
J. B. Bury. *Life of St Patrick and His Place in History.* Oxford University Press, New York, 1905.
James Carney. *The Problem of St Patrick.* Institute for Advanced Studies, Dublin, 1961.
T. F. O'Rahilly. *The Two Patricks.* Institute for Advanced Studies, Dublin, 1942.
Newport White. *St Patrick; His Writings and Life.* S.P.C.K., London, 1920.

BRENDAN

Geoffrey Ashe. *Land to the West.* Viking, New York, 1962.

Select bibliography

Magnus Magnusson and Hermann Palsson (trs.). *The Vinland Sagas*. Penguin, Baltimore, Md., 1965.

Denis O'Donoghue. *Brendaniana*. Browne and Nolan, Dublin, 1895.

J. F. Webb (ed.). *Lives of the Saints*. Penguin, Baltimore, Md., 1965.

COLUMBA AND SCOTLAND

A. O. and M. O. Anderson (eds.). *Adomnan's Life of Columba*. Nelson, Camden, N.J., 1961.

John A. Duke. *The Columban Church*. Oxford University Press, New York, 1932.

John A. Duke. *History of the Church in Scotland to the Reformation*. Oliver and Boyd, London, 1937.

W. Douglas Simpson. *The Historical Saint Columba*. Verry, Mystic, Conn., 1963.

W. Douglas Simpson. *Saint Ninian and the Origins of the Christian Church in Scotland*. Oliver and Boyd, Edinburgh, 1940.

W. F. Skene. *Celtic Scotland*. 3 vols. David Douglas, Edinburgh, 1876–80.

COLUMBANUS

Mrs Thomas Concannon. *The Life of St Columban*. Catholic Truth Society, Dublin, 1915.

Eleanor Shipley Duckett. *Gateway to the Middle Ages: Monasticism*. University of Michigan Press, Ann Arbor, 1938.

Gregory of Tours (ed. and tr. O. M. Dalton). *History of the Franks*. 2 vols. Oxford University Press, New York, 1927.

Jonas of Bobbio. *Life of Columbanus*. Translations and Reprints II, No. 7. University of Pennsylvania Press, Philadelphia, 1895.

Margaret Stokes. *Three Months in the Forests of France*. Bell, London, 1895.

Margaret Stokes. *Six Months in the Apennines*. Bell, London, 1892.

G. S. M. Walker (ed.). *Sancti Columbani Opera*. Institute for Advanced Studies, Dublin, 1957.

Index

Index

Index

Index

Index

Index